BEFORE YOU
QUIT YOUR JOB

10 Real-Life Lessons Every
Entrepreneur Should Know About
Building a Multimillion-Dollar Business

10 Real-Life Lessons Every Entrepreneur Should Know About Building a Multimillion-Dollar Business

By Robert T. Kiyosaki with Sharon L. Lechter, C.P.A.

The Authors of *Rich Dad Poor Dad*

WARNER
BUSINESS
BOOKS™

NEW YORK   BOSTON

CASHFLOW, Rich Dad, Rich Dad's Advisors, Rich Dad's Seminars, EBSI, and B-I Triangle are registered trademarks of CASHFLOW Technologies, Inc.

Visit our Web site at www.richdad.com

Warner Business Books
Warner Books

Time Warner Book Group, 1271 Avenue of the Americas, New York, NY 10020.
Visit our Web site at: www.twbookmark.com.

The Warner Business Books logo is a trademark of Warner Books.

Printed in the United States of America

First Edition: September 2005
10 9 8 7 6 5 4 3 2 1

Library of Congress Cataloging-in-Publication Data

Kiyosaki, Robert T.
    Rich dad's before you quit your job : ten real-life lessons every entrepreneur should know about building a multimillion-dollar business / Robert T. Kiyosaki, with Sharon L. Lechter.—1st ed.
        p.   cm.
    "Robert Kiyosaki provides first-hand accounts of his own start-up companies, how he learned from both his failures and successes, and the basics of entrepreneurship."—Provided by the publisher.
    ISBN 0-446-69637-4
    1. New business enterprises.   2. Entrepreneurship.   I. Lechter, Sharon L.   II. Title.
HD62.5.K96   2005
658.1'1—dc22

2005017421

Acknowledgments

Entrepreneurship is as much a spirit as it is a vocation. When Rich Dad partnered with Warner Books it was in large part due to Laurence Kirshbaum, Warner's CEO and Chairman. We recognized that entrepreneurial spark in his eyes. He energized his "Can Do" attitude throughout the entire organization. While publishing may not be a cutting-edge industry, Larry Kirshbaum is a cutting-edge leader and has been a joy to work with. Thank you, Larry.

Robert Kiyosaki
Sharon Lechter

Contents

Introduction

What Makes Entrepreneurs Different?

One of the most frightening days of my life was the day I quit my job and officially became an entrepreneur. On that day I knew there were no more steady paychecks, no more health insurance or retirement plan. No more days off for being sick or paid vacations.

On that day, my income went to zero. The terror of not having a steady paycheck was one of the most frightening experiences I had ever experienced. Worst of all, I did not know how long it would be before I would have another steady paycheck . . . it might be years. The moment I quit my job I knew the real reason why many employees do not become entrepreneurs. It is fear of not having any money . . . no guaranteed income . . . no steady paycheck. Very few people can operate for long periods of time without money. Entrepreneurs are different, and one of those differences is the ability to operate sanely and intelligently without money.

On that same day, my expenses went up. As an entrepreneur, I had to rent an office, a parking stall, a warehouse, buy a desk, a lamp, rent a phone, pay for travel, hotels, taxis, meals, copies, pens, paper, staples, stationery, legal tablets, postage, brochures, products, and even coffee for the office. I also had to hire a secretary, an accountant, an attorney, a bookkeeper, a business insurance agent, and even a janitorial service. These were all expenses my employer had once paid for me. I began to realize how expensive it had been to hire me as an employee. I realized that employees cost far more than the number of dollars reflected in their paychecks.

So another difference between employees and entrepreneurs is that entrepreneurs need to know how to spend money, *even if they have no money*.

The Start of a New Life

The day I officially left the company, I was in San Juan, Puerto Rico. It was June 1978. I was in Puerto Rico because I was attending the Xerox Corporation's President's Club celebration, an event recognizing the top achievers in the company. People had come from all over the world to be recognized.

It was a great event, a gala I will always remember. I could not believe how much money Xerox was spending just to recognize the top salespeople in the company. But even though it was a celebration, I was having a miserable time. Throughout the three-day event, all I could think about was leaving the job, the steady paycheck, and the security of the company. I realized that once the party in San Juan was over, I was going to go on my own. I was not going back to work at the Honolulu Branch Office or the Xerox Corporation.

When leaving San Juan, the plane I was on experienced some kind of emergency. In preparing to land at Miami, the pilot had us all brace, cradle our heads, and prepare for a possible crash. I was already feeling bad enough about this being my first day as an entrepreneur, but now I had to prepare to die on top of it? My first day as an entrepreneur was not off to a very good start.

Obviously, the plane did not crash, and I flew on to Chicago where I was going to do a sales presentation for my line of nylon surfer wallets. I arrived at the Chicago Mercantile Mart late because of the flight delays, and the client I was supposed to meet, a buyer from a large chain of department stores, was already gone. Once again I thought to myself, "This is not a good way to start my new career as an entrepreneur. If I don't make this sale there will be no income for the business, no paycheck for me, no food on the table." Since I like to eat, having no food disturbed me the most.

Are Some People Born Entrepreneurs?

"Are people born entrepreneurs or are they trained to be entrepreneurs?" When I asked my rich dad his opinion on this age-old question, he said, "Asking if people are born or trained to be entrepreneurs is a question that makes no sense. It would be like asking if people are born employees or trained to become employees?" He went on to say, "People are trainable. They can be trained to be either employees or entrepreneurs. The reason there are more employees than entrepreneurs is simply that our schools train young people to become employees. That is why so many parents say to their child, 'Go to school so you can get a good job.' *I have yet to hear any parent say, 'Go to school to become an entrepreneur.'*"

Employees Are a New Phenomenon

The employee is a rather new phenomenon. During the agrarian age, most people were entrepreneurs. Many were farmers who worked the king's lands. They did not receive a paycheck from the king. In fact, it was the other way around. The farmer paid the king a tax for the right to use the land. Those who were not farmers were tradespeople, aka small business entrepreneurs. They were butchers, bakers, and candlestick makers. Their last names often reflected their business. That is why today many people are named Smith, for the village blacksmith; Baker, for bakery owners; and Farmer, because their family's business was farming. They were entrepreneurs, not employees. Most children who were raised in entrepreneurial families followed in their parents' footsteps, also becoming entrepreneurs. Again, it is just a matter of training.

It was during the Industrial Age that the demand for *employees* grew. In response, the government took over the task of mass education and adopted the Prussian system, upon which most Western school systems in the world are today modeled. When you research the philosophy behind Prussian education, you will find that the stated purpose was to *produce soldiers and employees* . . . people who would follow orders and do as they were told. The Prussian system of education is a great system for mass-producing employees. It is a matter of training.

The Most Famous Entrepreneurs

You may also have noticed that many of our most famous entrepreneurs did not finish school. Some of those entrepreneurs are Thomas Edison, founder of General Electric; Henry Ford, founder of Ford Motor Company; Bill Gates, founder of Microsoft; Richard Branson, founder of Virgin; Michael Dell, founder of Dell Computers; Steven Jobs, founder of Apple Computers and Pixar; and Ted Turner, founder of CNN. Obviously, there are other entrepreneurs who did well in school . . . but few are as famous as these.

The Transition from Employee to Entrepreneur

I know I was not born a natural entrepreneur. I had to be trained. My rich dad guided me through a process of starting as an employee to eventually becoming an entrepreneur. For me, it was not an easy process. There was a lot I had to unlearn before I could begin to understand the lessons he was trying to teach me.

It was difficult hearing what my rich dad had to say because what he said was exactly opposite from the lessons my poor dad was trying to teach me. Every time my rich dad talked about entrepreneurship, he was talking about freedom. Every time my poor dad talked to me about going to school to get a job, he was talking about security. There was the clash of these two philosophies going on in my head and it was confusing me.

Finally I asked rich dad about the difference in philosophies. I asked, "Aren't security and freedom the same thing?"

Smiling, he replied, "Security and freedom are not the same . . . in fact they are opposites. The more security you seek, the less freedom you have. The people with the most security are in jail. That is why it is called maximum security." He went on to say, "If you want freedom you need to let go of security. Employees desire security and entrepreneurs seek freedom."

So the question is, can anyone become an entrepreneur? My answer is, "Yes. It begins with a change in philosophy. It begins with a desire for more *freedom* than *security*."

From Caterpillar to Butterfly

We all know that a caterpillar spins a cocoon and one day emerges as butterfly. It is a change so profound, it is known as a *metamorphosis.* One of the definitions of metamorphosis is *a striking alteration in character.* This book is about a similar metamorphosis. This book is about the changes a person goes through, when transitioning from *employee to entrepreneur.* While many people dream of quitting their job and starting their own business, only a few actually do it. Why? Because the transition from employee to entrepreneur is more than changing jobs . . . it is a true metamorphosis.

Entrepreneur Books Written by Nonentrepreneurs

Over the years, I have read many books about entrepreneurs and on the subject of entrepreneurship. I studied the lives of such entrepreneurs as Thomas Edison, Bill Gates, Richard Branson, and Henry Ford. I also read books on different entrepreneurial philosophies and what makes some entrepreneurs better than others. In every book, good or bad, I found some priceless bit of information or wisdom that has helped me in my quest to become a better entrepreneur.

Looking back at the books I have read, I noticed that they fall into two basic categories: books written by entrepreneurs and books written by nonentrepreneurs. Most of the books are written by nonentrepreneurs, people who are professional authors, journalists, or college professors.

While I have gotten something important from every book, regardless of who wrote it, I did find something missing. What I found missing was the "down in the gutter," "kick in the gut," "stabbed in the back," terrifying mistakes and horror stories that almost every entrepreneur goes through. Most of the books paint a picture of the entrepreneur as a brilliant, suave, cool businessperson who handled every challenge with ease. The books about great entrepreneurs often make it sound like they were born entrepreneurs, and granted, many of them were. Just as there are natural and gifted athletes, there are natural and gifted entrepreneurs, and most books are written about such people.

Books on entrepreneurship written by college professors have a different flavor. College professors tend to boil the subject to the bone, leaving only the static facts or findings. I find reading such technically correct books difficult because the reading is often boring. There is no meat left, nothing juicy, just the bones.

How This Book Is Different

This is a book about entrepreneurship, written by entrepreneurs who have experienced the ups and downs, the successes and failures, of the real world.

Today The Rich Dad Company is an international business with products in forty-four different languages, doing business in over eighty countries. But it all started as a company that my wife, Kim, and I started with our partner Sharon Lechter. It began on Sharon's dining room table in 1997. Our initial investment was $1,500. Our first book, *Rich Dad Poor Dad*, has been on the *New York Times* Best Seller List for over four and a half years, an accomplishment shared by only three other books. Maybe, as you read this book, it will still be on the list.

Rather than tell you how smart I am at business, which I am not, we thought it better to write a different type of book on entrepreneurship. Rather than tell you how I brilliantly sailed over the tallest peaks, and made millions, we thought you might learn more from how I dug many deep holes, fell into them, and then had to dig my way out. Rather than tell you about all my successes, we believe you will learn more from my failures.

Why Write about Failures?

Many people do not become entrepreneurs because they are afraid of failing. By writing about the things many people are afraid of, we hope to help you better decide if becoming an entrepreneur is for you. Our intent is not to frighten you off—our intent is to provide a little "real world" insight on the ups and downs of the process of becoming an entrepreneur.

Another reason for writing about failures is that humans are designed to learn by making mistakes. We learn to walk by first falling down and then trying again. We learn to ride a bicycle by falling off and then trying again. If we had never risked falling, we would go through life crawling like caterpillars. One of the missing elements we have found in reading many of the books about entrepreneurship, especially those written by college professors, is that they do not go into the emotional trials and tribulations an entrepreneur goes through. They do not discuss what happens to entrepreneurs emotionally when the business fails, when they run out of money, have to let employees go, and when their investors and creditors come after them. How would most college professors know how a failing entrepreneur feels? How would they know—since a steady paycheck, tenure, always knowing the right answers, and never making mistakes are highly prized in the academic world. Again, it's all a matter of training.

In the late 1980s, I was invited to do a talk on entrepreneurship at Columbia University. Rather than talk about my successes, I talked about my failures and how much I learned from my mistakes. The young audience asked a lot of questions and seemed genuinely interested in the ups and downs of becoming an entrepreneur. I talked about the fears we all face when starting a business, and how I faced those fears. I shared with them some of the more stupid mistakes I made and how those mistakes later became valuable lessons I would never have learned if I had not made the mistakes. I talked about the pain of having to shut a business down and lay people off because of my incompetence. I also shared with them how all my mistakes eventually made me a better entrepreneur, very rich, and most important, financially free, never needing a job again. All in all, I thought it was an objective and realistic talk on the process of becoming an entrepreneur.

A few weeks later, I found out that the faculty member who had invited me to speak at the university was called into her department head's office and reprimanded. His final words to her were, "We do not allow failures to speak at Columbia."

What Is an Entrepreneur?

Now that we have torn into college professors, it is time to give them some credit. One of the better definitions of an entrepreneur is from Howard H. Stevenson, a professor at Harvard University. He says, "Entrepreneurship is an approach to management that we define as follows: *the pursuit of opportunity without regard to resources currently controlled.*" In my opinion, this is one of the most brilliant definitions of what an entrepreneur is. It is bare bones . . . and brilliant.

The Power of Excuses

Many people want to become entrepreneurs but always have some *excuse* for why they do not quit their job, excuses such as:

1. "I don't have the money."
2. "I can't quit my job because I have kids to support."
3. "I don't have any contacts."
4. "I'm not smart enough."
5. "I don't have the time. I'm too busy."
6. "I can't find anyone who wants to help me."
7. "It takes too long to build a business."
8. "I'm afraid. Building a business is too risky for me."
9. "I don't like dealing with employees."
10. "I'm too old."

The friend who gave me this article by Professor Stevenson said, "Any two-year-old is an expert at making excuses." He also said, "The reason most people who want to become entrepreneurs remain employees is that they have some *excuse* that keeps them from quitting their job and taking that leap of faith. For many people, the power of their excuse is more powerful than their dreams."

Entrepreneurs Are Different

Mr. Stevenson had many other bare bone gems in his article, especially when he compares entrepreneurs to employees or promoters to trustees, as he labels them. A few of these gems of comparison are:

1. **When it comes to their Strategic Orientation:**
   PROMOTER: driven by *perception* of opportunity.
   TRUSTEE: driven by *control* of resources.

In other words, entrepreneurs are always looking for the opportunity without much regard to whether they have resources. Employee type persons focus on what resources they have or do not have, which is why so many people say, "How can I start my business? I don't have the money." An entrepreneur would say, "Tie up the deal and then we'll find the money." This difference in philosophies is a very big difference between employee and entrepreneur.

This is also why my poor dad often said, "I can't afford it." Being an employee he looked at his resources. Those of you who have read my other books know that my rich dad forbade his son and me to ever say, "I can't afford it." Instead he taught us to look at opportunities and ask, "How can I afford it?" He was an entrepreneur.

2. When it comes to Management Structure:
PROMOTER: *Flat* with multiple informal networks.
TRUSTEE: *Formalized hierarchy* with multiple tiers.

In other words, an entrepreneur will keep the organization small and lean, using cooperative relationships with strategic partners to grow the business. Employees want to build a hierarchy, which means a chain of command, with them at the top. This is their concept of building an empire. An entrepreneur will grow the organization horizontally, which means "outsourcing" rather than bringing the work "in house." An employee wants to grow the organization vertically, which means hiring more employees. Formal organizational charts are very important to employees climbing the corporate ladder.

In this book, you will find out how The Rich Dad Company stayed small yet grew big by using strong strategic partnerships with large hierarchies such as Time Warner, Time Life, Infinity Broadcasting, and major publishers throughout the world. We decided to grow in this manner because it cost us less time, people, and money. We could grow faster, grow bigger, become very profitable, have a global presence, and yet remain small. We used other people's money and resources to grow the business. This book will explain how and why we did it that way.

3. When it comes to Reward Philosophy:
PROMOTER: *Value driven*, performance-based, team-oriented.
TRUSTEE: *Security driven*, resource-based, job promotion-oriented.

In simple terms, employees want job security with a strong company, a steady paycheck, and the opportunity for promotion—a chance to climb the corporate ladder. Many employees consider a promotion and title more important than money. I know my poor dad did. He loved his title, Superintendent of Public Education, even though he was not paid much.

The entrepreneur doesn't want to climb the corporate ladder; he or she wants to own the corporate ladder. An entrepreneur is not driven by a paycheck but by results of the team. Also, as Howard Stevenson states, many entrepreneurs start a business because they have very strong values, values that are more important than simply job security and a steady paycheck. This book will go into values far more important than money. For many entrepreneurs, their values are more important than money. They are passionate about their work, their mission, and love what they do. Many entrepreneurs will do their work even though there is no money. Rich dad said, "Many employees are passionate about their work *only* as long as there is a paycheck."

In this book, you will also learn about the three different types of money; competitive money, cooperative money, and spiritual money. *Competitive money* is the type of money most people work for. They compete for jobs, promotions, pay raises, and against their business competition. *Cooperative money* is achieved by networking instead of competing. In this book you will also find out how The Rich Dad Company expanded rapidly with very little money, simply by working for cooperative money. Also, a significant part of this book is dedicated to the mission of a business, the values. While we all know that there are many entrepreneurs who are opportunists, working only for competitive money, there are others who build a business on a strong mission, working for *spiritual money*—the best of all money.

Different Styles of Management

There are two other points in the article that are refreshing, especially from a college professor. Howard Stevenson acknowledges that many people say that entrepreneurs are not good managers. Instead of agreeing with this commonly accepted point of view, he writes, *"The entrepreneur is stereotyped as egocentric and idiosyncratic and thus unable to manage. However, although the managerial task is substantially different for the entrepreneur, the management skill is nonetheless essential."* Right-on, Howard. In other words, entrepreneurs manage people differently. The next point explains why there are differences in management style between entrepreneur and employee.

Know How to Use Other People's Resources

The other point Stevenson makes tracks closely his definition of an entrepreneur, which is, "Entrepreneurship is an approach to management that we define as follows: *the pursuit of opportunity without regard to resources currently controlled."* He states, "Entrepreneurs learn to use other people's resources well." This is what causes the difference in management style. Employees want to hire people so they can manage them. It puts them in direct control over them. They will do as they are told or they are fired. This is why employee types want to build vertical hierarchies. They want the Prussian style of management. They want people to jump when they say, "Jump."

Since entrepreneurs are not necessarily managing employees, they need to manage people differently. Very simply put, entrepreneurs need to know how to manage other entrepreneurs. If you say, "Jump," to an entrepreneur, he or she usually responds with some rude comment or gesture. So entrepreneurs are not poor managers, as many people think; they simply have a very different management style because they are managing people they cannot tell what to do . . . or fire.

This difference in management style also explains why employee types work for *competitive money* and entrepreneurs tend to work for *cooperative money*.

Employee Looking for Employees

Some of the more common complaints heard from new entrepreneurs are, "I can't find good employees." Or, "Employees just don't want to work." Or, "All employees want is more money." This is a problem for a new entrepreneur with a confused management style. Management style is a matter of training. Again, compliments to Howard Stevenson, a college professor, for getting to the bare bones differences between entrepreneur and employee.

> ## How to Order the Article
>
> There is much more information packed into Howard H. Stevenson's article entitled, "A Perspective on Entrepreneurship," written in 1983. A copy of the article is available from Harvard Business School for less than $10.00. To order go to http:/harvardbusinessonline.org. It is a brilliant article, and useful for anyone who is interested in the subject of entrepreneurship.

Don't Wait till All Lights Are Green

Another reason many people are not as successful as they would like to be is fear—often the fear of making mistakes or the fear of failing. There is another reason, also a fear, but it appears a little differently. These people disguise their fears by being perfectionists. They are waiting for all the stars to line up before starting their business. They want all the lights to be green before they will pull out of the driveway. When it comes to entrepreneurship, many of these people are still stuck in the driveway with their engine idling.

Three Parts of a Business

One of the best entrepreneurs I have ever known is a friend and business partner of mine. I have formed several companies with him—three that went public and have made us multimillions. In describing what an entrepreneur does, he said, "There are three parts to putting a business deal together. One is finding the right people. Two is finding the right opportunity. And three is finding the money." He also said, "Rarely do all three pieces come together at the same time. Sometimes you have the people, but you do not have the deal or the money. Sometimes you have the money, but no deal or people." He also said, "The most important job of an entrepreneur is to grab one piece and then begin to put the other two pieces together. That may take a week or it may take years, but if you have one piece, at least you've gotten started." In other words, an entrepreneur does not care if two out of three lights are red. In fact, an entrepreneur does not care if all three lights are red. Red lights do not prevent an entrepreneur from being an entrepreneur.

Anything Worth Doing Is Worth Doing Poorly

Have you ever noticed that software, such as Microsoft's Windows, comes in versions such as Windows 2.0 and Windows 3.0? What that means is that they have improved their product and now want you to buy the better version. In other words, the first product they sold you was not perfect. They may have sold it knowing it had flaws, bugs, and needed to be improved.

Many people fail to get to market because they are constantly perfecting their product. Like the person who is waiting for all the lights to be green, some entrepreneurs never get to market because they are looking for, or working on, perfecting their product or writing the perfect business plan. My rich dad often said, "Anything worth doing is worth doing poorly." Henry Ford said, "Thank God for my customers. They buy my products before they are perfected." In other words, entrepreneurs start and continue to improve themselves, their businesses, and their products. Many people will not start unless everything is perfect. That is why many of them never start.

Knowing when to introduce a product into the marketplace is as much an *art* as a *science*. You may not want to wait for a product to be perfect; it may never be perfect. It just has to be "good enough." It merely has to work well enough to be accepted in the marketplace. However, if the product is so flawed that it doesn't work for its intended purpose, or otherwise does not meet marketplace expectations or causes problems, it can be very difficult to reestablish credibility and a reputation for quality.

One of the marks of a successful entrepreneur is being able to assess the expectations of the marketplace and know when to *stop developing and start marketing*. If the product is put on the market a little prematurely, then the entrepreneur can simply improve it, and take steps to maintain the goodwill in the marketplace. On the other hand, delay in introducing a product can mean opportunities irretrievably lost, a window of opportunity missed.

For those of you who remember the early versions of Windows, you'll recall how frequently your computer "crashed." (There were some who said that Windows was so full of bugs that it should have come with a can of in-secticide.) If an automobile broke down as frequently as Windows did, it would not have been acceptable in the marketplace. In fact, the automobile would have been a "lemon," and the manufacturer would have been forced to replace it. Windows, however, notwithstanding the bugs—the flaws—was phenomenally successful. Why was that? It filled a need in the marketplace and was not out of line with marketplace expectations. Microsoft recognized a window of opportunity and started marketing. As those of you who use the present version of Windows know, if Microsoft had waited for Windows to be perfect, it still would not be in the marketplace.

Street Smarts Versus School Smarts

In martial arts, there is a saying that goes, "A cup that is *full* is useless. Only when a cup is *empty* is it useful." This is true for the entrepreneur.

We have all heard people say, "Oh, I know all about that." Those are words coming from a person whose cup is full. Those are the words coming from a person who believes he or she knows all the answers. An entrepreneur cannot afford to know all the answers. Entrepreneurs know they can never know all the answers. They know their success requires that their cup is always empty.

To be successful as employees, people need to know the right answers. If they do not know the right answers, they may be fired or not promoted. Entrepreneurs do not need to know all the answers. All they need to know is who to call. That is what advisors are all about.

Employees are often trained to be *specialists*. Simply said, a specialist is someone who knows *a lot about a little*. His or her cup must be full.

Entrepreneurs need to be *generalists*. Simply said, a generalist is some-one who knows a little about a lot. His or her cup is empty.

People go to school to become specialists. People go to school to become an accountant, attorney, secretary, nurse, doctor, engineer, or computer pro-grammer. These are people who know *a lot about a little.* The more special-ized people are, the more money they make—or at least they hope they make.

What makes an entrepreneur different is entrepreneurs must know a little about accounting, the law, engineering systems, business systems, insurance, product design, finance, investing, people, sales, marketing, public speaking, raising capital, and dealing with different people trained in different special-ties. True entrepreneurs know there is so much to know and so much they *do not* know, they cannot afford the luxury of specialization. That is why their cup must always be empty. They must always be learning.

No Graduation Day

This means the entrepreneur must be a very proactive learner. Once I crossed the line from employee to entrepreneur, my real education began. I was soon reading every book on business I could get my hands on, reading financial newspapers, and attending seminars. I knew I did not know all the answers. I knew I had to learn a lot and learn it fast. Today, nothing has changed. I know that my education as an entrepreneur will never have a graduation day. I will always be in school. In other words, when I was not at work, I was reading or studying, and then applying what I learned to the business.

Over the years, this constant study and then application to the business has been one of my most important habits for success. As I said, I was not a natural entrepreneur, as some of my friends were. But as in the race between the turtle and the hare, I the turtle slowly but surely caught up with and passed some of my friends whose cups became full when they achieved suc-cess. A true entrepreneur has no graduation day.

Overspecialized

The following diagram comes from *Rich Dad's CASHFLOW Quadrant* (Warner Books), the second book in the Rich Dad series.

The E stands for *Employee.*

The S stands for *Self-employed, small business,* or *specialist*.

The B stands for *Big business owner (five hundred employees or more).*

The I stands for *Investor.*

One of the reasons so many entrepreneurs are in the S quadrant rather than the B quadrant is that they are overly specialized. For example, medical doctors in private practice are technically entrepreneurs but may find it hard to migrate from the S quadrant to the B quadrant because their training is too specialized—their cup is full. For a person to move from S to B, he or she will need more generalized training—and must always have an empty cup.

A side note on the CASHFLOW Quadrant. One of the reasons why rich dad recommended I become an entrepreneur in the B and I quadrants is that the tax laws are most favorable in those quadrants. The tax laws are *not* as favorable for employees or self-employed people, the E and S quadrants. The tax code offers greater incentives, i.e., loopholes, for people who either hire a lot of people in the B quadrant or invest in projects the government wants growth in, investments such as low-income housing. In summary, taxes are different in different quadrants.

This book will go into the differences in each quadrant and how an entrepreneur can migrate from one quadrant to another, especially from the S quadrant to the B quadrant.

A List of Differences

Before quitting their jobs, people need to decide if they want to make the transition from employee to entrepreneur. The transition or metamorphosis requires a change to some of the following traits.

1. Ability to change philosophy from *security* to *freedom*
2. Ability to operate without money
3. Ability to operate without security
4. Ability to focus on *opportunity* rather than *resources*
5. Having different management styles to manage different people
6. Ability to manage people and resources they do not control
7. Team and value oriented rather than pay or promotion oriented

8. Active learner—no graduation day
9. Generalized education rather than specialized
10. The courage to be responsible for the entire business

You may notice that farmers, possibly our earliest entrepreneurs, have had to develop most of these traits in order to survive as farmers. Most had to plant in the spring in order to harvest in the fall. Most had to pray the weather was in their favor and that pests, diseases, and insects left enough for the farmer's family to live on through a long hard winter. Rich dad often said, "If you have the mind-set and toughness of a farmer, you will be a great entrepreneur."

The Pot of Gold at the End of the Rainbow

While this book starts off describing the process of becoming an entrepreneur as a painful and time-consuming process, I also want to let you know that there is a pot of gold at the end of the rainbow. As with any learning process, even learning to walk or ride a bicycle, the start of the process is always the hardest. You may recall my first official day as an entrepreneur was not a good day. If you stick with the learning process, your world will change, just as your world changed when you finally learned to walk or ride a bike. The same is true with entrepreneurship.

For me, the pot of gold at the end of the rainbow has been greater than my wildest dreams. The process of becoming an entrepreneur has made me far richer than I could have become as an employee. Also, I have become somewhat famous and recognized throughout the world. I doubt if I would have become famous as an employee. Most important, our products have reached people throughout the world and in some way helped them make their lives a little better. The best part of learning to be an entrepreneur is being able to serve more and more people. Being able to serve more people has been my primary reason for becoming an entrepreneur.

The Philosophy of an Entrepreneur

Becoming an entrepreneur began with a change of philosophy. The day I left the Xerox Corporation in Puerto Rico, my philosophy shifted from the philosophy of my poor dad to the philosophy of my rich dad.

The shift looked like this:

1. From a desire for security to a desire for freedom
2. From a desire for a steady paycheck to the desire for great wealth
3. From seeing value in dependence to seeing value in independence
4. To make my own rules rather than obey someone else's rules
5. A desire to give orders rather than take orders
6. A willingness to be fully responsible rather than say, "It's not my job"
7. To determine the culture of a company rather than try to fit into someone else's company culture
8. To make a difference in this world rather than complain about the problems of the world
9. To know how to find a problem and turn it into a business opportunity
10. To choose to be an entrepreneur rather than an employee

The New Super Entrepreneurs

In 1989 the world went through perhaps the biggest change in history. In 1989, the Berlin Wall came down and the Internet went up. In 1989 the Cold War ended and globalization started to take off. The world went from *walls* to *Web*, from *division* to *integration*.

In his bestselling book *The World Is Flat* (Farrar, Straus and Giroux, 2005), Thomas Friedman states that when the wall came down and the Web went up, the world went to one Super Power (the U.S.), global Super Markets, and Super Individuals.

Unfortunately, one such super individual is Osama Bin Laden. Quoting Thomas Friedman:

> Osama Bin Laden declared war on the United States in the late 1990s. After he organized the bombing of two American embassies in Africa, the U.S. Air Force retaliated with a cruise missile attack on his bases in Afghanistan as though he were another nation-state. Think of that: on one day in 1998, the United States fired 75 cruise missiles, at $1 million apiece, at a person! That was the first battle in

history between a super power and a super-empowered angry man. September 11 was just the second such battle.

My prediction is there will soon be new Super Entrepreneurs whose wealth will dwarf the wealth of today's mega-rich entrepreneurs. In the 1980s, Bill Gates and Michael Dell were the hot young billionaire entrepreneurs. Today, the hot new billionaire entrepreneurs are Sergey Brin and Larry Page, founders of Google. My prediction is the next Super Entrepreneurs will not be from the United States. Why? Once again the answer is that walls have turned into webs.

In 1996, the Telecom Reform Act and money from Wall Street gave rise to such companies as Global Crossing, a bankrupt company that did one important task. It linked the world with fiber optics. Once this fiber optic network was in place, the brainpower from countries such as India did not need to emigrate to Silicon Valley to find work. The brainpower of India could now work from home, for much lower wages.

Due to the power of fiber optic cables and the Web, my prediction is the next Bill Gates or Sergey Brin will come from outside the United States, possibly from India, China, Singapore, Ireland, New Zealand, or Eastern Europe. Brainpower, innovation, technology, and access to the world's Super Markets will create the next teenage multibillionaire or trillion-dollar entrepreneur.

Today many Americans are panicked at the idea that our high-paying jobs are being *outsourced*, shipped not only to India, but all over the world. Today, even tasks performed by accountants, lawyers, stockbrokers, and travel agents can be performed somewhere else in the world for a lower price.

No More High-Paying Jobs

So what does this do to the Industrial Age advice, "Go to school so you can find a good secure job with high pay," or, "Work hard and climb the corporate ladder"? In my opinion, this old Industrial Age advice is *toast*. Many employees will have less work to find, much less, since the person competing for their job lives thousands of miles away. Most of us know that wages have not gone up for many workers. How can their wages go up when someone else is willing to work for so much less?

One big difference between an entrepreneur and an employee is that an entrepreneur is excited about the changes the change from *wall* to *web* is bringing. Many employees are terrified of the changes.

One Last Difference

The last difference I will mention is the difference in pay between employees and entrepreneurs. Looking at the list below of the highest-paid and the lowest-paid CEOs, you may notice that some of the most famous CEOs are the lowest paid. Could it be because CEOs who are employees work for a paycheck and CEOs who are entrepreneurs work for some other kind of pay?

Highest Paid:

1. John Wilder	TXU	$55.2 million
2. Robert Toll	Toll Brothers	$44.3 million
3. Ray Irani	Occidental Petroleum	$41.7 million
4. Bob Nardelli	Home Depot	$39.5 million
5. Edward Zander	Motorola	$38.9 million

Lowest Paid:

1. Richard Kinder	Kinder Morgan Energy	$1
2. Steve Jobs	Apple Computer	$1
3. Jeff Bezos	Amazon	$81,840
4. Warren Buffet	Berkshire Hathaway	$311,000
5. Paul Anderson	Duke Energy	$365,296

Source: Fortune magazine, May 2, 2005. The article includes salary, bonus, all stock grants, and other perks. Here I have included the first group, who appear to work primarily for salary, as *employees,* and the second group, who choose compensation in other forms, such as stock grants and other perks, as *owners* in the business.

Are You an Entrepreneur?

As you can tell, there are differences between employees and entrepreneurs. The purpose of this book is to go deeper into those differences so you can decide, before you quit your job, if being an entrepreneur is the path for you.

In Conclusion

In my opinion the biggest difference between an entrepreneur and an employee is found in the differences between the desire for security and the desire for freedom.

My rich dad said, "If you become a successful entrepreneur, you will come to know a freedom very few people will ever know. It is not simply a matter of having a lot of money or free time. It is the freedom from the fear of fear itself."

"Freedom from the fear of fear?" I asked.

Nodding, he continued, "When you look under the covers of the word *security*, you find *fear* hiding there. This is the reason most people say, 'Get a good education.' It's not out of the love of study or scholarship, it is out of fear—the fear you won't get a good job, or be able to earn money. Look at how a teacher motivates students in school—it is motivation by fear. They say, 'If you don't study you will fail.' So they motivate students to study by the fear of failing. When the student graduates and gets a job, once again the motivation is fear. Employers say verbally or nonverbally, 'If you don't do your job, you'll be fired.' The employee works harder out of fear, the fear of not putting food on the table, the fear of not having money to make the mortgage payments. The reason people crave security is fear. The problem with security is that it does not cure fear. It simply throws a blanket over the fear, but the fear is always there, like the boogeyman chuckling under the bed."

Being in high school at the time, I could really relate to the idea of studying out of fear. "In school, I only study because I am afraid of failing. I do not study because I want to learn. I am so afraid of failing I study subjects I know I will never use."

Nodding, rich dad said, "Studying for security is not the same as studying for your freedom. People who study for freedom study different subjects than people who study for security."

"Why don't they offer a choice of study in school?" I asked.

"I don't know," said rich dad. "The problem with studying for security is that the fear is always there, and if the fear is always there, then you rarely feel secure, so you buy more insurance and think of ways to protect yourself. You always quietly worry, even if you pretend you're successful and have nothing to worry about. The worst thing about living a life of security is that you often lead two lives—the life you live and the unlived life you know you could be living. Those are some of the problems with studying for security. The biggest problem of all is that the fear is still there."

"So becoming an entrepreneur means you will not have any fear?" I asked.

"Of course not!" smiled rich dad. "Only fools believe they have no fear. Fear is always present. Anyone who says he or she doesn't have fear is out of touch with reality. What I said is, 'Freedom from the fear of fear.' In other words, you don't have to be afraid of fear, you don't have to be a prisoner of fear, fear will not define your world, as it does most people's worlds. Instead of fearing fear, you will learn to confront fear and use it to your advantage. Instead of quitting because your business is out of money, because you are afraid of not being able to pay your bills, being a true entrepreneur will give you the courage to go forward, to think clearly, to study, to read, to talk to new people, to come up with new ideas and new actions. The desire for freedom can give you the courage to operate for years without needing a secure job or a steady paycheck. That is the kind of freedom I am talking about. It is the freedom from the fear of fear. We all have fear—the difference is whether fear causes us to seek security or to seek freedom. An employee will seek security; an entrepreneur will seek freedom."

"So if security is the result of fear, what is the driving force behind freedom?" I asked.

"Courage," smiled rich dad. "The word courage comes from the French word, *le coeur*—the heart." He paused for a moment and then finished this conversation by saying, "Your answer for choosing to be an entrepreneur or an employee is found in your heart."

Freedom Is More Important than Life

One of my favorite movies of all times is the classic *Easy Rider,* starring Peter Fonda, Dennis Hopper, and Jack Nicholson. In one of the scenes, just before Jack Nicholson is killed, he talks with Dennis Hopper about freedom. I believe it is appropriate to end this introduction with those lines, because it is why I chose to be an entrepreneur. I chose to be an entrepreneur to be free. For me, freedom is more important than life itself.

In this scene, the three of them are camped in a swamp after being teased, threatened, and run out of town by a bunch of good ole boys.

DENNIS HOPPER: "They're scared, man."

JACK NICHOLSON: "Oh they're not scared of you. They're scared of what you represent to them."

D.H.: "All we represent to them is somebody who needs a haircut."

J.N.: "Oh no. What you represent to them is freedom."

D.H.: "What the hell is wrong with freedom . . . man? That's what it's all about."

J.N.: "Oh yeah. That's right. That's what it's all about all right. But talking about it and being it—that's two different things. I mean it's real hard to be free when you're bought and sold in the marketplace. Of course don't ever tell anybody that they're not free because they're going to get real busy killing and maiming to prove to you that they are. Oh yeah, they're going to talk to you and talk to you and talk to you about individual freedom. But when they see a free individual it's going to scare them."

D.H.: "Well it don't make them running scared."

J.N.: "No . . . it makes them dangerous."

Right after this scene, the three of them are ambushed and beaten by the same good ole boys. Nicholson's character dies and Fonda and Hopper ride on, eventually to be killed, not by the same good ole boys, but by other good ole boys who share the same philosophy.

While the movie has different messages for different people, for me the movie was about the courage it takes to be free—the freedom to be yourself, regardless of whether you are an entrepreneur or an employee.

This rest of this book is dedicated to your freedom.

Get Started Today!

As a way of saying "Thank You" for reading this book,
we offer you the following free downloadable audio program.

"My Most Important Marketing Secrets."

Learn the marketing tips and strategies that I have found successful in
creating and building multimillion-dollar businesses

All you have to do to get this audio report is visit our website
www.richdad.com/beforeyouquityourjob
and the program is yours free.

In Addition:

You will find special resources to help you apply the principles from this book.
By actively applying the principles, you can make them a powerful reality in
your own life.

If you are serious about being a successful entrepreneur,
visit **www.richdad.com/beforeyouquityourjob** to find these resources now.

Thank you!

A Successful Business Is Created Before There Is a Business.

Chapter 1

What Is the Difference Between an Employee and an Entrepreneur?

Starting with the Right Mind-set

When I was growing up, my poor dad often said, "Go to school, get good grades, so you can find a good job with good benefits." He was encouraging me to become an *employee*.

My rich dad often said, "Learn to build your own business and hire good people." He was encouraging me to become an *entrepreneur.*

One day I asked my rich dad what the difference was between an employee and an entrepreneur. His reply was, "Employees look for a job after the business is built. An entrepreneur's work begins *before* there is a business."

99% Failure Rate

Statistics show that 90% of all new businesses fail within the first five years. Statistics also show that 90% of the 10% that survive the first five years, fail before their tenth anniversary. In other words, approximately 99% of all startup businesses fail within ten years. Why? While the reasons are many, the following are some of the more critical ones.

1. Our schools train students to be employees who look for jobs rather than train entrepreneurs who create jobs and businesses.
2. The skills to be a good employee are *not* the same skills required to be a good entrepreneur.
3. Many entrepreneurs fail to build a business. Instead they work hard building a job that they own. They become self-employed rather than business owners.
4. Many entrepreneurs work longer hours and are paid less per hour than their employees. Hence, many quit out of exhaustion.
5. Many new entrepreneurs start without enough real life experience and without enough capital.
6. Many entrepreneurs have a great product or service but don't have the business skills to build a successful business around that product or service.

Laying the Foundation for Success

My rich dad said, "Starting a business is like jumping out of an airplane without a parachute. In midair the entrepreneur begins building a parachute and hopes it opens before hitting the ground." He also said, "If the entrepreneur hits the ground before building a parachute, it is very tough climbing back into the plane and trying again."

For those of you familiar with the rich dad books, you know that I have jumped out of the plane many times and failed to build the parachute. The good news is that I hit the ground and bounced. This book will share with you some of my jumps, falls, and bounces. Many of my failures and successes were small ones, so the bounce was not that painful—that is, until I started my nylon and Velcro wallet business. I will go into further detail throughout the book because I made many mistakes, and learned from them along the way. The success of that business was sky high and so was the fall. It took me over a year to recover from that powerful bounce. The good news is that it was the best business experience of my life. I learned much about business and about myself through the process of rebuilding.

The Crack in the Dam

One of the reasons I fell so hard in the nylon surfer wallet business was that I did not pay attention to the little things. There is some truth to the age-old statement, "The bigger they are, the harder they fall." My little surfer wallet business grew so fast that the business was a lot bigger than the capabilities of the three entrepreneurs who created the business. Instead of creating a business, we had created Dr. Frankenstein's monster and did not realize it. In other words, our sudden success was accelerating our failures. The real problem was we did not know we were failing. We thought we were successful. We thought we were rich. We thought we were geniuses. To the extent that we bothered to consult expert advisors (like patent attorneys), we did not listen to them.

As three successful entrepreneurs in our late twenties and early thirties, we took our minds off the business and partied into the night. We actually thought we had built a business. We actually thought we were entrepreneurs. We actually believed our own story of success. We started bragging. Champagne started to flow. It was not long before we each had fast sports cars and were dating even faster women. Success and money had blinded us. We could not see the cracks forming in the wall of the dam.

Finally, the dam broke. The house of cards started tumbling down around us. Our parachute did not open.

Too Much Success

The point in sharing my entrepreneurial stupidity is that many people think that it is the *lack of success* that kills a business. And in many cases that is true. The failure of my surfer wallet business was a valuable experience because I found out early in my career as an entrepreneur that *too much success* can also kill a business. The point I am making is that a poorly conceived business can fail whether it is initially successful or not.

Hard Work Covers Up Poor Design

A poorly conceived business startup *may be* able to survive as long as the entrepreneur works hard and holds the business together with sheer determination. In other words, hard work can cover up a poorly designed business and keep it from failing. The world is filled with millions of small business entrepreneurs who are able to keep their leaky business afloat with hard work, sheer willpower, duct tape, and baling wire. The problem is, if they stop working, the business breaks apart and sinks.

All over the world, entrepreneurs kiss their families good-bye and head off to their own businesses, their pieces of the rock. Many of them go to work, thinking that working harder and longer will solve their business problems—problems such as not enough sales, unhappy employees, incompetent advisors, not enough free cash flow to grow the business, suppliers' raising their prices, insurance premiums' going up, landlords' raising the rent, changing government regulations, government inspectors, increasing taxes, back taxes, unhappy customers, nonpaying customers, and not enough time in the day, to name a few of the daily challenges. Many entrepreneurs do not realize that many of the problems their businesses face today began yesterday, long before there was a business.

One of the primary reasons for the high failure rate of small businesses is sheer exhaustion. It's tough to make money and to keep going when so much of your time is tied up in activities that do not make you any money or that cost you money without offsetting income. If you are thinking about starting your own business, before you quit your job, you might want to talk to an entrepreneur about how much time he or she spends on non–income-producing activities to run his or her business. Also ask how he or she handles this challenge.

As a friend of mine once said, "I'm so busy taking care of my business I don't have time to make any money."

Do Long Hours and Hard Work Guarantee Success?

A friend of mine quit his high-paying job with a large bank in Honolulu and opened a tiny lunch shop in the industrial part of town. He had always wanted to be his own boss and do his own thing. As a loan officer for the bank, he saw that the richest customers of the bank were entrepreneurs, and he wanted a piece of the action, so he quit his job and went for his dreams.

Every morning, he and his mom would get up at four o'clock to begin preparing for the lunch crowd. The two of them worked very hard, scrimping, cutting corners, in order to serve great-tasting lunches with generous portions at low prices.

For years I would stop by, have lunch, and find out how they were doing. They seemed very happy, enjoying their customers and their work. "Someday we'll expand," said my friend. "Someday we'll hire people to do the hard work for us." The problem was that someday never came. His mom passed away, the business closed, and my friend took a job as a manager of a fast-food franchise restaurant. He returned to being an employee. The last time I saw him he said, "The pay isn't great but at least the hours are better." In his case, his parachute did not open. He hit the ground before he built a business.

Now I can hear some of you saying, "At least he went for it." Or, "It was just bad luck. If his mom had lived, they might have expanded and gone on to make a lot of money." Or, "How can you criticize such good hardworking people?" And I agree with these sentiments. My intent is not to criticize them. Although not related to them, I loved the two of them dearly. I knew they were happy yet it pained me to see them work so hard and not get ahead, day after day. I only relate this story to make the same point. The business began to fail *before* there was a business. It was poorly conceived before he quit his job.

Is Being an Entrepreneur for You?

If this story about working long hours or failing if unsuccessful and possibly failing if successful or jumping out of a plane without a parachute and bouncing frightens you, then being an entrepreneur may not be for you.

But if the stories intrigue you or challenge you, then read on. After finishing this book, at least you will have a better idea of what entrepreneurs need to know to succeed. You will also have a better understanding of how to create, design, and build a business that grows with or without you, and possibly makes you rich beyond your wildest dreams. After all, if you are going to jump out of a plane without a parachute, you may as well win big if you are going to win at all.

The Job of an Entrepreneur

The most important job of the entrepreneur begins before there is a business or employees. The job of an entrepreneur is to design a business that can grow, employ many people, add value to its customers, be a responsible corporate citizen, bring prosperity to all those that work on the business, be charitable, and eventually no longer need the entrepreneur. Before there is a business, a successful entrepreneur is designing this type of business in his or her mind's eye. According my rich dad, this is the job of a true entrepreneur.

Failing Leads to Success

After one of my demoralizing business failures, I went to rich dad and asked, "So what did I do wrong? I thought I designed it well."

"Obviously you didn't," rich dad said with a smirk.

"How many times do I have to do this? I'm the biggest failure I know."

Rich dad said, "Losers quit when they fail. Winners fail until they succeed." Shuffling the papers at his desk for a moment, he then looked up at me and said, "The world is filled with want-to-be entrepreneurs. They sit behind desks, have important sounding titles like vice-president, branch manager, or supervisor, and some even take home a decent paycheck. These want-to-be entrepreneurs dream of someday starting their own business empire and maybe someday some of them will. Yet I believe most will never make the leap. Most will have some excuse, some rationalization, such as, 'When the kids are grown.' Or, 'I'll go back to school first.' Or, 'When I have enough money saved.'"

"But they never jump from the plane," I said, finishing his thoughts.

Rich dad nodded.

What Kind of Entrepreneur Do You Want to Be?

Rich dad went on to explain that the world was filled with different types of entrepreneurs. There are entrepreneurs who are big and small, rich and poor, honest and crooked, for-profit and not-for-profit, saint and sinner, small town and international, and successes and failures. He said, "The word entrepreneur is a big word and it means different things to different people."

The CASHFLOW Quadrant

As I mentioned in the introduction, the CASHFLOW Quadrant explains that there are four different types of people that make up the world of business and they are often technically, emotionally, and mentally different people.

E stands for *employee*.

S stands for *self-employed* or *small business owner*.

B stands for *big business owner (over five hundred employees)*.

I stands for *investor*.

For example, an employee will always say the same words, whether he or she is the president or janitor of the company. An employee can always be heard saying, "I'm looking for a safe secure job with benefits." The operative words are safe and secure. In other words, the emotion of *fear* often keeps them boxed in that quadrant. If they want to change quadrants, not only are there skills and technical things to learn, in many cases there are also emotional challenges to overcome.

A person in the S quadrant may be heard saying, "If you want it done right, do it yourself." In many cases this person's challenge is learning to trust other people to do a better job than he or she can. This lack of trust often keeps them small, since it's hard to grow a business without eventually trusting other people. If S quadrant people do grow, they often grow as a partnership, which in many cases is a group of Ss binding together to do the same job.

B quadrant people are always looking for good people and good business systems. They do not necessarily want to do the work. They want to build a business to do the work. A true B Quadrant entrepreneur can grow his or her business all over the world. An S quadrant entrepreneur is often restricted to a small area, an area he or she can personally control. Of course, there are always exceptions.

An I quadrant person, the investor, is looking for a smart S or B to take care of his or her money and grow it.

In training his son and me, rich dad was training us to first build a successful S quadrant business that had the capability of expanding into a successful B quadrant business. That is what this book is about.

What Kind of Business Do You Want to Build?

As part of my entrepreneurial training with rich dad, he encouraged his son and me to go out and study as many different types of business systems as we could. He said, "How can you be an entrepreneur designing a business if you do not know about the different types of businesses and entrepreneurs?"

Self-Employed Entrepreneurs

Rich dad was adamant in explaining that many entrepreneurs were not business owners but self-employed entrepreneurs—entrepreneurs who owned a job, not a business. He said, "You are probably self-employed when your name is the name of the business; your income stops if you stop working; if clients come to see you; your employees call you if there is a problem. You may also be self-employed if you are the smartest, most talented, or the best-educated person in your business."

He had nothing against self-employed entrepreneurs. He simply wanted us to know the difference between entrepreneurs who own businesses and those who own jobs. Consultants, musicians, actors, cleaning people, restaurant owners, small shop owners, and most small business people fall into owning jobs instead of businesses, or the S quadrant.

The main point rich dad was making about the difference between a self-employed entrepreneur and a big-business entrepreneur was that many self-employed businesses have a tough time growing into a big business. In other words they have a real challenge going from the S quadrant to the B quadrant. Why? Again the answer is that the business was poorly designed before there was a business. It was doomed before it was even started.

Rich dad himself started out as a self-employed entrepreneur in the S quadrant. Yet in his mind, he was designing a very large business, run by people much smarter and more capable than him. Before he started his business, he designed his S quadrant business to be able to grow into the B quadrant.

Professionals and Tradespeople

He also wanted us to know that many professional people such as doctors, lawyers, accountants, architects, plumbers, and electricians started a self-employed style of business based on a profession or a technical trade. Many of these professions and trades require government licenses to operate.

Also included in this category are professional salespeople, many of whom are licensed independent consultants, such as real estate, insurance, and securities salespeople. Many of these types of people are technically self-employed entrepreneurs, aka independent contractors.

The problem with this type of business is that there is not really a business to sell because there really isn't a business outside the individual owner. In many cases, there really isn't an asset. *The business owner is the asset.* If he or she does sell, he or she will not typically get the higher multiples a true B quadrant business can command. In addition, he or she may have to agree to "stay on" for the successful continuation of the business. *In essence they go from being the owner to the buyer's employee.*

In my rich dad's mind, it made no sense to work hard and not build an asset. This is why he advised his son and me against ever wanting to become employees. He said, "Why work hard building nothing?"

Later in this book, we will go into some ways this type of entrepreneur can create a business asset—an asset they can build and maybe sell someday.

Mom and Pop Operations

A very large category of entrepreneurs is often referred to as *Mom and Pop* businesses. This type of business gets its name because many small businesses are family businesses. As an example, my mom's mom owned a little convenience store that the family took turns working in.

The challenge for growth in a Mom and Pop operation is nepotism. Many people put their children in charge of the business, even though their children may be incompetent, because *blood is thicker than water.* Often the children don't share the passion for the business that their parents had or they don't have the entrepreneurial drive to lead the business.

Franchises

A franchise, such as McDonald's, is in theory a turnkey operation. The entrepreneur sells a ready-made business to a person who does not want to go through the creative and development phase of starting a business. It's like being an instant entrepreneur. One advantage to some franchises is that banks are more inclined to lend money to someone who wants to buy a franchise than to a person who wants to start a business from scratch. The banks are more comfortable with the successful track record of other similar franchises and the banks value the mentoring programs that most franchises have to assist the new entrepreneur.

One of the biggest problems with big-name franchises is that they are generally more expensive to get into and have little flexibility for a want-to-be entrepreneur. Franchises are the type of businesses that typically face legal issues and often end up in court. These fights are some of the most vicious fights in the business world.

Reportedly one of the main reasons for fighting is that people who buy a franchise business do not want to run it the way the franchisor, the person who created the business, wants them to run it. Another reason is if the franchise does not do well financially, the franchisee wants to blame the franchisor for the lack of business success. If you do not want to follow the directions of the franchisor to a tee, it is best you design, create, and start your own business.

Network Marketing and Direct Sales

The network marketing and direct sales industry is recognized by many to be the fastest-growing business model in the world today. It is also the most controversial. Many people still have a negative reaction, claiming that many network marketing organizations are pyramid schemes. Yet in reality, the biggest pyramid scheme in the world is the traditional big business corporation, with one person at the top and all the workers below.

Everyone who wants to be an entrepreneur should take a look at a network marketing business. Some of the biggest Fortune 500 companies, such as CitiBank, Avon, Levis, and Smith Barney, distribute their products through a network marketing or direct sales system.

We are not members of any one network marketing or direct marketing business, but we do speak favorably of the industry. People who want to be entrepreneurs should consider joining one of these businesses before they quit their jobs. Why? Many of these companies provide essential sales, business-building, and leadership skills not found anywhere else. One of the most valuable benefits from associating with a reputable organization is that it teaches the *mind-set* as well as the *courage* required to become an entrepreneur. You will also become more familiar with the systems required to build a successful business. The entry fee is typically quite reasonable and the education can be priceless. (To further explain the educational value of such types of business, we wrote a small book entitled *The Business School: For People Who Like Helping People* [Warner Books]. For more information on this book, please go to our website, www.richdad.com.)

If I were starting my entrepreneurial career all over again, I would start with a network marketing or direct sales business, not for the money but for the real world business training I could receive, training similar to the type of training my rich dad gave me.

Legal Thieves

One of the more interesting discussions Mike and I had with rich dad involved the subject of entrepreneurs stealing from other entrepreneurs. Rich dad

ng for an accounting firm as an example. One day
, an employee of the firm, resigned and started his
its he met while an employee of the firm. In other
walked out the firm's door, but took the business with
While this may not be illegal, it still is stealing." While this
ess design, it is definitely not the kind of entrepreneur he
wante.   me to be.

Creative Entrepreneurs

The type of entrepreneur he wanted us to be was a creative entrepreneur like
Thomas Edison, Walt Disney, or Steven Jobs. Rich dad said, "It is easy to be a
small entrepreneur, like a Mom and Pop sandwich shop. It is also relatively
easy to be an entrepreneur in a trade or a profession, such as a plumber or
dentist. Also it is easy to be a competitive entrepreneur, someone who sees a
good idea, copies the idea, and then competes against the entrepreneur who
created the idea." (In the Rich Dad's Advisors book *Protecting Your #1 Asset*
[Warner Books], Michael Lechter refers to this type of competitor as "spoilers" and "pirates.") This is what happened to me when I pioneered the nylon
and Velcro wallet business. Once we created the market and the awareness of
this new product line, competitors came out of the woodwork and my little
business was squashed. Of course I cannot blame them. I can only blame myself because once again, I designed the business poorly before there was a
business.

Even though I took a pounding, rich dad was happy that I was learning to
be a creative entrepreneur, rather than a competitive one. He said, "Some entrepreneurs win by creating. Other entrepreneurs win by copying and competing." He also said, "The riskiest of all types of entrepreneur is the creative
entrepreneur, also known as an innovator."

"Why is the creative entrepreneur the riskiest type to be?" I asked.

"Because being creative means you are often a pioneer. It is easy to copy
a successful and proven product. It is also less risky. If you learn to innovate,
create, or invent your way to success, you are an entrepreneur creating new
value rather than an entrepreneur who wins by copying."

Public and Private

The vast majority of businesses large and small are *private* companies. A large private company is often referred to as a *closely held* company. That generally means a company owned by just a few owners, and ownership interests are not available to the public at large.

A public company is a company that sells shares of the business to the public at large, most often through stockbrokers and other licensed securities dealers. A public company sells its shares on a stock exchange like the New York Stock Exchange and operates under much more stringent rules than private companies.

Rich dad never formed a public company, yet he recommended that Mike and I create one, as part of our development as entrepreneurs. In 1996, at the same time we were forming The Rich Dad Company, I was also an investor and involved in forming three public companies. One company was created to explore for oil, one for gold, and one for silver. The oil company failed even though it struck oil, which is a story in itself. The gold and silver companies did find substantial amounts of the gold and silver they were looking for. Although the oil company failed, the gold and silver companies made the investors a lot of money.

Working on developing the public companies was a great experience. As rich dad suggested, I learned a lot and became a better entrepreneur in the process. I found out that the rules are a lot tougher for a public company, that a public company is actually two different companies serving two different customers—the real customers and the investors—as well as serving two bosses, the board of directors and the government securities agency, such as the SEC, the Securities Exchange Commission. I also found out about tougher accounting standards and tougher reporting standards.

When I was first starting out as an entrepreneur, rich dad said, "The dream of many entrepreneurs is to see the company they formed listed on the stock exchange." Yet, after the Enron, Arthur Anderson, Worldcom, and Martha Stewart scandals the rules became tighter and the compliance requirements much more complicated and expensive. The government was breathing down public companies' backs. Building a public company business wasn't as much fun as I had expected. Even though I learned a lot, made myself and our investors a lot of money, became a better entrepreneur, learned how to design a public company, and was glad I went through the learning process, I doubt if I will ever form a public company again. That type of business is for a different type of entrepreneur. I can make more money and have more fun in small closely held private businesses. (If you are interested in more information on the pros and cons of private businesses and public companies we recommend the Rich Dad's Advisors book *OPM: Other People's Money*, by Michael Lechter (Warner Business Books, 2005).

Can Anyone Be an Entrepreneur?

Rich dad wanted his son and me to understand that anyone could be an entrepreneur. Being an entrepreneur was not that special. He did not want the idea of being an entrepreneur to go to our heads. He did not want us looking down on anyone or thinking we were better than other people if we became successful entrepreneurs.

To this he said, "Anyone can be an entrepreneur. Your neighborhood babysitter is an entrepreneur. So was Henry Ford, founder of the Ford Motor Company. Anyone with a little initiative can be an entrepreneur. So don't think entrepreneurs are special or better than other people. Your job is to decide which entrepreneur you most want to be like—the babysitter or Henry Ford? They both provide a valuable product or service. Both are important to their customers. Yet they operate in very different spectrums, different bandwidths of entrepreneurship. It's like the difference between sandlot football, high school football, college football, and professional football."

With that example, I understood the point rich dad was making. When I was in college in New York, playing college football, our team had the opportunity to practice with a few players from a professional football team, the New York Jets. It was a very humbling experience. It was soon obvious to all of us on the college football team that while we played the same game as the pro players, we were playing it at a completely different level of play.

As a linebacker, my first rude awakening was trying to tackle a New York Jets running back coming through the line. I doubt if he even knew I hit him. He ran right over me. It felt like I was trying to tackle a charging rhino. I did not hurt him but he definitely hurt me. That running back and I were about the same size. But after trying to tackle him, I realized the difference was not physical. It was spiritual. He had the heart, the desire, and gift of natural talent to be a great player.

The lesson I learned that day is that we both played the same game, but we were not playing at the same level of play. The same is true in the business world and the game of entrepreneurship. We can all be entrepreneurs. Being an entrepreneur is not that big a deal. A better question to be asked in designing a business is, "At what level of play do you want to play the game?"

Today, older and wiser, I do not have illusions that I would ever be as great an entrepreneur as Thomas Edison, Henry Ford, Steven Jobs, or Walt Disney. Yet I can still learn from them and use them as mentors and role models.

And that is rich dad's entrepreneurial lesson #1: "A successful business is created before there is a business."

The most important job of an entrepreneur is to design the business before there is a business.

Laying the Foundation for Success—Design the Business

Most new entrepreneurs get excited about a new product or an opportunity they think will make them rich. Unfortunately, many of them focus on the product or opportunity rather than invest the time designing the business around the product or opportunity. Before quitting your job, it might be a good idea to study the lives of entrepreneurs and the different types of businesses they created. Also you might want to find a mentor who has been an entrepreneur. All too often, people ask business advice from people who have business experience as an employee but not as an entrepreneur.

Later in this book, we will introduce the B-I Triangle, which outlines what components are required to create any business, regardless if it is big or small, franchise or individually owned, Mom and Pop or publicly owned. Once a person understands the different components that make up a business it becomes much easier to design businesses as well as evaluate good ones and bad ones.

Also, we always recommend keeping your daytime job while starting a part-time business—not for the money but for the experience. That means, even if your part-time business does not make any money, you are gaining something far more important than money—real life experience. Not only will you learn about business, you will learn a lot about yourself.

A Bonus

One of the reasons for the success of The Rich Dad Company was that the business was started by three already successful entrepreneurs, Sharon, Kim, and me. Each of us brought our own experiences and perspectives to the team. Sharon came from the background of the proverbial A student, a certified public accountant who had migrated into the realm of entrepreneurship. She had started and grown several companies of her own prior to starting The Rich Dad Company with Kim and me. As a bonus for you, Sharon will provide her unique perspective and will share her own insights and experiences related to each lesson.

SHARON'S INSIGHTS

Lesson #1: A Successful Business Is Created Before There Is a Business.

The path to entrepreneurship is like a trek through the wilderness. If you want to survive and successfully reach your destination you must prepare beforehand. Before you go hiking through the woods, you pack carefully to make sure that you have all of the things you need to survive the trip. You think about the obstacles and dangers that you are likely to encounter. You check the weather report. You make sure you bring the right clothing, equipment, food, and water. The journey into entrepreneurship requires the same sort of careful planning. What preparation is necessary to put yourself in the best position to succeed?

- *You start by being sure that you have the right mind-set—that you think like an entrepreneur instead of an employee.*
- *You do your homework—study the market, your target customers, and the competition.*
- *You identify the skills needed for a successful business in that market, and assemble a team of coventurers and advisors that provide the skills you need.*
- *You identify some advantage over the competition and ways to distinguish yourself from them in the minds of potential customers.*
- *You put together a business plan mapping out your route to success.*
- *You lay the proper legal foundation for your business.*

What do we mean by legal foundation? Here are some examples:

- *You choose a form of legal entity for the business that provides the best limitation of liability and minimizes taxes (refer to Garrett Sutton's Rich Dad Advisor book* Own Your Own Corporation, *Warner Books).*
- *You obtain all necessary licenses and permits, making sure that clear and complete written agreements are in place to avoid any future misunderstandings.*
- *You put the appropriate legal protections in place so that you can sustain your competitive advantage. As my husband, Michael Lechter, puts it: You build a fort around your intellectual property so that you can fight off the spoilers and pirates among your competitors (refer to Michael's Rich Dad Advisor book* Protecting Your #1 Asset, *Warner Books).*

ENTREPRENEUR VERSUS EMPLOYEE

What are the characteristics of an entrepreneur? How does an entrepreneur differ from someone with an employee mentality? Certainly, a willingness to take calculated risks is one element. Another element is a willingness to fly in the face of conventional wisdom. As Michael also likes to say, an entrepreneur will "suspend disbelief" and try something even when all the people around him or her say that it can't be done.

However, from my perspective, the defining characteristics of true entrepreneurs are creativity and the ability to accomplish things beyond their own resources. They are masters at solving problems, converting those problems into valuable intellectual property, then leveraging the intellectual property into a business. They are masters at using other people's money and other people's resources. An entrepreneur's mantra is, "Let's figure out how we can do it," and never are heard the discouraging words, "We can't do it," or, "We can't afford it."

GETTING STARTED

Create a Business or Buy a Business?

I can't tell you how many people tell us that they want to start their own business. Most often the conversation goes something like:

"Sharon, I am so excited about starting my own business," Susan says.

I reply, "Wonderful, what type of business are you interested in?"

Without hesitation Susan answers, "I want a business that provides good cash flow and that my employees can run, so I have a lot of free time to spend with my family. Oh, and I don't want to have to pay a lot for it."

At this point, I know that Susan is not really an entrepreneur and may not be able to become one. She truly does not understand the commitment required to build a successful business. Her comments, "I don't want to have to pay a lot for it," and, "I want a business that provides a good cash flow," tell me that she really wants to acquire a business that has already been built by a successful entrepreneur. The value has already been created by the seller. The seller is entitled to compensation from Susan for the value created. She will have to pay for that existing value. In this case, unless Susan knows how and is able to take this business to the next level or knows how to enter a new market, she is buying a job, not creating a business.

There is a big difference between being an entrepreneur who creates and builds a business and buying a business. In the example with Susan, it is clear that she wants to "buy" a business, not "create" a business.

There is nothing wrong with buying a business. However, it is CREATION that energizes an entrepreneur. To build a business from nothing that is successful, creates value, and is sustainable is the true goal of an entrepreneur. It is the CREATION part that provides maximum leverage and sometimes essentially infinite return on investment. When you buy someone else's creation, typically they, not you, achieve the leverage. Of course, that does not mean that the acquisition of an existing business is "wrong," particularly if you are bringing in additional talent or something to the table to take the business to the next level, or when the acquired business is only one component of a larger plan.

For example, the purchase of a franchise is not the "end game" for a true entrepreneur. A franchise may well be a great stepping stone—a source of education for an entrepreneur—but there is typically little room in a franchise for entrepreneurship and entrepreneurial efforts. When someone (the franchisee) buys a franchise, he or she is buying the right to use goodwill and business systems that have already been developed in connection with someone else's (the franchisor's) business (and sometimes the right to participate in collective marketing or purchasing programs). One advantage of a franchise business is that it has immediate credibility (with, for example, lenders) because the systems have already been tested and proven to work by the franchisor. (Of course, in order for the franchise to be successful, the franchisee must contribute significant efforts.)

However, consistency from franchise to franchise is one of the primary factors that makes franchising viable. In fact, the franchisor is, as a matter of law, required to control the way the franchise does business, or the franchisor will lose valuable rights. While there are some franchisors that will agree to adopt suggestions from their franchisees, it is the franchisor that makes the ultimate decisions. This tends to leave very little room for creativity on the part of the franchisee, and can sometimes be stifling to his or her entrepreneurial spirit.

From a Franchisor

With all of our franchises over the years I have noticed that there are four big-picture issues. Understanding the relationship among these four issues is what I focus on in training new franchisees.

1. Words: What words drive the way our franchise is heading?

How do I greet my customers? How do I sell to the customer? What words are used to conduct the business and establish its culture?

The Words in and of a business always tell you a story.

2. Numbers: What numbers do I use to test the words that I'm using?

Sales talk and blue sky floats by. How much time, how many sales leads, what is the cost, can I measure the in- and outflows of my cash?

The Numbers measure the franchise story.

3. Symbols: What are the symbols that I want the world to see representing the business?

Words, numbers, and/or pictures can be symbols, logos, uniforms, people—anything that leverages who and what your franchise is.

Symbols leverage your franchise story.

4. Focused action: This is the driver of all franchise and business stories. This is what makes or breaks any business. What am I doing? No matter what you are doing, it will work for you or against you in building your franchise.

I have come up with a formula that I use in all the businesses that I design to combine the impact of these four issues:

(Words + numbers) $\times$ symbols / focus

The bottom line is that a franchisee must focus on the established business systems, including what words they use, how their numbers perform, and the symbols they use in order to reach their greatest success in the franchise. One of the greatest benefits of buying a franchise is that the franchisor has already established the successful track record of the business system.

Kelly Ritchie
Franchise Control Systems

Create a Business or Create a Job?

Robert talks about the self-employed entrepreneur who builds a small business around him- or herself. This is probably an entrepreneur who owns a job, not a business. Rich dad has a rule of thumb about this distinction between a job and a business. If you can leave your business for a year and come back and find it stronger and bigger, you have created a big business, a B quadrant business. If you cannot, you may have created a job, or an S quadrant small business. For example, many lawyers or accountants become so successful that their clients *only* want to do business with them. The more successful they become, the less time they have. They own a job, not a business. There's a distinct difference between the two.

This is not to say that you cannot build a business around your expertise and creativity. You simply have to find a way to leverage your expertise and creativity—create systems that let others (your employees or coventurers) apply your expertise and creativity.

WHAT IS YOUR PERSONAL REASON FOR STARTING A BUSINESS?

As we begin this book about becoming an entrepreneur, it is important to understand your personal motivation for wanting to build a business. Ask yourself the following questions:

1. Why do I want to own my own business?
2. How badly do I want to own my own business?
3. At what level of play do I want to play the game?
4. At what level of play am I willing to extend myself to play the game?
5. Am I willing to spend the time to learn about other successful entrepreneurs and their businesses?
6. Am I afraid to fail?
7. Can I turn my fear of failing into a strength that will help me drive the business?
8. Can I learn from my mistakes?
9. Can I build a team, or do I like to work by myself?
10. Am I willing to pay the price?
11. Am I willing to put in the time now to be rewarded later?
12. Am I willing to delay financial rewards until the business succeeds, or do I need a paycheck?

As you are answering these questions, if you are still determined to start a business, take it one step further and ask yourself the following questions:

- *What have been your greatest successes?*
- *What have been your greatest failures?*
- *How many times have you worked for free?*
- *Would you work for this company even if you were not paid?*
- *Are your family and friends emotionally supportive of your efforts in this venture?*
- *Are you willing to educate yourself in all the areas of the B-I Triangle (essential components of a successful business—to be discussed and reviewed throughout this book)?*

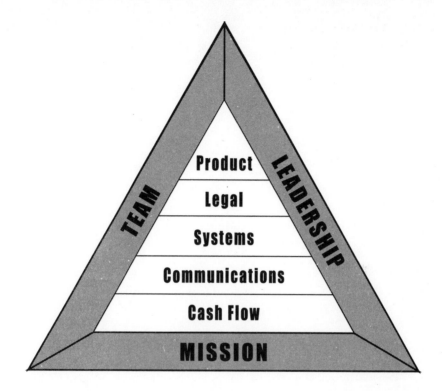

If after answering all of these questions you are still eager to become an entrepreneur, you may have just what it takes to be a very successful entrepreneur.

Congratulations for seeking freedom!

Learn How to Turn Bad Luck Into Good Luck.

*The irony is that what makes people smart
also makes them less smart—that is,
they learn from their mistakes.*

Chapter 2

Dumb and Dumber Gets Rich and Richer

My First Business

My first business failed in 1956. I was nine years old.

My second business succeeded in 1956. I was still nine years old. If not for the failure of my first business, my second business would not have succeeded.

Failing as a Strategy

Failing in business early in life was a defining experience. It was instrumental in developing a success strategy for my future. At the age of nine, I started to realize that making mistakes was the best way for me to learn about business. Although I did not make much money, I realized that the smarter I became by failing and learning from those failures, the richer I would become. Today in business, I will often do something, knowing I might fail. Why? *Because at the age of nine, I learned that failing was essential to succeeding.*

There are two primary reasons why entrepreneurs fail. One is that the would-be entrepreneur is so afraid of failing he or she freezes, and then does nothing. He or she gets up and goes to work—always with some excuse why he or she is not ready to quit his or her job and start his or her business. The usual excuses include not enough money, too risky, the time is not right, kids to feed, and many others.

The second reason entrepreneurs fail is that they do not fail enough. Many small business owners and self-employed business owners succeed to a point and then stop growing. The business plateaus or begins to die. The business reaches a certain size and then fails to grow. Once again, the entrepreneur needs to risk failing before the business can begin growing.

The fear of failing is the primary reason why so many people do not succeed in life or are not as successful as they would like to be. This occurs not only in business, it occurs in all aspects of life. I remember in high school never going on a date because I was so afraid of being rejected. Finally, just before graduating, I asked a beautiful classmate for a date to the senior prom, and to my surprise, she said, "Yes." We had a miserable time but at least I was making progress.

Another Difference between an Employee and an Entrepreneur

Recently, during a radio interview, I was called a "risk taker" by a radio host. In response, I replied, "In today's rapidly changing world the people who are *not* taking risks are the risk takers. People who are *not* taking risks are falling behind."

The program was a half-hour show that regularly interviewed different people from different walks of life. It could have been called *The Secret to My Success* show. When the host asked me for my secret, I told her about my first business failure at the age of nine and how that failure led to the success of my second business. I then said, "I realized that failing was the way to success."

"You learned this at nine?" the host asked.

"That's correct," I replied. "Like most people, I do not like failing. I hate it. Yet, that business failure early in life gave me a glimpse into the future. I saw my process for success. Some people get ahead by knowing all the right answers. These people generally do well in school. That is not my process. I get ahead by failing. That is why I have started so many different businesses. More have failed than succeeded. Yet the ones that have succeeded have been pretty big successes, like the success of The Rich Dad Company, my real estate company, and the two public gold- and silver-mining companies I helped found. Also, I did not make much money early in my career as an entrepreneur, but now later in life I make more money than most people."

"So the secret to your business success is being willing to make mistakes and then learning from them."

"Yes. That is my job as an entrepreneur. My job is to set new goals, create a plan, make mistakes, and risk failing. The more mistakes I make, the smarter I become and hopefully the company grows and prospers from the lessons learned."

"I'd get fired if I made too many mistakes on the job," replied the radio interviewer. "To me, making mistakes and failing is *failing*. I do everything possible not to make mistakes. I hate making mistakes. I hate feeling stupid. I must know the answers. I feel it is important to do everything the right way, the way the company tells me to do it."

"And that is why you are a good employee," I replied kindly. "Employees are hired to *not* make mistakes. An employee's job is to follow the rules, do as they are told; do their job the right way. If employees want to do things *their own* way or they do not follow the rules, or make too many mistakes, they are fired because they are not doing the job they were hired to do."

"So my job as an employee is to *not* take risks and your job as an entrepreneur *is* to take risks, to make mistakes, to sometimes fail. Is that what you are saying?"

"Yes," I replied. "That difference is the key difference between an entrepreneur and an employee."

"So you take risks. Is that what you do as an entrepreneur?"

"No, not quite," I said, chuckling. "I don't randomly take any risk that comes along. First of all, I had to learn the *science of making mistakes* and learning from mistakes. Second, I had to learn how to choose the risks I took. The better my skills as an entrepreneur became, the better my judgment at taking calculated risks. Today, I look at taking risks as part of my job. I do not want my employees to take risks."

"Sounds like a double standard," said the host.

"It's business," I replied. "Failing is not fun but it is necessary for progress."

"So do you like failing?" asked the host.

"No, on the contrary. I hate failing as much as the next person. The difference is I know that failing is part of the process of my businesses success. The moment I fail, I know I am at the point of a breakthrough in learning. It's the point where the *new me* emerges."

"The new you?" shrieked the radio host. "What kind of hocus pocus is that?"

"Well," I replied slowly, "we have all experienced this *new me* experience. For example, when we were babies and could not walk, we stood and fell, stood and fell. Then one day we stopped falling and began to walk. The moment we could walk, we were no longer babies. People called us children, not babies. When we learned to drive a car we became young adults. Each time we learned a new skill a new person emerged and our worlds changed. That is what I mean by a *new you* or a *new me*. We are new because we have new skills and are better able to face a new world."

"So there is a *world* of difference between an employee and an entrepreneur?" asked the host sarcastically.

"Oh, absolutely," I replied, working hard not to get caught up in her skepticism. "We live in very different worlds because we are very different people. One of us lives in a world that thrives on risk. The other lives in a world that avoids risk. Different worlds, different people."

There was a silence for a moment. The host seemed to be gathering her thoughts. "And that is why so many employees do not make it as entrepreneurs?"

"It's one of the reasons but not the only reason," I said gently. "It's not easy transitioning from a world of avoiding mistakes to a world of actively making mistakes."

"But you make it sound easy," said the host. "You seem so nonchalant about failing."

"I never said it was easy, but it does get easier," I replied. "Look, the point is an entrepreneur has a lot to learn and needs to learn quickly. There is not the luxury of a steady paycheck for an entrepreneur. He or she must make mistakes and correct quickly. If he or she avoids making mistakes, or pretends he or she hasn't made a mistake or blames someone else for his or her mistakes, the learning process will overwhelm the entrepreneur and the business fails."

"You have to learn quickly because you're making something out of nothing," added the host. "There is nothing there to support you."

"Especially in the beginning of your development as an entrepreneur. Yet as you get better, you can go from nothing to something very quickly. One of the great joys of being an entrepreneur is the ability to take an idea and turn that idea into a successful business in a short period of time. Centuries ago, alchemists were trying to turn lead into gold. An entrepreneur's job is to turn an idea into gold."

"It's almost money for nothing," said the radio host.

"Almost," I replied. "If you can do that, you'll never need a job. You can go just about anywhere you want in the world and strike it rich. I do business in over eighty countries. One of my mining companies operates in China and the other operates in South America. An employee or a self-employed person's scope of business is often limited to a town, state, or country."

"So it is a different world," conceded the host.

"Yes," I replied. "That is the world of an entrepreneur. If you are good, you are free to travel the world and do business. Most employees need to apply for a work visa before they can work in another country. An entrepreneur may enter a country as a corporation, or form a joint venture with another corporation in that country. Training yourself to be an entrepreneur is developing your potential to access a world of nearly unlimited wealth."

"And to do that, you need to learn to turn your failures into successes."

"That's correct," I replied.

"And what if you fail and lose money?" she asked.

"It's just part of being an entrepreneur. I do not know many entrepreneurs who have not lost money at one time or another."

"But if an employee lost the company's money, the employee would be fired," said the host with an edge in her voice.

"In many companies they would be," I replied quietly. "My point is that it is the fear of losing money that costs people the most money. They are so afraid of losing . . . they lose. They settle for a steady paycheck. They may not lose much money in their life, but they lose out on the potential for great wealth."

Truth During the Commercial Break

"I need to take a commercial break," said the host as she shut down the studio. The sound engineer then took over and began to play the commercials that supported the show.

"I've wanted to quit my job for years," said the host, feeling safer in her soundproof room and not broadcasting to the world.

"But you are paid too much to quit," I said, completing her thoughts.

Nodding, she said, "Yeah, that's it. I'm not paid a lot, just enough so I won't quit and go somewhere else. I need my paycheck. My husband and I make a lot of money but with four kids in school, there is no way we can do what you are talking about."

Although I did not agree with her point of view, I did let her know I understood how she felt.

"So, what would you say to me? How do I break out? I need that paycheck. I need this job, even if it doesn't pay much. I feel I am trapped in a room, with walls that are closing in around me. What can I do?"

Taking a moment to collect my thoughts, I finally asked, "Do you remember the example I used of the baby learning to walk?"

"Yes, I do," said the host. "And once they can walk the baby becomes a child. And once they learn to drive they become a young adult."

"And that is how we learn anything in life. We learn by first having a desire for a change, we want something better. You may have enjoyed your work at one time but now you know it is time for a change, it's time to move on, just as a baby somehow knows it is time to change, it's time to stop crawling. At some magical point in time, the baby knows when the time is right, when it's time to do something different. The baby begins by clinging to something, like a pants leg of a parent or the leg of a table. Babies wobble as they are learning to bridge the gap between crawling and walking. They do this repeatedly, and then one day they let go and fall down. The baby failed. Instead of quitting, which is what many adults would do, the baby repeats the process again and again. Then one day, the baby's mind, body, and spirit come into alignment and the baby can stand. Soon after standing, the baby learns to walk. The baby becomes a child."

"Then comes bicycles and then comes cars," said the host. "Babies become children and children become adults."

I completed the thought by saying, "Yes, and the same process is similar for entrepreneurship. I just happened to start at nine, failed at nine, and succeeded at nine. You can do the same if you are willing to risk going through your learning process."

"So you are confident in your skills as an entrepreneur?" asked the host.

"No, not really. I am confident in my ability to make mistakes, correct, and improve my business. I am a better entrepreneur today and I plan on getting better. But no, I am never fully confident in my skills as an entrepreneur, because I do not rest on my laurels, or my past successes. I constantly put myself in situations where I am beyond my skills. I am always on edge, always tentative, always testing myself. That is the way I continually get better."

"And that is why you start new businesses even if you fail?" asked the host.

"I start new businesses even if I succeed. That is why I have so many businesses, businesses that run without me. That is my secret to great wealth. Most employees have one job. As an entrepreneur, I have multiple businesses."

"That's why you do not want to be self-employed or run the business."

"Yes, and that is why I am glad I failed at the age of nine. At the age of nine, I learned how to start businesses that ran without me. I wrote about those businesses in *Rich Dad Poor Dad*."

"Yes, I remember," said the host. "I just did not get the significance of those businesses. I did not realize those tiny businesses would have such a profound impact on your life."

Nodding again, I said, "I found my strategy for life at the age of nine."

The sound engineer then informed us the commercial break was over and it was time to continue the interview. The host turned on her microphone and said, "We only have a few minutes left, so let's wrap this up. You're telling us that an entrepreneur's job is to make mistakes and an employee's job is to not make mistakes. Is that your message?"

"Yes, it is. At least that is the way I see it. If I am not taking calculated risks, not making mistakes and growing the company, I should be fired. If my employees make too many mistakes, I might have to let them go. That is why I hire smart employees who hate making mistakes. They do their job, I do mine."

"That is why we say to our kids, 'Go to school so you can get a good job,'" said the host. "Schools are training our kids to be employees."

"Yes," I replied. "If you do well in school you'll probably do well in the corporate world or in government."

"Did you like school?" asked the host.

"Not really," I replied. "I did not do well in school because I made too many mistakes. I was a C, D, and on several occasions, an F student. So in school, I figured out that since I was already good at making mistakes I might as well become an expert at making mistakes. That is why I am an entrepreneur, not an employee. I am not that academically smart. No one would hire me for a high-paying job. I don't like following orders, so I'd probably never be promoted. I like changing things and doing things my way rather than doing what I am told to do."

"You would definitely not get a job at this radio station," said the host.

"I might not get a job here—but I do know how to buy this radio station and hire people smarter than me to run it for me," I added with a hint of humor in my voice.

"Okay, we have to wrap this up," said the host. "Do you have any other examples that show that making mistakes and failing is essential to being an entrepreneur? Is there anyone else, another example besides you that can support this point of view?"

"Oh, sure," I replied. "Thomas Edison was asked to leave school because teachers complained that he was *addled* or scatterbrained. Later in life, he was criticized for having failed over a thousand times before inventing his version of the electric light bulb. When asked how he felt about failing over a thousand times, he said something to the effect of, 'I did fail over a thousand times. I believe it was a thousand and fourteen experiments that failed before we finally succeeded. It takes at least a thousand failures to qualify you to invent a light bulb.'"

"What does he mean it takes at least a thousand failures to qualify you to invent the light bulb?" the host asked.

"It means, if you or I wanted to invent a light bulb today, instead of just buying one from the store, we would probably fail at least a thousand times before we knew how to make a light bulb."

"So he was labeled a scatterbrain in school and failed a thousand times before inventing the light bulb," said the host. "That means he is an inventor. How does that make him an entrepreneur?"

"Do you know what company he founded?" I asked.

"No. I do not."

"He founded General Electric, one of the most powerful companies in the world. Originally known as Edison General Electric, one of the original twelve members of the Dow Jones Industrial Average, and of the original twelve only GE has survived to this day. Not bad for an addle-minded scatterbrain who failed a lot."

The interview was over.

Learn from Your Mistakes

My rich dad believed in learning from your mistakes. He did not view mistakes as bad but simply as opportunities to learn something about business and yourself. He said, "Mistakes are like stop signs. Mistakes say to you, 'Hey, time to stop . . . take a moment . . . you don't know something . . . It's time to stop and think.'" Rich dad also said, "A mistake is a signal that it's time to learn something new, something you did not know before." Along that line of reasoning he also said, "Too many people are too lazy to think. Instead of learning something new, they think the same thoughts day in and day out. Thinking is hard work. When you are forced to think you expand your mental capacity. When you expand your mental capacity your wealth increases.

"So every time you make a mistake, stop, and take the opportunity to learn something new, something you obviously need to learn. When something does not go your way, or something goes wrong, or you fail, take the time to think. Once you find the hidden lesson you will be thankful for the mistake. If you are upset, angry, ashamed, blaming someone else for the mistake, or pretending you haven't made a mistake, you haven't been thinking hard enough. Your mental capacity hasn't expanded enough. You haven't learned the lesson. So keep thinking."

Poor Dad's Philosophy on Mistakes

My poor dad, being an educator, had a different point of view on mistakes. To him making a mistake also indicated you did not know something, but to him, making a mistake meant you were stupid or intellectually challenged. When my poor dad made a mistake, he often pretended he did not make one, denied making one, or blamed someone else for the mistake. He did not view making mistakes as an opportunity to learn and increase one's intellectual capacity. He did his best to avoid making mistakes. *He did not view making mistakes as a good thing, as my rich dad did.*

Bad Luck to Good Luck

Lesson #2, *Learn How To Turn Bad Luck Into Good Luck,* is the second lesson because of the differences I noticed between my rich dad and my poor dad when it came to making mistakes. In my opinion, it was each man's personal philosophy on the subject of mistakes that determined his ultimate success in life.

His First Big Failure

In earlier books, I wrote about coming home from the Vietnam War and having to decide in which dad's footsteps I would follow. I was about twenty-five at the time and both my dads were just turning fifty. At the time, my poor dad had just lost his bid as the Republican candidate for lieutenant governor of the State of Hawaii. Since he ran for office against his boss, the governor, my dad was informed that he would never work in state government again. So he was unemployed and out of work at the age of fifty.

The problem was, all he knew was the world of education. He entered the academic world at the age of five and did not leave that world until the age of fifty. Out of work, he had to take early retirement. He took his retirement money, entered the world of business as a reluctant entrepreneur, and purchased a big-name ice cream franchise. He purchased this big-name franchise because he thought it was a *cannot-fail* business. In less than two years the *cannot-fail* franchise failed and my father was once again out of work and now out of money.

Blaming Not Learning

My poor dad was angry, depressed, upset, and blaming the franchisor as well as his partners for the failure of the business and the loss of his money. It was during this period that I understood why my rich dad stressed the importance of stopping, thinking, learning, and correcting. It was obvious from my dad's mental and emotional state of mind that he had gone through many stop signs and was *blaming* instead of *learning.* He was continuing to think with the mental capacity of an employee, not an entrepreneur.

Within just a few months of opening his ice cream business, my dad knew it was in trouble. Once friends stopped coming by to buy a cone, the store was virtually empty. My dad would sit there for hours, all by himself, without customers. Instead of taking a moment to stop, think, and ask for guidance, he fired his employees to reduce costs, worked longer and harder in the business, fought with his partners, and then spent the remainder of his money by hiring an attorney, and went after the franchisor. In other words, he used up his money blaming the franchisor for his problems. Out of money, the business finally closed. It was obvious that my real dad had taken bad luck and turned it into more bad luck. Instead of stopping, learning, and correcting, he could not admit that he might be making mistakes. Instead of making things better, he made matters worse.

With his political campaign loss and the loss of his first and only business, he remained angry and defeated until he died, nearly twenty years later. That is why this lesson on mistakes, bad luck, and being dumb and dumber yet getting richer and richer is so important to me.

Show Me a Happy Loser

I once heard Vince Lombardi, the famous coach of the Green Bay Packers professional football team, say, "Show me a happy loser and I will show you a loser." Over the years, I have taken the time to look deeper into the multiple meanings his saying has. On the surface, Vince Lombardi's words seem to mean that people who take losing lightly are losers. I have been that happy loser many times in life, saying such things as, "Oh, it doesn't matter. Winning is not that important to me. It's how I played the game that matters." On the surface I may appear nonchalant or happy about losing, but truthfully deep down inside, I hate losing. In other words, when I pretend to be okay about losing, I am lying to myself.

The more I thought about Lombardi's quotation the more meanings came to the surface. Some of the other things he might have meant are:

1. Nobody likes to lose. Losing is not something we look forward to.
2. Losing should inspire winning.
3. Some people avoid losing at all costs because it is so painful.

In my opinion, it was the third meaning that caused my poor dad's business failure. For years, he operated in a world where losing, making mistakes, and failing was to be avoided at all costs. As an employee, he was used to and wanted his steady paychecks and guaranteed benefits. To many workers, like my dad, *security* is far more important than *opportunity.* That is why so many employees, as a personal philosophy, will avoid making mistakes at all costs. One of the reasons my dad failed was simply that he had avoided making mistakes for too long.

High-Speed Learning

In March 2005, my wife, Kim, and I signed up to take Bob Bondurant's four-day formula-one racing school, located in Phoenix, Arizona. Don't ask us why we signed up for it. We just did simply because it sounded fun and exciting. We are not professional racecar drivers and have no intention of becoming professional racecar drivers.

All my life, I loved movies about Grand Prix races and Formula car racing. I envied Paul Newman and his hobby of auto racing. Starting with my very first car, a 1969 Datsun 2000, I have almost always owned high-performance street cars. After the Datsun, I purchased a Corvette, several Porsches, and a Ferrari. My problem has always been the cars had more power than I had talent. That problem was one of the reasons why Kim, who also owns a very fast Porsche, and I decided once and for all to learn to drive racecars on a racetrack.

From day one of the class, we realized that we had made a mistake. There were two classes. One class was for High-Performance Driving. This is the class we should have been in. In that class were everyday people, who simply wanted to learn to drive regular cars at high speed. The second class was titled Grand Prix Driving, which is the class Kim and I were in. In this class were professional racecar drivers and amateur drivers with years of racing experience. Kim and I did not realize we were in the wrong class until we noticed the first class driving high-performance Cadillacs, while we were driving high-performance Corvettes.

The thought of asking for a transfer crossed our minds, but we decided hanging out with professional drivers might be a great way to learn a lot faster. But a knot formed in my stomach once we decided to stay with our class. I knew I was about to face some of my greatest fears. Kim was feeling the same. After lunch on the first day, we were racing those souped-up Corvettes. My fear had turned into terror. I was in way over my head.

On the morning of the second day, the knot in my stomach was worse. My logical mind was chattering away, trying to find a way to quit gracefully. In the classroom, my instructor came up to me and kindly said, "You're driving too slowly. You need to drive much faster." At that moment I was ready to quit and I would have, except the instructor then said, "Your wife Kim is catching on. She's driving much faster than you are." Immediately, my male pride kicked in, logic went out the window, and I had no choice. If Kim was driving faster than me, I had to stay. As a side note, Kim was the only woman in our class of twelve people. She was very excited about passing men.

Burn Out the Fear

For three full days, the knot in my stomach grew worse as speeds kept increasing, turns came faster, and my mind went into sensory overload with all I had to learn and do at high speeds. At lunch on the third day, I finally asked my instructor why he kept insisting I increase my speed. After all, I wanted to drive slowly so I could learn the lessons before adding speed. He smiled and said, "I want you to go fast because speed will burn that fear out of you. Your fear keeps you stuck. You get up to your fear and then back off on the throttle. Your fear is still driving the car. That is why, when you get up to that fear, I want you to go full throttle."

Again, I wanted to quit. Again, I was being told I was not going fast enough. Again, I thought that the way to learn was to practice at slow speeds, not fast speeds. "Look," said Les, my instructor, "you have to trust that there is a Grand Prix driver inside you. If you don't go fast, you'll never meet the driver inside you. I want you to push yourself, push that throttle, so the driver in you comes forward and takes over the car. If I let you go slowly, the coward in you is still driving the car. There is only one way the professional driver can come out and that is by pushing hard on the accelerator. When you go to full throttle, you have to trust that the professional racecar driver in you will take over."

On the fourth day, the knot in my gut was even worse and my mind was coming up with every reason why I did not have to do this course. The fourth day is when the class stops driving the Corvette and gets into Formula One open-wheeled racers. On this day we had red jumpsuits and helmets on. Being overweight, I had trouble sliding down into the car. It felt like I was sliding into a coffin. I couldn't move. Again, the coward in me almost took over. I wanted to quit. I could hear my mind saying, "You don't need to do this. You don't have anything to prove. You'll never be a racecar driver. Why are you doing this? This is nuts."

In less than an hour, I was happier than I have been in years. I was at home in the car. Suddenly, all three days of lessons, fears, and frustrations clicked and I was driving the car at full throttle. Instead of fear, it was exhilaration. The driver in me had pushed the coward aside and taken over the car.

As we left the class, late that afternoon, high as kites, one of the students who was in the high-performance sedan driving course instead of the Formula One racing class we were in came over to us and said, "I loved the class I was in, but I really wish I was in your class."

Thanking him, I replied, "That's funny, because up until today, I was wishing I was in your class."

Two Different Worlds

The reason I mention the driving school is not to brag about my new driving skills. I mention it because the school is about a process—a process very similar to an employee becoming an entrepreneur, a process of going from one world to another.

One of the first lessons I learned is that what I need to do on the streets and highways is opposite to what I have to do on the racetrack. For example, on the highway, if you see a wreck directly in front of you, most people step on their brakes. In the driving school we were taught to step on the throttle.

In the real world, when a car begins to skid, most people step on their brakes. In driving school we have to know when to step on the brake and when to step on the throttle. In other words, with different skids, there are different responses. Trust me, stepping on the brake is easy. Stepping on the throttle in a skid is hard. It goes against everything I know. In order to do it, I definitely needed to increase my mental and physical capacity. In the normal world of driving, most people are asked to drive at or below the speed limit. In driving school, we were taught to step on the throttle and go beyond our personal limits to speed. Speed and fear definitely increased my capacity.

A Great Curriculum

My four days at the Bob Bondurant High-Performance Racing School were four days of the steepest learning curve I have ever gone through in my life. The learning curves at the racing school were even steeper than the learning curves I went through at the Navy Flight School. Obviously, Bob Bondurant is not only a great Formula One driver, he is also a wonderful teacher. As a fellow teacher, even though terrified most of the time, I did spend a lot of time evaluating his teaching methodology. I was impressed with the curriculum in the classroom and on the track. For four days, he and his instructors kept us going through our fears as well as our mental and physical limitations with a high degree of safety. Once on the track, I did not have much concern for my physical well-being. The primary concern I had was my wife Kim passing me at higher speeds, which she did on several occasions. Physically I was fine, but my ego was severely bruised each time her car flew past mine.

The Entrepreneurial Process

The process of going from street driver to racetrack driver required that I un-learn many things. In other words, the *right* things to do on the street will get you killed on the racetrack. Also, the *smart* thing to do on the street, such as slow down, is often the *stupid* thing to do on the racetrack. The same is true with going from employee to entrepreneur. They are two different worlds and what is *right* in one world is *wrong* in the other.

The reason I tell the story of my poor dad's transition from the world of government to the world of entrepreneurship is to illustrate this point—the point that what he did *right* in the world of government was *wrong* in the world of entrepreneurship.

Since a new entrepreneur is creating something out of nothing, it is obvious that mistakes will be made. In order to succeed, a new entrepreneur needs to be committed to going through these steps as quickly as possible.

1. Start the business.
2. Fail and learn.
3. Find a mentor.
4. Fail and learn.
5. Take some classes.
6. Keep failing and learning.
7. Stop when successful.
8. Celebrate.
9. Count your money, the wins and the losses.
10. Repeat the process.

The Dreaded Disease

In my estimation, 90% of want-to-be entrepreneurs do not get to step one. They may have a plan, they may have created the perfect business in their head or on paper, but that dreaded disease known as *Analysis Paralysis* infects them. Instead of going forward, I have seen many want-to-be entrepreneurs design and redesign their plan. Or they find some excuse why the time or the plan is not right. Instead of taking action and failing, they work hard at trying not to fail. They enter the world of Analysis Paralysis.

It is impossible to become an entrepreneur without starting a business. It would be like trying to learn how to ride a bicycle without a bicycle or me wanting to learn to be a racecar driver without a racecar and a track. My rich dad said, "The main reason to start a business is to have a business to practice on. If you do not have a bicycle to practice on, how can you learn to ride a bike? If you do not have a business to practice on, how can you learn to be an entrepreneur?"

Different Schools of Thought

At the Bondurant High-Performance driving school, the course curriculum did not focus on doing things *right*. The course focused on making driving *mistakes* at higher and higher speeds. As our ability to make mistakes and to correct them at high speeds increased, our confidence went up. On the fourth day of the course, I could make a horrible mistake at high speed, lose control of the car in a turn, regain control, get the car back on the track, get back to full throttle, and race on. If I had attempted that on the first day, I would probably be in the hospital.

Once again, I mention this driving school because it reflects a contrast in different schools of thought. My poor dad came from the school of thought that focused on the avoidance of mistakes. That is why he was a good employee. My rich dad came from the school of thought that encouraged the making of mistakes. That is why he was a good entrepreneur.

Dumb and Dumber

This chapter is entitled Dumb and Dumber Gets Rich and Richer as a tribute to Jim Carrey. For those of you who have ever watched a Jim Carrey movie, you may have noticed that the dumber he is on screen, the richer he becomes. The same is true with entrepreneurship. If you are a person who needs to always look good, sound smart, never make mistakes, and have all the right answers, then being an employee or a self-employed person might be a better path for you.

When I first started out, I looked like the biggest clown in town. My businesses would go up and come crashing down. Soon my reputation as an entrepreneur in the business community of Honolulu was laughable. If not for my rich dad guiding me and encouraging me to learn from my mistakes and go out and make more, I might have quit my process. I found it painful to play Jim Carrey's screen characters in real life.

Yet as the years went on, the mistakes were bigger but not as painful, simply because I was becoming an expert at making mistakes. Instead of running through five or six stop signs, I did stop, think, learn, correct, and expand my capacity as an entrepreneur before going on. Today I can honestly say I am richer than many of my peers, many who did well in school or had higher-paying jobs early in life, simply because I was willing to be dumb and dumber for years. That's part of paying the price to succeed.

Turning Bad Luck into Good Luck

When we were just entering high school, rich dad taught his son and me how to turn bad luck into good luck. At the time, both Mike and I were sinking fast in our sophomore year of high school because we were flunking English. Mike and I were not great writers.

Instead of being upset with us, rich dad said, "Let this setback in school make you stronger, not weaker. If you can turn this bad experience into a good experience you will be further ahead of your classmates who passed the course."

"But we both have Fs on our report cards," Mike protested. "That record travels with us all the way through college."

"Yes, the grade travels with you, but so does the lesson in life. In the long run, this lesson in life can be far more important than your grades if you take this bad incident and turn it into a good incident."

Mike and I were really angry with our English teacher. We were depressed and felt like failures. Looking at us, rich dad chuckled and said, "Your teacher is winning. You guys are losing because you're acting like losers."

"What can we do?" I asked. "He's got the power. He's already flunked us and the whole school knows it."

"He only has the power to flunk you," smiled rich dad. "You have the power to take your anger and do something even more stupid, like slash the tires on his car, which I suspect has crossed your minds, or do something good, like take your anger and do well in school, or do well in football, or in surfing. Take your anger and turn it into greatness. Then you will win. If you take your anger and slash the tires on his car, you will take a bad situation and make it worse. You'll probably spend time in jail if you do what you are thinking."

The Power of Emotions

That day rich dad taught us that as humans we have four basic emotions. They are:

1. Joy
2. Anger
3. Fear
4. Love

He also explained that there were many other emotions, but these were the basic ones. Many of the other emotions were combinations of two or more of these basic emotions. For example, *sadness* is often a combination of anger, fear, and love . . . and occasionally joy.

He then taught us that each emotion could be used in two basic ways, for good or for bad. For example, I could feel joy and use the joy to go out and drink heavily, which would be using the emotion of joy for a bad purpose. I could also use the emotion of joy and send thank-you notes to everyone who helped me in life. The same is true with all four basic emotions, even love.

Today, I still do not like my English teacher, yet I am grateful that he flunked me. If not for that F, I might not have studied harder to get through college and I might never have become an international best-selling author.

In other words, that F at the age of fifteen, combined with my first business failure at the age of nine, has made me a millionaire over and over again. Best of all, not only did I learn many lessons about life and myself; I learned to turn my anger into joy, and I learned that being dumb and dumber can make me become richer and happier.

And that is one of the steps in turning bad luck into good luck. As rich dad said, "If you can turn bad luck into good luck, you will have twice the luck and be twice as lucky in love, life, health, and money."

Before Quitting Your Job

Before quitting your job, you may want to practice turning bad luck into good luck or turning any anger you might have into joy. Those skills are important skills to possess, before embarking upon the journey from the world of an employee, a world of avoiding mistakes, into the world of an entrepreneur, a world of making mistakes.

Later in this book we will explain how and when I decided to make "making mistakes" my specialty. A reason why I decided to get ahead by failing was simply that I was failing in school. Academically, I have never been that bright. Although I read a lot today, I am still a slow reader, moving my lips as I read, and when I count, I still need my fingers and toes to count my money. Although I did graduate from a great school, all through my years in school, I was always a C, D, and F student, always graduating at the bottom of my class.

Sharon Lechter, who founded The Rich Dad Company with my wife and me, is the A student, a CPA, and an entrepreneur, and she will supplement the lessons in this book with the smarter approach to being an entrepreneur. In other words, she did not follow the *dumb and dumber* approach to being an entrepreneur, as I did. The businesses she founded are more successful than mine. Nonetheless, Sharon had her own lessons to learn along the way.

Regardless, if you are considering being an entrepreneur or have already started your own business, I believe you will find some of these real life lessons entertaining and even a little educational.

=================

SHARON'S INSIGHTS

Lesson #2: Learn How to Turn Bad Luck Into Good Luck.

Rich dad said, "There are no mistakes, just learning opportunities!"

THE ENTREPRENEUR'S JOB IS *TO* MAKE MISTAKES.

THE EMPLOYEE'S JOB IS *TO NOT* MAKE MISTAKES.

I might put it a little differently: AN ENTREPRENEUR CANNOT AND WILL NOT BE DETERRED BY THE FEAR OF MAKING A MISTAKE. He or she will not let his or her fear of making a mistake get in the way.

Nobody likes making mistakes. From my perspective, it is not an entrepreneur's *goal* to make a "mistake." However, experimentation and making wrong choices are natural parts of being an entrepreneur. Successful entrepreneurs are not afraid to risk being wrong, and if they make a mistake they learn from it, and sometimes put it to work for them and capitalize on it.

IS MAKING A WRONG CHOICE A MISTAKE?

Whether something is a "mistake" is a matter of perspective. The perspective of an entrepreneur is different from that of a worker/employee. To try new things, particularly things that other people think unlikely to work, is part of the essence of being an entrepreneur. Because the entrepreneur tends to follow untraveled paths, there is a much higher likelihood of missteps. Most entrepreneurs recognize that and accept it. Experimentation means trying something to see if it will work. Obviously, not all experiments will work. If it was a sure thing, it would not be an experiment. Sometimes things go wrong. Sometimes you make a wrong choice. When someone tries an experiment that goes wrong, is it a mistake to have tried the experiment? Entrepreneurs typically do not view that as a mistake at all, but merely as experimentation, a calculated risk. Remember Robert's story about Thomas Edison.

DEALING WITH MISTAKES

When entrepreneurs make a mistake, they typically do not fixate on the consequences of the mistake. They typically are not particularly concerned that making the mistake might make them look bad. The true entrepreneur focuses instead on learning from the mistake. How do you solve any problems resulting from the mistake? How do you avoid making the mistake in the future? How do you minimize the adverse consequences of the mistake if it does occur again in the future? Is there a way to capitalize on the mistake and turn it into an advantage?

How do you capitalize on a mistake? I like to think in terms of turning problems into opportunities. You identify a problem and come up with a solution for it—how to avoid or minimize the consequences of the mistake. That solution may well be a valuable asset (often called intellectual property) around which a business can be built or which can be used as a tool to grow your existing business. Of course, you would want to put legal protections in place so that you have exclusive rights to that solution to the greatest extent possible.

For example, let's take a trip back in time and assume that you were in the process of developing one of the first transistor radios. You found out the hard way that if you made a mistake in the way that you connected the battery to the circuit (reversed the polarity), the transistors had a tendency to go up in smoke. At that point in time, transistors were very expensive, and it was a costly mistake. But you learned from the mistake. You identify a problem—and come up with a solution: a plug with a key that prevents it from being inserted the wrong way. Assume that you are able to obtain patent protection on your solution to the problem. Do you think that you could build a business around the solution to that mistake?

THE ANATOMY OF A MISTAKE

There are actually two primary aspects to the fear of making a mistake—fear of the consequences of a mistake and fear of looking bad (perception). We are not saying that it is wrong to consider the consequences of an action. Even entrepreneurs generally think through the potential consequences of an action. *Being an entrepreneur does not mean acting irresponsibly.* (Being an entrepreneur does not mean that you would test out a new vehicle braking system for the very first time by running a car full speed to within ten feet of an animal and jamming on the brakes.) The difference between an entrepreneur and a worker/employee is that the entrepreneur is not paralyzed by remotely possible consequences, but will find a way to minimize likely adverse consequences.

The other aspect of fear of making a mistake—a fear of looking stupid—is, well, stupid. It is not surprising that someone is afraid to make a mistake because he or she might look stupid. As we have discussed in our other books, our public schools tend to condition us to be afraid of looking stupid. As a straight A student this was a very big issue for me. I wanted to be right and didn't want it to ever appear that I didn't know something. I even felt that asking a question would be admitting that I didn't know something. It took me nearly twenty years to break through this mental roadblock and to realize that asking questions is how we learn. I must admit that I still catch myself "wanting to be right." I also recognize this same mental hurdle in many highly educated people, and it makes me feel sad for them. Being able to "look stupid" occasionally and ask questions freely opens up a whole new world to top students. I now call myself a "recovering A student" and invite all of you other straight A students to join me.

Having said that, there are situations where the entrepreneur has to be concerned with credibility. Your reputation in your profession or business community can be harmed by *too* many mistakes. But when people are too afraid of making a mistake, they often simply are unwilling to take any risk, and never even consider becoming an entrepreneur. And if they do start the process, they concentrate their focus so much on avoiding risk that they fall victim to "analysis paralysis," as Robert described. They are so focused on trying to gather information and identify and eliminate all of the risks that they never feel comfortable actually moving forward with the business. Analysis paralysis stops them in their tracks.

We are not suggesting that you move forward without regard to the consequences. You need to act responsibly and do your homework. You need to set the foundation for your business to keep it from collapsing in the future. You need to plan. As rich dad said, A SUCCESSFUL BUSINESS IS CREATED BE-

FORE THERE IS A BUSINESS. But you must also recognize the point of diminishing returns. There is a broad spectrum between moving forward blindly and falling victim to analysis paralysis. In truth, you will never be able to eliminate all the risks.

At some point, you will have enough information to go forward, and additional planning is simply wasting time. Once you have identified the opportunity and the major risks, set the foundation and developed a business plan to minimize the risks, then move forward to implement the plan.

Analysis paralysis is not the only obstacle to taking the first step into entrepreneurship. There is also the "inertia" factor. It's easy to do nothing, so that is exactly what many people do—nothing. This is particularly true if you are comfortable the way you are. There generally is some sort of perturbation that initiates one's journey into entrepreneurship, something that makes you want to change the status quo.

THE TRANSITION PROCESS

Let's look at the stages you might go through in transitioning from employee to entrepreneur.

Stage 1—You become unhappy as an employee.

Now, we are not saying that there is anything wrong with being an employee. For this world to operate, we need people who are happy being employees. The problem with being an employee is when you no longer want to be one. The Sunday Night Blues set in and you dread going to work on Monday morning. You may say or think the following:

1. "I don't want to go to work. Besides, my job description begins with the words *dead end.*"
2. "I like my job, but I'm not getting ahead. When I look up the corporate ladder, all I see is my supervisor's rear end above me."
3. "I'm not being paid what I'm worth. Regardless if I work hard or fall asleep on the job, I don't get paid any more or any less. Many of my fellow workers do not work as hard as me, yet they make

the same amount of money as me. To me, this is not fair. If I work harder, I want to make more money."

4. "I used to enjoy what I did but now I'm bored. I want a more challenging job but my boss says I'm not qualified. He says I need to go back to school before I can be promoted."

5. "I don't want to go from job to job. Besides, it's time I worked for myself and built my own business."

6. "I have too much seniority to quit. If I quit, I'll have to start at the bottom in a different company and take a cut in pay."

7. "The company I work for isn't going anywhere."

8. "I do all the work and my boss gets all the credit."

9. "Why am I working for this guy, running his company, making him rich? He's never here. All he does is play golf. I should run my own business and make myself rich."

10. "Why am I working so hard to make all my clients rich when all I get paid is an hourly rate?"

11. "I want to do my own thing. I want to be my own boss."

12. "The writing is on the wall. They promoted someone younger than me."

13. "I can't afford to leave my job or retire. I don't have enough money in savings and my 401(k) was wiped out in the stock market crash."

If you have thoughts like these, it may be time for you to become an entrepreneur. You may want to start a part-time business while you are still employed. But the important word here is "start."

Stage 2—Overcome the Fear of Getting Started

Over the years, I have met many people who wanted to quit their jobs but were terrified of failing. Instead of quitting their jobs and getting started on their own business, they continue going to work day after day, using such excuses as:

1. "I'll do it tomorrow."

2. "I'll do it when the perfect opportunity appears."

3. "I'll do it when I have the money."
4. "I'll do it when the time is right."
5. "I'll do it when I have more time."
6. "I'll do it when I find the right partner."
7. "I'll do it when the kids are out of school."
8. "I'd do it but my wife wants me to keep my job."
9. "I'll wait to see if I get the next promotion. If I don't, then I'll start my own business."
10. "I'll go back to school and take a few classes first."
11. "What happens if I fail?"
12. "I'll be too embarrassed if I fail!"
13. "I'm not smart enough."
14. "What will my friends say?"

Stage 3—Just Start!

You have made the decision to get past the fear and to start your business. You have the business plan, the product or service, and you are ready to start. Commit yourself to going through the steps rich dad shared with Robert as quickly as possible.

1. Start the business.
2. Fail and learn.
3. Find a mentor.
4. Fail and learn.
5. Take some classes.
6. Keep failing and learning.
7. Stop when successful.
8. Celebrate.
9. Count your money, the wins and the losses.
10. Repeat the process.

You have heard the saying, "Getting started is half the battle." Use your fear as a motivator to succeed.

WHY NOT?

When I left public accounting, many of my friends and family were shocked and asked me, "Why? Why in the world would you risk leaving the fast track to become a partner at a large international accounting firm, to do something so risky as to start a new business?" I really spent a lot of time soul-searching. I was twenty-five at the time (and thought I knew everything). The conservative accountant in me asked the same question, "Why?" However, it was the entrepreneur in me that said, "Don't ask yourself, Why? Ask yourself, Why not?"

I have never regretted my decision at age twenty-five, because I listened to the entrepreneur in me, "Why not?"

I could always get another job with an accounting firm, but I might not ever have the same opportunity to own equity in a company. As it turned out, the company I joined for ownership was a tremendous LEARNING OPPORTUNITY—and I learned a lot. Within a year I had moved on, but I have never regretted my decision to listen to the entrepreneur in my head. My *big* bonus was that I met my husband, Michael, through that company.

When looking at new opportunities today, I still ask myself, "Why not?" instead of "Why?"

So I challenge you to ask yourself, "Why not? Why not get started today?"

Know the Difference Between Your Job and Your Work.

Chapter 3

Why Work for Free?

Differences Between Job and Work

"Do you know the difference between your job and your work?" asked rich dad one day.

Puzzled, I asked, "Aren't they the same thing? Isn't a *job* the same as *work?*"

Rich dad shook his head and said, "If you want to be successful in life, you need to know the difference."

"What's the big deal?" asked Mike as he and I shrugged our shoulders and waited for the lesson we knew was coming, whether we wanted the lesson or not.

"What does your dad always say to you about getting a job?" asked rich dad.

Thinking for a moment, I replied, "He says things like go to school and work hard so you can get a good job."

"Does he say, 'Do your homework so you can get a good job'?"

"Yeah," I replied. "He does say things like that."

"So what is the difference between your job and your work?" asked rich dad again.

"I don't know," I replied. "It all sounds like work to me."

"Oh, I get what you're saying," said Mike. "A job is something I get paid for. I do not get paid for work such as my homework. Work is what I do to prepare me for my job."

Rich dad nodded. "That's it. That's the difference between your work and your job. You get paid for a job but you do not get paid for doing your work." Looking at me, he asked, "Do you get paid for doing yard work at home, or does your mom get paid for doing her housework?"

"No," I replied. "Not in my family. I don't even get an allowance."

"Do you get paid to do your homework?" asked rich dad. "Does your dad give you money to read books?"

"No," I replied a little sarcastically. "Are you saying that my homework is what prepares me for my job?"

"That is what I am saying." Rich dad smiled. "When it comes to money, the more homework you do, the more money you earn on your job. People who do not do their homework make less money, regardless if they are an employee or an entrepreneur."

Thinking for a long while, I finally said, "So it is true that if I do not do my homework at school, I won't get a high-paying job?"

"Yes, I would say that is true," said rich dad. "At least, if you don't do your homework you will not become a medical doctor, accountant, or lawyer. If you are an employee, it's tough to get promoted and earn more money if you don't have a trained skill or a college degree."

"And if we want to be entrepreneurs, we need to do a different type of homework?" I asked.

Rich dad nodded and said, "And many entrepreneurs quit their job without doing their homework. That is why so many small businesses fail or struggle financially."

"So you're having us do our homework to become entrepreneurs."

"Exactly," rich dad said. "And that is why I am *not* paying you. Working for me for free is doing your homework. Many employees do not understand working for free. They expect to get paid for anything they do. That is why they fail. They continue to think like employees. They want that steady paycheck."

Lots of Work but No Jobs

"In many poor parts of town, there is a lot of *work* to be done . . . but there are very few *jobs*," rich dad continued.

Thinking for a moment, I finally repeated what he said. "There is a lot of work but no jobs?" To me it was puzzling and I needed to think more about what he said.

"Why is that?" asked his son Mike.

"Well, one reason is that we are trained in school to look for jobs. If there are no jobs, people are out of work, even if there is a lot of work to do. When a factory closes or moves overseas, it usually leaves behind a lot of unemployed employees."

Rich dad continued to explain, "Employees see no jobs so they do nothing. On the other hand, an entrepreneur sees a lot of opportunity. The entrepreneur knows that the jobs will come if the work is done."

"So they need to be retrained. They need to do their homework," I added. "That's the work that needs to be done."

"That is some of the work," said rich dad. "Look . . . the point I am making is that too many people confuse work and job. Too many people expect to get their job training for free. Even if a person has a job, too many employees expect their employers to provide them with training and pay them at the same time."

"They want the company to pay for their education?" I asked. Being a teenager and not having worked in a big company, the idea of expecting to be paid for training was strange to me.

"Many people also expect the government to provide them with job training for free," added rich dad.

"And that is why you say they are poor people," said Mike. "It's more than financial, it is a poor attitude toward the value of education, training, and preparing oneself to have a skill people will pay for."

Rich dad agreed. "I've seen employees attend training classes keeping one eye on their watch. At quitting time, they jump up and leave the class even if the instructor has not finished the lesson. Or I've seen employees who are outside, smoking and gossiping; or drinking in the bar and watching sports on TV; or flirting with other workers, rather than attending the class the employer is paying them to attend. That is why so many people do not get ahead in life financially. Too many won't learn anything even if it is free or if they are paid to learn it. And this applies to both employees and entrepreneurs."

Since I came from a family of government educators who believed in free education, I asked, "Would you explain a little further the relationship between work and jobs?"

Doctors Worked for Free

"Sure," said rich dad. "Medical doctors spend a lot of money and a lot of time learning to be doctors before they get paid as a medical doctor. That is one reason why they earn more money than most people."

"The doctors did their homework before they get paid," Mike added.

Professional Athletes Worked for Free

"They certainly did," said rich dad. "But also look at great athletes who earn a lot of money. I do not know of a single great athlete who got paid for practicing his or her sport. Most professional athletes started young, practiced longer and harder than the average athlete. Most professional athletes practiced for years, many paid for lessons, and they put in long hours, long before they got paid. They had to do their homework before they got their jobs as pros."

"That is why you don't pay us," I said softly. "We work for you for free."

Rich dad smiled. "Even the Beatles worked for free before they became world famous and rich. Like the medical doctor or professional, they paid their dues. They did their homework. They did not ask for a guaranteed record contract, a steady paycheck, and medical benefits before they began practicing."

"I've bought a lot of their records," said Mike. "I've helped make them rich."

"They made themselves rich," said rich dad with a smile. "Doing your homework applies to more than just money. It also applies to your health. Many people are unhealthy because they do not work out."

"They don't exercise," I said. "So they have poor health."

"Notice the word poor?" asked rich dad. "Poor financially and poor in health. People who are lazy and lack discipline are often the people with the worst health and the worst wealth."

"So we need to do our homework if we want to become entrepreneurs," I summarized.

"That is why you boys have been working for me for free for all these years. You've been doing your homework to become entrepreneurs. If I were training you to be employees I would be paying you by the hour."

"So that is why my dad, a government school teacher, got so angry when you had me work for you for free," I added.

Chuckling and nodding again, rich dad said, "Your father thinks like an employee. That is why he thinks I should pay you. He does not understand working for free. He does not understand that you are receiving a priceless education. It's just not the kind of education he values. The type of education an employee needs is different from the type of education an entrepreneur requires."

"That is why he thinks you're cheating us," I added.

"I know," smiled rich dad. "Look, years from now, you'll be a lot richer because of what I am teaching you. What you are learning is much more valuable than a small paycheck."

Before You Quit Your Job

Before quitting your job, you will need to find out how many different jobs make up a business.

Rich dad said, "That a person is a highly successful employee—let's say in sales—does not mean he or she will be successful in business." The reason he said this was that selling is only one of many jobs required by a business. His other point was that a struggling business is a business where a job or several jobs are not being done at all or are not being done well. He said, "An entrepreneur may be working hard but only working hard at one job at a time. That is why so many self-employed business owners struggle or eventually burn out from overwork. They may be working hard but they may not be doing all the jobs a business requires."

The Basic Jobs of a Basic Business

In the third of the Rich Dad series, *Rich Dad's Guide to Investing* (Warner Books, 2000), the B-I Triangle is introduced. The B and I refer to the Business Owner and Investor quadrants of the CASHFLOW Quadrant.

The following is the B-I Triangle that rich dad shared with me.

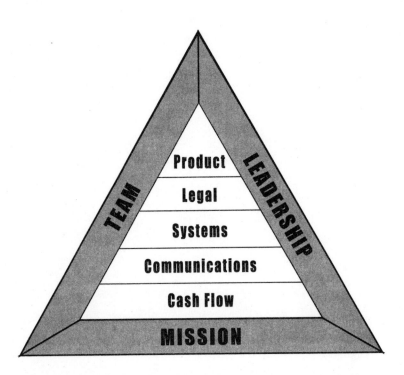

Rich dad said to me, "If you are going to be an entrepreneur or an investor, fully understanding the B-I Triangle is essential to your success." As a teenager I did not really believe or appreciate rich dad's respect for the importance of the triangle. Today I do.

A Great New Product

Many times individuals will say, "I have an idea for a great new product." As you can tell from the B-I Triangle, the product is only the tip of the iceberg.

The Jobs

You can think of the different aspects of a business as job descriptions. To be successful, the business needs someone with the skills to fulfill each of those functions. Starting with the level *product,* you will see the list of jobs required to bring the product to market. In simple terms the levels *product, legal, systems, communications*, and *cash flow* are technically all jobs required for a business to function successfully. If one or more of these jobs are not being done, or are being done poorly, the business will struggle and often will fail.

When my poor dad's ice cream business began to fail, it was not because it was not selling a good ice cream product; in fact it was a great ice cream product. In my opinion, the reason the business failed was that my dad was not a good sales or marketing person. He was a great communicator as a speaker, yet he failed to fill the job description known as *communications.*

Taking my poor dad's ice cream lesson a little further, my dad did not realize that sales and marketing involve more than simply running advertising or being able to sell an extra scoop of ice cream to a customer. His problems began when he thought the *brand* of ice cream was all he needed for success. His problems began when he rented a cheap location in a remote shopping mall. His ice cream shop was located in an obscure corner of a so-so shopping mall. That meant he did not have foot traffic or car traffic passing in front of his shop. No one knew where his ice cream shop was. He thought the brand of the ice cream was strong enough to pull customers in. As stated in Chapter One, his business began failing before there even was a business.

He Almost Made It

In retrospect, he did well when it came to choosing a good *product.* The *legal* work for the franchise was also done well. The *system* for making the ice cream was excellent. The franchisor made sure there was a good accounting package as part of the business, so the *cash flow* job description was covered. There just wasn't enough cash to count. So my dad did a good job in covering four out of five jobs. He almost made it.

Where my dad did a poor job was at the *communications* level of the B-I Triangle. He did not fully understand the intricacies of sales and marketing. When sales did not happen, the whole business began to fail. Instead of cutting his losses and purchasing a better location immediately, my dad did what many people do when sales decline and cash becomes tight. He cut back on staff. He cut back on advertising. He went cheaper instead of spending more money.

When he did spend money, he spent it on legal bills, blaming the franchisors for his problem. Few things are a bigger waste of money than a lawsuit. Yet that is what happens when people blame rather than learn. Instead of looking at his own actions and taking personal responsibility for the mistake, my dad insisted he was right. Eventually he went broke. There is a poem that describes people who are willing to die being right. It goes:

> *Here lies the body of Justin Grey.*
> *He died defending his right of way.*
> *He is right . . . his case is strong,*
> *But he's as dead as if he was wrong.*

Every time I see people taking their sweet time in a crosswalk, expecting all cars to stop as they cross a busy street, I think of this poem. When I meet people who need to be right; people who habitually blame other people when things go wrong; people who would rather argue than listen; people who know all the answers; and people who think they are the center of the universe, I think of this poem. I also repeat this poem to myself, whenever I become Justin Grey.

The Triangle of Financial Success

The B-I Triangle applies to more than just the B and I side of the CASHFLOW Quadrant. Looking at the quadrant below you can see that there is a triangle in each of the quadrants.

For example, if an employee is a receptionist for a business, his or her *product* is defined as *a well-answered phone.* That is the product of the job. In my opinion, the receptionist of a company has one of the most important jobs in the company. If the receptionist does his or her job well, the company actually runs smoother. If the receptionist delivers a bad *product*, for example, by being rude over the phone, then his or her value to the company goes down. The receptionist should be counseled, retrained, or terminated. I am sure we have all experienced a rude receptionist at one time or another.

The receptionist also has *legal* rights. If the company violates those rights, the receptionist can take action. The receptionist is an essential part of the entire business *system*. At home, the receptionist may be the leader of a *system* known as a home and a family. If life at home is happy, then the chances are the receptionist does a better job at work. If the systems at home are breaking down, such as no heat, no water, leaky roof, problem family members, the failing *systems* at home may affect the *systems* at work.

Since the receptionist is an integral link in the *communication* system of a business, if he or she has poor *communication* skills, once again the entire business system suffers. Retraining or removal is essential. If the receptionist has loving *communications* at home, this reflects in the receptionist's life. If *communications* at home are abusive, it can greatly affect the job performance of the receptionist.

Managing *cash flow* at home is very important. If the receptionist spends too much money, this not only affects life at home but may also affect the receptionist's attitude at work. The number one reason for arguments in a marriage is money. Sadly, many divorces are caused by problems in the *cash flow* of the family.

An Entrepreneur's Homework

Before quitting his or her job the entrepreneur should do his or her homework. That means making sure that the five jobs of the CASHFLOW Quadrant for his or her new business are covered.

1. Product
2. Legal
3. Systems
4. Communications
5. Cash flow

If the entrepreneur is weak in covering just one of the five jobs, the business may fail or struggle financially, or fail to grow. That is why the lesson in Chapter One is: *A successful business is created before there is a business.*

A *Simple Checklist*

A business is far more complex than this overly simplified list of five jobs. Nonetheless this simple list has served well over the years. I often use these five jobs as a checklist. Whenever a business begins to struggle, this list of five jobs can help analyze and identify where the problem or problems may lie.

I Have an Idea for a New Product

Whenever someone says, "I have an idea for a new product," this simple checklist can be used to bring some reality to what may be required to bring the product to market. In most instances, the want-to-be entrepreneurs give up on their idea because they are not willing to do their homework. They soon realize why a new *product* is just the tip of the iceberg, or in this case, the tip of the B-I Triangle.

Why They Give Up

One reason why so many want-to-be entrepreneurs give up is that they start to realize they are only trained for one out of the five jobs. For example, a creative artist may only be formally trained at product design. An attorney may only be formally trained for the legal level of a business. An engineer may be formally trained for products or systems but not the other levels. A person with a sales and marketing degree may only be trained for the communications level. And an accountant may only be prepared for the cash flow level.

When want-to-be entrepreneurs look at the five job levels, they often realize they have more homework to do before their hot new product makes them rich.

Professional Self-Employed

Highly educated professional people often have a higher rate of success because their education often prepares them for more than one level. For example, consider an attorney's business in terms of the B-I Triangle:

1. **Product:** The attorney is the product. You hire attorneys for the services they have been trained to perform.

2. **Legal:** Attorneys are licensed (which protects them from nonlicensed competitors). Generally, agreements are in place defining the rights and duties of the members of the law firm, and their relative compensations. In addition, most lawyers enter into engagement agreements (letters) to define their relationship with their clients.

3. **Systems:** Lawyers are trained to establish business systems for performing services, and for invoicing and collecting payment for those services. Systems for leveraging the expertise of more experienced attorneys are tried and true within the legal profession. For example, to provide for efficient and cost-effective legal research, less experienced, less expensive attorneys will do the initial research to find applicable case law on an issue, which is then provided to a more experienced attorney for analysis. Commercially available software packages are often used to implement billing and collection systems.

4. **Communications:** Attorneys understand that to be successful they need to maintain a good reputation and a good relationship with their clients. Most law firms market through word of mouth, although some are now resorting to advertising. Most people have an understanding of what an attorney does, which means they need to communicate less or explain less.

5. **Cash flow:** People expect to pay for an attorney's services. However, this does not mean an attorney can ignore issues of cash flow. Very often services are not invoiced until the end of a month during which they are provided, and clients often delay paying attorneys' fees. It is not uncommon for 90 or 120 days to pass from the time an invoice for services is sent out before receipt of payment. In the meantime, the attorney's payroll must be met and bills paid.

Again, this is oversimplified. Yet it does explain why people such as attorneys, accountants, medical doctors, dentists, plumbers, electricians, truck drivers, cab drivers, and babysitters may have an easier time setting up a business. There is a market in need of their services and willing to pay for their services.

For professionals such as schoolteachers and social workers, the road to becoming highly paid self-employed entrepreneurs may be a little tougher. It can be done, yet it is a sad reality that someone will be more likely to hire and pay money for the services of a self-employed attorney than a self-employed schoolteacher.

One reason why highly educated people such as my poor dad, a schoolteacher, suffer as entrepreneurs is that their professional education does not prepare them for multiple levels of the B-I Triangle. Many people such as firemen, nurses, librarians, or secretaries are trained to perform essential services but not the services required by the five job levels of a business. Before they quit their job, I strongly recommend they do their homework.

You Do Not Have to Be First to Win

Many people think Thomas Edison was the *first* person to invent the electric light bulb and being first helped him found General Electric. The facts are he was not first. The records show that he was actually twenty-third on the list of people who invented working light bulbs. So why does history recognize Edison as the inventor and why did his company become the biggest in the world? The answer is found once again in the B-I Triangle, his life, and the five job levels of a business.

1. Edison was born in 1847.
2. From twelve to fifteen, he works on the railroad selling snacks and printing his own newspaper.
3. From fifteen to twenty-two, he works for the telegraph company.
4. In 1869, at age twenty-two, he receives his first patent.
5. In 1876, he constructs his own laboratory in New Jersey.
6. In 1878, he invents tinfoil phonograph.
7. In 1879, he invents electric light.
8. In 1882, he installs complete electrical system in New York City.

Raising Money: Communications

You may notice that instead of attending school, from the age of twelve to fifteen, Edison worked in sales. He would go up and down the train selling candies and a newspaper he printed. He was working on the communications job level.

When I left the Marine Corps, in 1974, my rich dad said, "You must get a job in sales. Being able to sell is the basic skill of all entrepreneurs." In 1974 I went to work for the Xerox Corporation and suffered for two years because I was shy and I hated rejection. But by 1977 and 1978, I was consistently in the top five of all salespersons.

Today, I meet many want-to-be entrepreneurs who have a great idea for a new product or new business. The problem for most of them is that they cannot sell, which means they cannot raise money. The inability to raise money may be reason number one why most want-to-be entrepreneurs give up and go back to their jobs.

If You Cannot Sell You Cannot Be an Entrepreneur: Cash Flow

If you cannot sell, you cannot be an entrepreneur. If you cannot sell, you cannot raise money. If the thought of sales terrifies you, get a job at a department store and begin there. Or get a job with a company like Xerox that requires that you go around to businesses and knock on doors. As your courage increases, you may want to try a network marketing or direct sales company that is willing to train you.

An entrepreneur raises money in these ways.

1. From friends and family
2. From banks and organizations that support entrepreneurs
3. From customers
4. From suppliers
5. From investors
6. From public markets

Michael Lechter has written a Rich Dad Advisor book entitled *OPM: Other People's Money* (Warner Books). It is a very important book for all entrepreneurs. It covers each of these various ways to raise the needed capital for your business.

In other books I have read about Edison, they say his ability to sell allowed him to have a constant stream of venture capital flowing into his projects. They say he was ahead of his time in understanding and integrating the concepts of self-promotion. His ability to self-promote is one of the reasons he was given credit for having been the first to invent the electric light bulb, when he was in reality number twenty-three.

Who Owns the Company

Typically the person who raises the money, or puts up the money to start the business, owns the lion's share of the business. So learn how to sell and keep learning. For me, learning to sell was much like learning to drive racecars. It was my own fear that I had to overcome.

I am saddened by the fear in the eyes of people who want to be entrepreneurs, but are afraid of selling.

Secures Patent: Legal

In 1869, Thomas Edison receives his first patent at the age of twenty-two. He was doing his job by legally protecting his asset. Later in this book, I will go into why this step is so important for any entrepreneur.

Works for the Telegraph Company: System

By working for the telegraph company, Thomas Edison learned to understand the power of a system. That is why, when inventing his electric light bulb, he was also designing the electrical system that would power his light bulbs. If he had not worked for the telegraph company, he might not have known the importance of this system.

Another word for system is network. That is why the richest people on earth control networks, such as television networks, radio networks, gasoline networks, network marketing networks, and distribution business networks.

A big difference between a small business owner and a big business owner is the comprehension of the importance of a system or a network. Just looking at The Rich Dad Company, our success is largely due to network systems. For example, Warner Books distributes our books through their network system of booksellers. Our TV shows travel through the airwaves of television networks all over the world. Our investment seminars are joint ventures with large radio networks.

Overly Simple

As you can tell, this overly simplifies the importance of making sure all five jobs of the B-I Triangle are done. Once again, if one or more of the five jobs is not being done, the business suffers. If an entrepreneur designs a business and forgets one of the five jobs, the business suffers or even fails. The business succeeds or fails before there is a business. That is why it is important to do your homework, even if it means working for free.

Before You Quit Your Job

As this books goes on, we will further develop the B-I Triangle. Before you quit your job, it is important to look deeper into each job level of the B-I Triangle. This does not mean you have to be an expert at each level. This does mean as an entrepreneur, you do not have just one job, you have five jobs. So before quitting your job, spend a little time learning a little more about each level.

SHARON'S INSIGHTS

Lesson #3: Know the Difference Between Your Job and Your Work.

Rich dad said, "Work to learn, not to earn." With that advice he was telling Robert to do his homework, to learn the skills that would help him build a strong B-I Triangle around his business. He encouraged Robert to learn how to sell.

What are your skills? Look at the five jobs of the B-I Triangle and rate yourself as to where you are strongest and where you are weakest.

- *Product*
- *Legal*
- *Systems*
- *Communications*
- *Cash flow*

What if you find that you are totally lacking in one or another of those skills? A savvy investor will recognize if one of these areas is lacking and will likely not invest with you, no matter how good a "sales job" you do on him or her. Does that mean that you are doomed to failure? Of course not. You bring someone that has the skills that you lack on to your team. That person can be an equity participant in (part owner of) your business, an employee, or an advisor. No one can be an expert in everything. In planning your business, you bring together *a team* that covers all five jobs to ensure a strong B-I Triangle. That is why "Team" is part of the framework of the B-I Triangle

At Rich Dad, our partnership was great because we all brought different skills to the table. Robert, Kim, and I were all strong entrepreneurs, with skills in all five jobs. But it was the combination of our strengths that propelled the business forward.

Product—The CASHFLOW game was the original signature product with *Rich Dad Poor Dad* written as the "brochure" for the game. Robert and Kim had created the game and Robert and I have written *Rich Dad Poor Dad* and the Rich Dad series of books. While these original two products remain our core products, we continue to produce additional multimedia products and services to supplement them. The Rich Dad Advisor series of books was created to share the advice that we received from our advisors with you so that you might benefit from them in building your own team.

Legal—None of The Rich Dad Company founders were attorneys, so we relied on our advisors to fill that function. Michael Lechter is an integral part of our team and protected our rights in the products through patents, copyrights, trademarks, and tight and strong agreements with our suppliers and partners as outlined in his Rich Dad Advisor book *Protecting Your #1 Asset* (Warner Books). In addition Michael helped us develop the joint venture and international licensing strategies that we used and still follow today. Our growth has been through using licensing and strategic partnerships using other people's money and resources. This strategy is covered in Michael's Rich Dad Advisor Book *OPM, Other People's Money*.

Garrett Sutton is a corporate attorney and the author of Rich Dad Advisor books *Own Your Own Corporation* (Warner Books), and *How to Buy and Sell a Business* (Warner Books), which relate to the legal section of the B-I Triangle. It is imperative that you choose the right entity structure for your business. Garrett's books will help you understand your choices so you can better discuss your options with your own corporate attorney.

Spending the time and money to set up your business and protecting your assets in the beginning is crucial. As Robert learned in his wallet business, you may not get a second chance. Trying to save money on these important steps at the beginning can end up costing you so much more later on.

Systems—I had experience in designing and building the business systems needed to support the company. Having years of experience in book and game publishing, I knew how to create the manufacturing, ordering, inventory, sales fulfillment, customer service, and accounting systems to make the business operate smoothly and to position the company for growth. We also found strategic partners who already had the systems in place in certain markets to support us so we didn't have to re-create those same systems. If one system fails to operate correctly, it can cause your entire business to implode.

Communications—Robert is a brilliant communicator. He can take complex subjects, like accounting and investing, and make them easy to understand. He can talk to a group of twenty-five thousand people, and each of them will leave feeling he or she has had a personal conversation with him. Robert and Kim had years of experience in creating and presenting investment seminars. Kim oversaw the public relations and promotions arm of the business, making sure we were in the public eye as much as possible. I oversaw communications with our partners and strategic alliance partners. All three of us are strong salespeople.

To read more about sales, refer to Blair Singer's Rich Dad Advisor book *SalesDogs* (Warner Books). Blair reviews the various types of salespeople and how each type can become more effective in sales.

In addition, we recognized the importance of trademarks and brand recognition. Trademarks are the symbols that *communicate* to our customers that the Rich Dad products and services originate with us. Trademarks tie the company's reputation and the goodwill with its customers to its products and services.

We relied on our advisors to develop and protect our trademarks. Today, the Rich Dad trademarks and trade dress are recognized as identifying Rich Dad products and services throughout the world. That did not happen by accident.

Keeping in communication with your customers is very important. Through our website, www.richdad.com we provide free information, both a free and a subscription community, and information about our CASHFLOW clubs, special promotions, and upcoming events.

Cash flow—As an accountant by training and an entrepreneur in spirit, I managed the cash flow of the company. All three of us shared the philosophy that no money was to be spent until we knew where new revenues would come from to pay for the expense. It was this shared philosophy that made our partnership so strong. The three of us did not need money and took no salary for the first several years of the company, until the cash flow was strong enough to support it. The cash flow section of the B-I Triangle is extremely important because a business's cash flow is similar to a human body's need for oxygen for its blood stream. A lack of sufficient cash flow is one of the most common reasons for business failures.

HOW DO I BUILD A TEAM?

This is by far one of the most often asked questions I hear. The best way to build your team is to start by looking at the five jobs of the B-I Triangle. You don't need to make your team members partners with ownership in the business, but you need the skills on board to complete the B-I Triangle.

HOW DO I PAY THEM?

In the early stages of your business, you may need to be creative in how you bring your team together. You may agree to pay an advisor more than he or she asks for, if he or she agrees to wait to be paid until the sales can support the payment. You may add the talent through an advisory board instead of bringing the person on full-time. In some instances, you may need to bite the bullet and find the money now to pay for the appropriate guidance and legal protection.

It is important when you find partners or strategic partners that you be open about the financial arrangements. Try to find partners who are not "financially needy." Financial need has brought many wonderful partnerships to an abrupt and bitter end.

ENTREPRENEURS AND THEIR TEAMS

Rich dad said, "Business and investing are team sports." It is so much fun to have the right team, the right mission, and the right people covering the five jobs of the B-I Triangle. When all of these roles are covered by the right people, your business will have a great chance of success.

We are taught to be individual players in school. But in the world of business, it is all about having the right team and cooperating to propel the business forward.

(For more information on building a strong team, read Blair Singer's Rich Dad Advisor book *The ABC's of Building a Business Team That Wins,* Warner Books.)

USING OTHER PEOPLE'S MONEY AND RESOURCES
TO BUILD YOUR BUSINESS

As I mentioned earlier, an entrepreneur is a master at using other people's money and other people's resources to build his or her business. There are a number of different types and sources of OPM. The concept of OPM includes more than the traditional mechanisms for funding a business—obtaining a loan, or selling equity interests to investors. It also includes nontraditional forms, such as in-kind contributions and cooperative ventures. By strategically choosing the appropriate types of OPM, and strategically timing fund-raising efforts, you can build your business but still minimize your loss of control.

NEW MANAGEMENT

As The Rich Dad Company has grown so has our need to bring in new management. While Robert, Kim, and I as owners will always be ultimately responsible for the company, we recognized the need to bring in new leadership and management to oversee each of the areas of the B-I Triangle. As your company grows so will your need for the right team and advisors. It is important to recognize when you need to step aside to provide for future growth of your business.

GETTING STARTED

Go back to your personal assessment of your skills and how they relate to the B-I Triangle for your business. Do you have the team to cover the essential skills of each job of the B-I Triangle? If not, start looking for the rest of your team. If so, you are one step closer to building a successful business.

Success Reveals
Your Failures.

Chapter 4

Street Smarts versus School Smarts

Good Grades in the Real World

"If I do well in school, will I do well in the real world?" I asked my rich dad.

"That depends upon what you define as the 'real' world."

The B-I Triangle became more meaningful to me after my poor dad shut down his ice cream franchise. In his fifties he had taken his early retirement money and his life savings and lost it all. Instead of rebounding, which many entrepreneurs do after the loss of a business, my dad seemed to go downhill.

Rather than start a new business, he took a job as the head of the Teachers Union and went after his ex-boss, the governor of Hawaii, demanding better wages and benefits for teachers. Instead of continuing, learning from his mistakes, and becoming a better entrepreneur, he once again became an employee and an advocate for employee rights.

One reason why he did not rebound was because he was out of money. Instead of learning to raise capital for his next business venture, he just took a job. In effect, he was starting all over again, doing what he knew, which was to *work for and save money*, rather than learn something new, such as learn how to *raise money.* He went back to the world of employees where he felt more comfortable.

My Education Continues

Realizing that it was the lack of skill in the *communications* level that brought my dad down, I applied for a job in sales at IBM and the Xerox Corporation. It was not the paycheck but the *sales training* that I was applying for. Rich dad had told me that if I wanted to be an entrepreneur, I had best do my homework at the *communications* level of the B-I Triangle.

After two interviews, it was obvious that IBM was not the company for me, and I am certain they knew that I was not the employee for them. After five interviews at Xerox, however, I was on the short list of ten candidates applying for four positions. The final interview was with the Honolulu branch manager. On that day, six of the ten finalists sat outside his office, a scene much like the scenes from Donald Trump's hit TV show, *The Apprentice*. The other four candidates had already been interviewed.

At the time of the interview, I was still in the Marine Corps, and was dressed in my Marine Corps uniform. Sitting outside the branch manager's office, I nervously surveyed my competition. All of them were younger than me, fresh out of college, very attractive men and women, and dressed like corporate executives.

The Vietnam War was still on and very unpopular in some circles, which meant men in uniform were unpopular in those circles as well. Being off the military base and in downtown Honolulu among civilians was not fun. I had never been spit on but I had been spit at several times. So I felt really out of place, sitting next to these young people in business attire, in my Marine Corps uniform, which consisted of a short-sleeved khaki shirt, green slacks, short haircut, and military decorations.

Finally, the secretary notified me that the big boss was ready to talk to me. Entering his office, I took a seat in front of him. Reaching across the desk to shake my hand, he wasted no time in saying what he had to say. "I've reviewed your file. You come highly recommended by the rest of my staff who interviewed you. They believe you could be a valuable asset to our sales team."

With that I took a deep but quiet breath and waited for the good or the bad news. Although he was saying nice things, I noticed that he had trouble looking at me. His eyes were constantly buried in my file folder.

Finally he looked up and said, "I hate to tell you this, but I am going to be the one who turns you down." Standing, he extended his hand and said, "Thank you for applying."

Standing and shaking his hand, my blood was boiling. I wanted to know why. Why was I turned down? Figuring that I had nothing to lose, I asked, "With all due respect, sir, would you mind telling me why you're turning me down? You haven't even given me the courtesy of an interview. Can you give me a specific reason why you're so sure I'm no longer a candidate?"

"Now is not the time," said the branch manager. "At this moment, we have ten excellent applicants and only four openings. I wish we had more openings but we don't. Why not wait a year and reapply? Maybe your chances will be better then. Now, if you'll excuse me, I need to continue interviewing the other candidates."

Looking directly at him I said, "Just give me a reason. How can you tell which one of us is better than the other without an interview? Besides, I believe this is a very rude way to treat me. You have me come all the way over here and then do not even have the courtesy to interview me. So just tell me how you can make a decision without an interview. That is all I want to know."

"Okay, if you must know, you are the only applicant without an MBA. You only have a bachelor's degree." With that, the branch manager walked to the door to show me out.

"Just a minute," I said. "After graduating from the Merchant Marine Academy, where I earned my bachelor's degree, I've spent five years in the Marine Corps, fighting a war no one wanted to fight. I did not have to go to war, because I was sailing for the oil industry. I was employed by Standard Oil, which made me draft exempt, yet I volunteered anyway. And now you're telling me that you are not going to hire me because I didn't go back to college to get my master's degree? I had other things to do. There was a war to fight. And you're telling me that you'd rather hire draft dodgers who went to school?"

"That is not what we are here to discuss. We are *not* here to discuss the war or our political inclinations," said the manager, who was about my age. "And yes I am hiring people who went back to school. The job market is tight. We have many qualified applicants so we can afford to be choosy. Right now, we are only hiring applicants with MBAs. That is how we are making our decision. Go back, get your MBA, and maybe then we'll talk."

"So why wasn't I told this earlier?" I asked. "Why let me go through this process only to tell me now?"

"We make exceptions for exceptional people," said the manager. "Even though you did not have a master's degree, our screeners thought you might have other qualities we are looking for. So far, my other managers thought you were good, but not exceptional."

At that moment, I decided to become exceptional, or at least memorable. The manager, holding the door open, once again extended his hand for a weak handshake with a weak smile. Refusing to shake his hand, in a loud voice I asked, "Tell me something. What does a college degree have to do with sales?" With those words, all the other applicants with their MBAs turned their heads and stared at the open door.

"It shows character. It shows dedication and a high degree of intelligence."

"So what does a college degree have to do with sales?" I repeated.

"Okay," said the manager. "What makes you think you can sell, Mr. Marine? What makes you think you're better qualified to sell than these applicants who have more education than you?"

"Because I have spent five years getting a different kind of education, an education you cannot find in school. While these kids were cramming for college exams, I was flying a helicopter into Viet Cong machine-gun nests. My education has been in leadership, to bring out the best in my troops even though we were all terrified. Not only have we been trained in classrooms to think under pressure, we have had to think under pressure in actual combat. Most important, I have been trained to think of the mission before I think of myself; to think of my men before I think of myself. These college kids have been trained to merely kiss butt for a higher grade."

To my surprise, the branch manager was listening. I had his attention. At that moment, I decided to go for the *close*.

"Even though I do not have an MBA, I know I have the guts, the courage, and the ability to think under pressure. I know because I have been tested, not in the classroom but on the battlefield. I know your job is to beat IBM, just as my job was to beat the Viet Cong. For a year, I have been flying my gunship against the Viet Cong, a competitor far tougher and more determined to win than any IBM sales rep. My training for the past five years has allowed me to beat the Viet Cong. That is why, even though I do not have an MBA, my Marine Corps education has prepared me to beat IBM. If you think an MBA program trains these kids to beat IBM on the street, by all means hire them. I have my doubts. But I do not have doubts about me. If I can beat the Viet Cong, I know I can beat an IBM sales rep—even if they have an MBA and I don't."

The entire office area was silent. Looking down the row of hopeful applicants, briefcases carefully placed at their sides or on their laps, I could see the MBAs shaking a little. They had heard everything I said.

Turning to the branch manager, I shook his hand and thanked him for listening. I had said my piece. Smiling, I said, "I think I'll go work for your competitor."

"Just a minute," the branch manager said softly. "Please step back into my office. I do have the power to make an exception in spite of our current hiring policy."

Nothing to Lose

After being hired, I went over to rich dad's office to tell him the news. I also told him what I said once I knew I was not going to be hired. He smiled and said, "Sometimes we win the most when we have nothing to lose." He also said, "The hard part for most people is getting to nothing. Most people would rather hang on to a little than let go and get to nothing."

Four Years of Misery

Learning to sell was much harder for me than learning to fly. In fact, there were many days I wished I were back in Vietnam flying against Viet Cong machine-gun nests instead of being on the streets of Honolulu, knocking on doors. Basically, I am a very shy person. Even today, parties and social events are painful for me. So knocking on the doors of strangers was a terrifying daily experience.

For two years, I was the worst salesperson on the Xerox sales team. Every time I saw the branch manager in the hallway, I was embarrassed. Every time

I saw him, I remembered the Vietnam hero speech I gave to get the job. At my semiannual reviews, my branch manager always reminded me that he had hired me on faith and how his faith in me was slipping.

Finally, on the verge of being fired, I called rich dad and asked for a meeting. Over lunch, I explained to him that I was failing. My sales numbers were down, my income was down, and I was always at the bottom of the list of salespeople. "What do you think my problem is?"

You're Not Failing Fast Enough

Rich dad laughed his usual laugh. His laugh was his way of letting me know that I was okay and just stuck in the learning process. "How many cold calls do you make a day?" he asked.

"Three or four on a good day," I replied. "Most of the time, I am doing busywork at the office or hiding in some coffee shop, working up the courage to go knock on another door. I hate making cold sales calls. I hate rejection."

"I do not know anyone who likes rejection or making cold calls," said rich dad. "Yet I do know people who have learned to overcome their fear of rejection and the fear of making cold calls. They became very successful people in spite of their fears."

"So how can I stop failing?" I asked.

Again, rich dad laughed and said, "The way to stop failing is to fail faster."

"Fail faster?" I whined. "Are you kidding me? Why would I want to fail faster?"

"If you don't fail faster, you'll fail anyway," smiled rich dad. "Look, you're in the middle of a learning process. The process requires that you make many mistakes and learn from those mistakes. The faster you make mistakes, the faster you get through the process and get to the other side. Or you can quit. Then the process spits you out."

Rich dad was saying the same thing Thomas Edison said about failing a thousand times before inventing the electric light bulb. Rich dad was also saying the same thing my driving instructor was saying to me when I was learning how to drive a racecar at high speed. They were saying that if I wanted to get through the process faster, I had to be willing to fail faster.

Failing at Failing

For a few weeks I took rich dad's advice to heart and did my best to make more cold calls. I knocked on door after door at high speed. The problem was, I was still not getting in front of the person I needed to talk to. Their secretaries were very skilled at keeping pesky salespeople like me away from their bosses.

Failing at failing faster, I called rich dad again and asked for advice. I called him because I realized I was even failing at failing. Again, he laughed and said, "Keep your daytime job and find a sales job at night. But find a sales job that will let you fail faster."

Naturally I whined and complained. I didn't want to work at night. I was single and this was Hawaii. I wanted to be in the nightclubs of Waikiki. I did not want to be selling at night. After listening to me moan and complain, rich dad simply asked, "How badly do you want to be an entrepreneur? *The number one skill of an entrepreneur is their ability to sell.* If you do not get through this part of the process, you'll be better off as an employee. It's your life, it's your future, it's your choice. You can fail now or you can fail later."

It was an old lesson. I had listened to the same lesson before. The subject changed—this time it was the subject of sales—but the lesson was always the same. The lesson was if I wanted to succeed, I had to be willing to fail.

With my own dad's business failure still fresh in my head, I knew this lesson about sales was especially important. I knew that if I wanted to become an entrepreneur in the B quadrant, I had to learn to sell. But I hated knocking on doors. I dreaded it, day in and day out. One day, after hearing four replies of, "We're not interested," and one, "If you do not get out of my office, I'll call the cops," I hit the depths of depression. I went home rather than go back to the office. Sitting in my little apartment in Waikiki, I contemplated quitting. I even considered going back to school and getting my law degree, but I lay down, took a couple of aspirin, and that idea soon passed. It was time to fail faster in a new way.

Working for Free

Rather than find a job at night, I remembered rich dad's advice that it was easier to find work if you were willing to work for free. I found a charity that needed people to dial for dollars at night. Leaving my job at Xerox, I would go uptown and dial for dollars from 7:00 P.M. to 9:30 P.M. For two and a half hours, I failed as fast as I could over the phone. Instead of only making three to seven sales calls a day, I was sometimes making over twenty sales calls in two and a half hours at night. My rejection rate and failure rate went up. But curiously, as my failure rate went up, so did my success in raising money. The more calls I made, the better I became at handling the rejections. I learned what worked with the calls that succeeded and started changing my pitch based on the rejections and the successes. The faster I failed at night for charity, the more I succeeded at Xerox by day. Soon I was climbing up the list of salespeople, rather than being at the bottom of the list. Even though I was not being paid at night, my income by day was going up.

Working those extra hours even had an impact on my fun hours. The higher the number of *rejections* went at the charity, the more fun I had in the nightclubs of Waikiki. Suddenly I was not as afraid to talk to the pretty women in the clubs. I was less awkward; less terrified about being rejected. Soon I was even becoming cool and popular, and women were actually hanging around me. After four years at an all-male military school, and then years in the Marine Corps, being around so many pretty women was quite a treat. It was a lot better than being the lonely nerd at the end of the bar staring at the pretty women from a distance.

From 10:00 P.M. to one in the morning, I was the disco duck, just like John Travolta in the movie *Saturday Night Fever*. I even had a white suit, long-collared shirts, disco boots on my feet, and shells around my neck. Everywhere I went, I walked to the sounds of the Bee Gees song "Staying Alive," playing in my head. My hours were ridiculous and I am sure I looked ridiculous, but it worked. I was failing fast and doing my homework for the communications level of the B-I Triangle.

Failing Pays Off

In my third and fourth years at Xerox, instead of being at the bottom of the sales pack, I was at the top of the pack. I was also making a lot of money. My failing was paying off. In the fourth year, I was consistently number one in sales. Once I made it to the top, I knew it was time to move on. My school days in sales were over. It was time to learn something new. But little did I know that my success in sales was setting me up for the biggest business failure of my life.

The Four Business Schools

Rich dad explained to his son and me that there are four different types of business schools. They are:

1. The Traditional Business Schools. These schools are located at accredited colleges and universities and offer degreed programs, such as an MBA program.
2. The Family Business School. Many family businesses, such as my rich dad's business, are great places to get a business education—if you are a member of the family.
3. The Corporate Business School. Many businesses offer intern programs for promising young students. After graduation, the company hires and then guides their career development. In many cases, the company will pay the tuition and even allow time off for further study. After receiving a formal education, promising employees are often rotated through different divisions of the company, so they get to see the entire business and get hands-on experience.
4. The Business School of the Streets. This is the school entrepreneurs attend when they leave the security blanket of school, family, or the corporate world. This is the school where your street smarts are developed.

Going to School

All four schools have their merits, their strengths and weaknesses. I am not here to say one is better than the other. In my life, I have been fortunate enough to attend all four, in one way or another.

A Traditional Business School

While at Xerox, I did attend a local university night school, with the intent of receiving my MBA. That lasted less than a year. It was not for me. The instructors were either employees of the school or employees of a corporation. The students, for the most part, were seeking to become high-paid, well-educated employees, just like their instructors. They were looking to climb the corporate ladder, whereas I wanted to build and own corporate ladders. It was a different culture and a different curriculum, so I left.

A Family Business School

My friendship with Mike allowed me to attend a Family Business School via rich dad's businesses. That was a great school for me, simply because it lasted for years and rich dad was not only a successful real world entrepreneur, he was also a great teacher.

A Corporate Business School

Through the Xerox Corporation, I attended one of the best corporate sales training programs in the world. Soon after I was hired, in 1974, the company flew me first class from Honolulu to Leesburg, Virginia, to spend two weeks at their sales training facility. It was fantastic. After receiving our classroom training, we immediately hit the streets to practice what we learned in the classroom. Our sales managers were great teachers and mentors. They kept us on track with classroom theory applied to real world challenges found on the street. We studied hard, not only learning sales skills but also studying our competitor's products and strategies. We had one objective at that time and that was to beat IBM. They were tough competitors and a worthy opponent, so we knew we had to be up for the challenge.

The Business School of the Streets

But the toughest business school for me was the Business School of the Streets. Once I left Xerox and hit the streets, I literally hit the streets. The Business School of the Streets was a horrible school, a harsh teacher, and tough on grades. Many times I came face to face with my greatest fears and the depths of personal self-doubt. Yet, it was also the best business school for me. It was just what I needed. Instead of As and Bs as grades, street grades are measured in dollars earned or dollars lost.

Graduation Day

In 1978, I "graduated" from the Xerox Corporate Business School and entered the Business School of the Streets. It was an emotionally tough transition for me. I went from the world of flying first class, having nice offices, a steady paycheck, and everything paid for by the company, to a world where I paid for everything, including paper clips, travel, and other people's salaries and benefits. Before I left the Corporate Business School, I had no idea how much running a business cost. For two years, in order to reduce expenses, my two partners and I did not take salaries. Once again, I was working for free and I knew why rich dad insisted his son and I work for him for free. He was preparing us for the world of entrepreneurship—a world where everyone gets paid first and you get paid last . . . if you get paid at all.

Lesson #4: Success Reveals Your Failures

Another of rich dad's lessons was "success reveals your failures." In other words, your strengths will reveal your weaknesses. Again, I did not know what he meant until my own business had became successful.

Our nylon surfer wallet business was successful in two out of the five levels. We were successful at the communications level and the product level. The three partners had trained for years to be successful at those levels. The problem was we were too well-trained at the two levels and our success was too great too soon. It was like hooking up a plastic garden hose to a fire hydrant. As soon as international success put pressure on the system, the whole business blew. Our strong points blew out through our weak points. Our strengths had revealed our weaknesses. Our success had revealed our failures. We had failed to strengthen the legal, the systems, and the cash flow levels of the B-I Triangle. We had them covered, but we failed to strengthen them as our success increased.

Back to the Drawing Boards

After our venture collapsed, two of my partners left the business. I wanted to quit also, but rich dad said, "Rebuild the business. It will be the business school you have been waiting for."

For the next six years, I went back to the drawing board many times. Each failure was less painful and the recovery was quicker. Each time I failed, I knew what to work on. I knew what I had to study next. The Business School of the Streets was guiding me. Each failure was actually making me smarter and more confident. Each failure made me less afraid of failing and more excited about learning what I needed to learn next. Each failure was a challenge, the door to the next world. If I was successful, the door to the next world opened. If I failed and the challenge beat me, the door slammed in my face. If the door slammed in my face, it meant I needed to get smarter. I needed to think harder. I needed to use my creativity to find a way to get into the next door. In many ways, it was like being a salesman on the street again, knocking on doors once more.

When people ask me how we survived through all those years without money, my answer is, "I do not know. I simply took it one day at a time." After my first two partners left, and things looked bleakest, two new partners showed up, and one of them was my brother Jon. They brought in some money but more important, they brought in a new vitality and new skills. One new partner, Dave, brought experience in the systems level of the business. He was excellent at manufacturing. My brother Jon came in to handle the cash flow level. He was excellent at keeping our creditors happy and suppliers supplying. We also brought in a new advisor, a retired senior auditor from an accounting firm, to help us straighten out our mess. He was happy to work for free since his wife wanted him out of the house anyway. He was happy to have an office to go to. I also believed he found our struggles entertaining. He would chuckle a lot as my two new partners and I moaned and groaned about our problems. More than work for free and straighten out our mess, he also helped us raise more capital by teaching us how to raise capital in a more professional manner.

As I said, "We survived by taking it one day at a time." All I knew was that I did not want to go back to a job as my poor dad had, once his ice cream business failed. In many ways, my philosophy was, "I had gone too far to turn back."

Rich dad was correct. It was the best ten-year business school I could have gone to. Starting with Xerox in 1974 and finally having built a successful business by 1984, it was a ten-year process of building, failing, correcting, rebuilding, and failing. For me, it was the best way to learn. Many times, I felt like I was building a racecar instead of a business. Our team would work on the business, take it out to the racetrack, step on the gas, blow an engine or hydraulic line, and return to the shop.

A System of Systems

In many ways, building a business is very much like building a car. A car is a system of systems. A car consists of an electrical system, fuel system, brake system, hydraulic system, and so on. If one of the systems breaks, the car shuts down or becomes unsafe.

The human body is also a system of systems. We have the blood system, respiratory system, digestive system, skeletal system, and more. If one of the systems breaks, the body may also shut down.

In many ways, learning to be an entrepreneur is like going to school to become an auto mechanic or a medical doctor. Just as a medical doctor will look at X-rays or your blood tests, an entrepreneur will look at the B-I Triangle to assess the overall health and vitality of his or her business.

After building and rebuilding my nylon wallet business several times, and building and rebuilding other businesses, analyzing businesses became easier and easier. Today, instead of fear, there is excitement. Today, instead of great risks I see great opportunities. Today I know that if I lost everything I could rebuild it. That is why going through all four of the business schools, gaining school smarts as well as street smarts, was a great education.

Which Is More Important?

Often I am asked, "What is more important for an entrepreneur, school smarts or street smarts?" Today, my answer is both. To be a successful entrepreneur, you and your team need to be school smart and street smart. When you look at the B-I Triangle, you can see why. While all five levels require street smarts, the legal and cash flow levels really do require a school-trained professional. Obviously, for the legal level you want an attorney, and for the cash flow level, you want an accountant, preferably a CPA. As obvious as this may sound, you would be surprised how many people come to me wanting advice on how to build a business without an accountant or attorney on their team.

Team Smarts

An entrepreneur needs to know the difference between school smarts and street smarts. More important, an entrepreneur needs to have team smarts, which means finding the best combination of people required by the task at hand. To win in business, ultimately, it is team smarts that wins.

In Jim Collins's bestselling book *Good to Great* (HarperCollins, 2001), he talks about the need to make sure you have the right people on the bus and that they are in the right seats on the bus. It is important to have a team with the talent necessary for all the jobs in the B-I Triangle. More important, Jim talks about how important it is to get the wrong people *off* your bus.

Three Big Mistakes

When it comes to legal and accounting professionals, I have noticed three basic mistakes entrepreneurs make:

1. The entrepreneur does not have or does not seek proper legal and accounting advice before setting up his or her business.
2. The entrepreneur listens to his or her accountant or attorney too much. Many times I have asked the entrepreneur who was running the business, the entrepreneur, the accountant, or the attorney? Always remember, even if they are smarter than you in certain subjects, it's you who pays their bills. You need to decide the course of your business.
3. The entrepreneur has an accountant or attorney who is not part of the entrepreneur's team. This does not mean you have to employ

them full-time. It simply means you need to trust them. They need to know everything and want to know everything. You need to be intimate. Rich dad used to say, "Having a part-time accountant or attorney is like having a part-time husband or wife."

The Difference between School Smarts and Street Smarts

A-Thinker	**C-Thinker**
Analytical skills/critical thinker	Creative thinker/flexible logic
T-Thinker	**P-Thinker**
Technical skills/expertise	People skills/personal leadership

On the left side are characteristics generally associated with school-smart people. The right side is generally associated with street-smart people. My rich dad said, "If you are to develop as an entrepreneur, you will need to develop all four areas of yourself."

I will refer again to these traits, and they should become clearer with each example. For now, I will briefly explain each quadrant.

A-Thinker: We all know people with great analytical skills. They enjoyed solving math problems in school. If you offer a new idea they will probably be critical or cynical more than open to the new idea. Rather than make a quick decision, they will usually think and analyze the situation for a long period of time before deciding. Before making a decision they will come back to you and ask for more details.

C-Thinker: We all know people who are creative artists in their work. This does not mean they are artists who paint. It's just that they are creative. They could be accountants or attorneys. They like to see the big picture. They think outside the box. C-Thinkers often drive A-Thinkers crazy. Flexible logic means they are flexible in what makes sense to them. For example, when I say, "I can make more money when the market is crashing," C-Thinkers may be better able to grasp that logic more than an A-Thinker. In other words, C-Thinkers can take something illogical and make it fit their logic. They are more open-minded. A-Thinkers often just reject anything that does not fit their way of thinking.

T-Thinker: We all know people who are technical wizards. They may be computer wizards who speak a language found only on Mars. Or they may be motorheads who think everyone knows how to drop a transmission and fix it. T-Thinkers are often the exact opposite of P-Thinkers. Why? Because T-Thinkers seem to be most comfortable with people who enjoy the same technical subject they do. They attend computer conventions just to meet other computer geeks. They hang out in auto parts stores just to meet someone they can talk to.

P-Thinker: In high school, the strongest P-Thinkers often ran for student body officer or were voted Most Popular. These people can start a conversation with anyone, unlike the T-Thinker. At a party, P-Thinkers are the stars. Everyone invites them to their parties because they make the party fun. In business, the staff and employees love this person. They will do anything for a P-Thinker. In business P-Thinkers can make great leaders if they also possess the necessary business skills. When they speak, people listen.

Different Thinker Different Entrepreneur

As you may have already guessed, each different type of thinker will be attracted to different types of entrepreneurial businesses. For example, a T-Thinker motorhead may enjoy opening an auto parts store. An A-Thinker lawyer may like opening a law practice. A C-Thinking medical doctor may want to become a cosmetic surgeon. And P-Thinkers may become perpetual politicians, always running for office. They may also become a minister, ministering to their flock. Or they may become entertainers, getting paid to be the center of attention.

All Four Are Important

Rich dad said, "All four types of thinkers are important for a business. Small businesses stay small or fail because they lack one or more of the different types of thinkers." One of the reasons why my nylon surfer wallet business failed was that we were too strong in the C and P categories and very weak in the A and T categories.

Many self-employed entrepreneurs are very strong in the A or T category. A person may be a great lawyer in the A category or a great electrician in the T category. These people are very smart and experts in one market niche, and do best on their own. They may struggle to grow because they are weak in the C or P category.

In the world of investing, an A or T person will invest differently from a C or P person. A and T people want a precise formula to follow. They want to see the numbers and analyze them repeatedly. C or P investors are more interested in exotic deals or want to know who the other *players* are in the deal. Notice the word *player,* which means people are important in the investment equation. This is important for P-Thinkers.

When I do my classes on investing, I will often have a group of people ask, "Tell me what to do. What is the formula you followed?" When I hear such questions, I know they are probably A- or T-Thinkers. It drives them crazy when I say, "We just created the investment. We got together with a group of people and put the deal together and made a lot of money." It drives them crazy because our way of investing does not fit their logic system. It is easy for A- and T-Thinkers to follow a formula such as "Save money, get out of debt, invest for the long term, and diversify." This formula soothes their need for a logical formula for investing, even though it is not the greatest investment formula. They may get frustrated with my formulas since they may not have minds that allow flexible logic.

Rich Dad's Advice

Rich dad was concerned about my becoming an entrepreneur because I was weak in all four categories. I was not strong as an A-, T-, P-, or C-Thinker. He said, "You have to find one category and become good at it."

On a legal tablet, he wrote down the five jobs of the B-I Triangle.

Product
Legal
Systems
Communications
Cash flow

He then said, "I don't think you have a realistic chance in the legal, systems, or cash flow levels of the B-I Triangle. You have not done well in school and you probably never will. I don't think you'll ever go back to school and become a lawyer, accountant, or engineer. That leaves the product level and the communications level. Choose one and commit the rest of your life to being the best at that level." And that is how I decided to leave the Marine Corps and work for the Xerox Corporation. In 1974, I decided my best chance for success as an entrepreneur was to be an expert at communicating to *people.* I was not a natural P-Thinker but I decided it was a category I was willing to study for the rest of my life.

Today, I have tremendous respect for people with school smarts, people who are creative and can design products, or legal minds who have made the study of law their life, or engineers who are great at systems. I have tremendous respect for smart accountants who know how to keep track of where the cash has been flowing.

Why Become an Expert at Only One Level

When I asked my rich dad why I should become an expert at one level his reply was, "If you want to have the best team around you, you need to be the best at something as well. If you are only mediocre at communications, then you will never need the best attorneys, engineers, designers, or accountants. You will only need mediocre ones because you are mediocre."

An Expert at All Levels

Some self-employed people do not do as well as they could because they feel they have to be experts at all five levels. They are often smart, and good at all five levels, but they may not be strong at all levels. This may be why they often stay in the S quadrant. If you want to be a success in the B quadrant, you need to be the best at one of the levels, and then build a team of experts around you that fill in the rest of the levels.

Overcoming my shyness, I would say I became pretty good at sales, marketing, writing, speaking, and creating informational products. If not for years of training at the communication level and developing my P-Thinking abilities, I doubt if The Rich Dad Company would have become as successful as it has become.

Today, The Rich Dad Company has strong product design teams, aggressive and smart legal teams, and established international distribution systems, as well as internal systems, marketing communication systems throughout the world, and a world-class accounting team keeping the cash flowing. As a business, we have thousands of people throughout the world working for us, or our products. As the old saying goes, The Rich Dad Company was an overnight success, but it took years to get there.

Before You Quit Your Job

The Business School of the Streets is a very tough school. I still have memories of walking around New York City, running out of money, knocking on doors, hoping to find someone who would say "yes" to my nylon wallets. I love New York City, yet I always know that it can be a very cruel city if you are poor, unsuccessful, and unknown.

Although The Rich Dad Company's offices are in Scottsdale, Arizona, the engines of the business are located in New York City and cities all over the world. It is exciting to have access to the offices of some of the most powerful companies in the world, companies such as Time Warner, Viacom, American Express, ABC, NBC, CBS, *Fortune, Businessweek* magazine, Forbes magazines, the *New York Times, New York Post,* and CNN. It is even more exciting to do, or propose to do, business with them. Yet as successful as we have been over the last eight years, I always remember the streets of New York, and how cold the city can become if one of the levels of the B-I Triangle becomes weak.

So before quitting your job, know that your most important job is to develop yourself. If you will dedicate yourself to becoming a great entrepreneur you will find it easier to find great people to be members of your team. If you can put together a great team, you will find it easier to be successful wherever you are. So it is not a matter of which kind of smarts is more important. Just remember it is very important to strive to be as smart as you can be, both in street smarts and in school smarts.

SHARON'S INSIGHTS

Lesson #4: Success Reveals Your Failures.

As Robert explained, rich dad described four different types of business schools. They are:

1. The Traditional Business School
2. The Family Business School
3. The Corporate Business School
4. The Business School of the Streets

While all four of these can provide valuable training, as they did in Robert's case, do you have to have *all* four to succeed as an entrepreneur? The answer is "it depends." While each of the four provides valuable education and training, they are not prerequisites for success. But how do we succeed without them?

If you do not have traditional business school experience, you can still work toward gaining the education through alternative methods. Community colleges offer business and entrepreneurial programs. The Small Business Association offers seminars and local organizations offer seminars and mentoring services to entrepreneurs.

There are many books and online resources to support an entrepreneur's desire for education.

FOCUS ON THE FIVE JOBS OF THE B-I TRIANGLE

Without traditional business school education, finding and using these other sources can speed your path to success. By focusing on education specific to developing the skills of the five jobs of the B-I Triangle, you can better prepare yourself in building a team that can support you.

BECOME AN EXPERT IN ONE JOB

As rich dad advised Robert, you may want to consider focusing your efforts on becoming an expert in one of the five jobs. Like Robert, you may want to focus on the *communications* level. Generally the entrepreneur will be the most passionate and effective salesperson for his or her company. Being able to sell is essential in convincing investors to invest in your company as well as selling your company's products to consumers. As both rich dad and Robert advise, being able to sell is a very important business skill for an entrepreneur.

EXPERT ADVISORS

As we have discussed in many instances you can leverage the experience and education of your advisors to fill in areas in which you may be weak. For instance, during my years in public accounting, I was exposed to many successful companies as well as many companies that were not so successful. This experience, combined with my education as a CPA, has been invaluable in the businesses I have started over the last twenty-five years. Your accountant may be able to provide this expertise to you and your business.

Find and engage good advisors, then *listen* to them. Ask as many questions as you want—those questions are the key to making sure that the advisor takes all of the important questions into account when providing their advice—but make sure that the advice from the experts factors in your decisions. One of the mistakes that I have seen entrepreneurs make is to ignore any advice that they don't like. It makes no sense to pay good money for advice, and then ignore it. You may not always follow the advice, but it should be a factor in your considerations. In the end, it's your job to make the decision—but it is the advisor's job to make sure that the decision that you make is an informed decision. It is your job as an entrepreneur to determine whether to assume a risk. It is the advisor's job to make sure that you understand the risk that you are assuming.

I also recommend that you bring your various advisors together regularly for brainstorming sessions. While this may seem obvious, many business owners consult their advisors independently. The best way to leverage your advisors' education and experience is to get them together and learn how each approaches an opportunity or challenge and how they bounce ideas off each other. In the end, it is of much greater benefit to you. You are still the leader and ultimately responsible for your company.

STREET SMARTS

Even with my education and my experience in public accounting, there was still plenty to learn from real life business experience. There is nothing like learning from your mistakes to realize how much there is to know in building and running a successful business. It just makes you realize how important it is to build the right team around you. As rich dad said, "It is not only what you know, but who you know." When you encounter a problem in business it is a great relief to know who to call for instant assistance. It is through cooperation and collaboration that the successful businesses of tomorrow will be built.

TEAM SMARTS

The combination of school smarts and street smarts will help you build a successful business. But "team smarts" is the true formula of success. It combines school smarts and street smarts from your entire team. All of your team's shared education and experience combined to work on your business collaboratively will surely propel your business forward.

The Process Is More Important than the Goal.

Chapter 5

Money Talks

Success?

"We were rich for six months," I said. "Money was pouring in, and then the roof caved in."

"Well, at least you were millionaires, even if it was only for six months," said rich dad, chuckling. "Many people will never know what it feels like to be rich."

"Yes, and now I'm financially ruined," I whined. "Six months of success and years to pay it back."

"Well, at least you had a taste of the good life." Rich dad smiled, doing his best to cheer me up. "Most people will never know what it feels like to build an international business and be an international success. Most people will never know what it feels like to have money pouring in the door."

"And most people will never know what it feels like to be an international failure with money pouring out the door," I said, now beginning to laugh.

"So why are you laughing?" asked rich dad.

"I don't really know," I replied. "I guess I am laughing because as painful as it is right now, I would not trade this experience for anything. As you said, I caught a glimpse of a different world, a world very few people will ever see, a world I would like to see again. It was all so very exciting, for a while."

Rich dad leaned back in his chair. For a long period of time, he seemed to sit there silently reflecting upon his life, the battles won and battles lost. Finally he came out of his thoughts and said, "Most people dash from home to work seeking security from this world. For many, work and home are where they hide from the harsh realities of a competitive world. All they want is a steady paycheck and a place to call home away from home." Rich dad again paused and then said, "And others seek something else."

"You mean something more than just security and money?" I asked.

With a wistful look in his eye rich dad said, "Yes. If all I wanted was a secure job, a steady paycheck, and a home away from home, I would never have become an entrepreneur."

"And what were you looking for?" I asked. "Beyond security and money?"

"A different world . . . a different way of living. As you know, I came from a very poor family. I wanted more than just a lot of money. I wanted more than just a big house and nice cars. I wanted a life few people ever live. I knew I faced greater chances of failing than succeeding. I knew there would be highs and lows as an entrepreneur. And like everyone else, I was concerned by the highs and lows. Yet, it was the thought of a different level of life that made the risks seem worthwhile. It was not just about making money, it was about a life's adventure." Rich dad then stopped for a long moment, thinking his private thoughts.

Finally continuing he said, "When my life is over, I already know the highs and lows will become memories of just one great adventure, of deals won and deals lost, friends made and friends lost, and of money made and money lost. It will be memories of total strangers walking in your door, just to join you on your next adventure, and walking out your door once the adventure is over. And along the way, hopefully you find that place, a place with the quality and beauty of life you knew in your heart existed; you knew in your dreams would come true."

"And have you found your place?" I asked.

Rich dad simply nodded and smiled contentedly.

A *Glimpse of Your Future*

With that, there really was not much more to talk about. I knew what I had to do. I had creditors to talk to; a business to repair and rebuild. I still had many things to learn, so I knew it was time to get back to work. Picking up my things, I shook rich dad's hand and headed for the door.

"One more thing," said rich dad.

Turning at the door, I asked, "And what is that?"

"You know those six months when you were on top of the world?"

"Yes, I do," I replied.

"That was a glimpse of your future."

"A glimpse?" I repeated. "What do you mean? A glimpse of what future?"

"In 1974, when you decided to follow my advice rather than your dad's, you began a journey, a process. The process has a beginning and an ending. It may take years, but it does have an ending. Someday this struggle you are in will suddenly end and a new life and new process will begin. You will win if you remain faithful to this process. During this current process, you will be given many more challenges, and more lessons to learn. The process is testing you as well as teaching you. If you pass the test and learn the lesson, you get to go on to your next process. If you fail a test and quit rather than retake the test, the process spits you out. So those six months of the good life were giving you a glimpse of your future, a glimpse of the world you seek, a glimpse of a world that awaits you. A glimpse of your future and a way of saying to you, 'Keep going. You're on the right track.' It's giving you a shot of courage to face the process to come and the motivation to keep going and to keep learning."

"And how do you know this?" I asked. "Did you also receive a glimpse of your future when you needed it?"

Once again, rich dad simply nodded and grinned.

A *Ten-Year Process*

Rich dad's lesson on the subject of process has proven to be a very important lesson in my life. Looking back, it seems that my personal processes ran in approximately ten-year cycles, with each ten-year cycle a different process. For example:

1. 1974 to 1984: *The Learning Process.* This is the period of time when I was learning the real world skills of an entrepreneur. Classroom days were over and the Business School of the Streets was doing the teaching. I was making many big mistakes simply because I had a lot to learn. During this period of time, I was practicing my entrepreneurial skills building a company that manufactured nylon wallets in the Far East and marketed them throughout the world. We also designed merchandise products for rock bands such as Duran Duran, Van Halen, Judas Priest, Pink Floyd, and Boy George. At this time, I was learning as much as I could about all levels of the B-I Triangle. This was the *real world* business school I referred to earlier in the book.

2. 1984 to 1994: *The Earning Process.* During this period of time, I began to make a lot of money as well as build a foundation of wealth. The lessons learned from the mistakes were paying off in money. Investing that money in real estate gave Kim and me not only a foundation of assets generating passive income but also more experience as real estate investors. During this period I was following my passion, which was to teach entrepreneurship and investing. Our company put on courses entitled The Business School for Entrepreneurs and The Business School for Investors. At this point, I was combining my poor dad's profession, teaching, with my rich dad's lessons on business and investing. This was also my time to advance my skills on the communication level of the B-I Triangle by learning to teach in ways far different from the traditional methods of teaching. As stated in a previous chapter, I had to decide which level I wanted to become an expert at. After learning the basics of all five levels, I decided that my best chance of developing my skills was at the communication level. By being the best I could be at this level, I would have a better chance of attracting a higher caliber of team members at the other levels.

3. 1994 to 2004: *The Giving Back Process.* After Kim and I had enough money to survive on without working, I knew it was time to give back. In selling our education business, I took time to design a business that could teach my rich dad's lessons to more people at lower prices. That was the conception of The Rich Dad Company. Instead of teaching via seminars, that at times cost over $5,000 to attend, I decided to create

the CASHFLOW Game. During this period of time, my focus shifted from making money to asking myself the question, "How can I serve more people?" Ironically, I have made more money focusing on serving more people rather than focusing on how to make more money. In 2004, Kim, Sharon, and I decided that we had taken the business to a point where we needed to bring in additional management to take it to the next level—and the business has much further to go. Our job as entrepreneurs is done.

The ten-year cycles were not planned. It just seemed to happen that way. It was only when I looked back over my shoulder that I recognized the ten-year pattern.

Catching Up to My Future

Today, I live the life I caught a glimpse of in 1978. The process had kept its promise to me.

Who Wants to Be a Millionaire?

LESSON #5: The process is more important than the goal.

Most of us have heard that it is important to set goals. Yet rich dad had a different take on goals. He said, "Goals are important, but the *process* of obtaining the goal is far more important than the goal." Explaining, he would say, "If you ask most people, 'Who wants to be a millionaire?' most people would raise their hand. That would mean they have a goal of becoming a millionaire but now they need to choose the *process* for achieving that goal. There are many ways a person can reach their goal of becoming a millionaire."

Different Processes to Become a Millionaire

Rich dad said, "The reason the process is more important than the goal is that the process determines who you become in attaining your goals. Some examples of this are:

1. You can become rich by inheriting money. But most of us know if we stand to inherit money—and finding a rich person willing to adopt you may prove quite difficult.

2. You can become rich by marrying for money. The problem is we all know who and what you become in the process. It is the oldest profession in the world.

3. You can become rich by being cheap. The problem is, if you become rich by being cheap, at the end of the process you are still cheap—and the world hates rich cheap people. In fact the rich cheap people of the world give rich people a bad name.

4. You can become rich by being a crook. The problem is, at the end of the process you are a rich crook with crooked friends. Honest rich people do not like crooked rich people.

5. You can become rich by being lucky. There are many ways to be lucky when getting rich. You can be born with great talent, as many athletes and actors are; you can win the lottery; you can be born rich; or you can just happen to be in the right place at the right time. The problem is if you lose the money, you have to count on luck to get the money back.

6. You can become rich by becoming a smart entrepreneur. To become a rich entrepreneur you need to become a smart entrepreneur. The reason I like this process of becoming rich is that the process requires you to become smart, and becoming smart is much more important than making money. If you lose your money, this process will teach you how to get it back and become even smarter in the process.

Money Does Not Make You Rich

Lottery prizes are often in the millions of dollars simply because there are millions of people who want to become rich by being lucky. I find it interesting that this process of getting rich is not only the riskiest of all methods with the worst odds of winning; it is a process that does not increase your financial intelligence at all. In fact, winning the lottery often reveals how low a person's financial intelligence really is. The following are recent stories from the MSN website about people who used *the process of luck* to become millionaires.

Two-Time Lottery Winner—Living in a Trailer

"Winning the lottery isn't always what it's cracked up to be," says Evelyn Adams, who won the New Jersey lottery not just once, but twice (1985, 1986), to the tune of $5.4 million. Today the money is all gone and Adams lives in a trailer.

"I won the American dream but I lost it, too. It was a very hard fall. It's called rock bottom," says Adams.

"Everybody wanted my money. Everybody had their hand out. I never learned one simple word in the English language—'No.' I wish I had the chance to do it all over again. I'd be much smarter about it now," says Adams.

A Poor Boy Who Got Lucky

Ken Proxmire was a machinist when he won $1 million in the Michigan lottery. He moved to California and went into the car business with his brothers. Within five years, he had filed for bankruptcy.

"He was just a poor boy who got lucky," explains Ken's son Rick.

Living on Food Stamps

William "Bud" Post won $16.2 million in the Pennsylvania lottery in 1988 but now lives on his Social Security.

"I wish it never happened. It was totally a nightmare," says Post.

A former girlfriend successfully sued him for a share of his winnings. It wasn't his only lawsuit. A brother was arrested for hiring a hit man to kill him, hoping to inherit a share of the winnings. Other siblings pestered him until he agreed to invest in a car business and a restaurant in Sarasota, Florida—two ventures that brought no money back and further strained his relationship with his siblings.

Post even spent time in jail for firing a gun over the head of a bill collector.

Within a year he was $1 million in debt. He admits he was both foolish and careless, trying to please his family. Now he lives quietly on $450 a month and food stamps.

What If You Lost a Billion Dollars?

Years ago, a reporter asked Henry Ford, a billionaire when a billion dollars was worth much more than it is today, "What if you lost everything?"

Ford's response was, "I'd have it back in less than five years."

When you contrast Henry Ford's response to the responses of the lottery winners, I believe you get the difference between the process of becoming a millionaire by luck and that of becoming a billionaire by being an entrepreneur.

A Question to Think About

After reading about Henry Ford's response, I often ask myself, "If I lost it all, how much would I recover in five years?" If my past is any indicator, each time I hit zero—and I did hit zero a number of times—I came roaring back making much more money than I lost. I've not made a billion dollars, as Henry Ford did, but my businesses have had income in the hundreds of millions of dollars. So the entrepreneur's process, in my opinion, is the best process to get rich because it is also an educational process to achieving great wealth, if you have the heart, mind, and stamina for it.

Pouring the Foundation

The educational process of becoming an entrepreneur requires the entrepreneur to learn and gain experience in the five levels of the B-I Triangle. Once a person becomes somewhat proficient in all five levels, life is pretty good. As stated earlier, it took me about ten years as an undergraduate student of the Business School of the Streets to attain a basic level of proficiency. Can a person attain proficiency at all five levels faster? Absolutely. One of the reasons for writing this book was to simply inform you of the levels. If you know about the levels, it makes it easier to focus your learning activities and personal development, level by level.

Why Cash Flow Is the Base Level

Most want-to-be entrepreneurs focus on the product level, the top level of the B-I Triangle. While the product is important, looking at the B-I Triangle, you notice that cash flow is the base level with the most area allocated to it in the diagram.

When I first started out as a professional entrepreneur, I used to get excited looking at new products or ideas. That is how I got caught up in the nylon wallet business. The nylon wallet was just one of about fifty different product ideas we considered. Some of the other ideas were wooden puzzles, sugar packets with Hawaiian pictures on the packets wrapped in a burlap box, a magazine, and even candy bullets packaged in a box that said, "Bite the Bullet." As you can tell, our C-Thinking ability was unlimited.

As soon as we decided on the nylon wallet as our product, the three of us began designing its packaging. Again, this required C-Thinking, which all three of us enjoyed. It was not long before we were hitting the streets looking for investors. Most potential investors were polite and took time to look at our product and its packaging. Then, if they were interested, they all asked the same questions. "May I see your numbers? What are your projections?" When we did not have them, we were turned down and turned down quickly.

Even rich dad turned us down, but he did not turn us down politely. He was furious. Kicking my two partners out of his office, he closed the door behind them and gave me one of the most severe reprimands I have ever had from either of my dads. I have written about this incident in other books, so I will not retell the details of the story, yet the lesson is worth repeating. The lesson is, for successful business people and investors, the numbers are very important.

Today, older, wiser, and much wealthier, whenever I am asked to evaluate a new product or business, I do the same thing those investors did to me years ago: I ask for the numbers.

This does not mean I am any better at reading or producing numbers today than I was in 1978. The difference is I ask for them and then ask someone who is trained at reading the numbers to go over the numbers with me. My level of expertise is the communications level, and I do go over that portion of the business plan carefully. That I am pretty good at the communications level and not that good at the cash flow level is not an excuse for me to ignore the cash flow level, or any level for that matter. As an entrepreneur and an investor, I need to know the entire business, not just the parts of the business I am interested in.

If a want-to-be entrepreneur asks to show me a new product, the first question I ask is, "Do you have financial projections?" Or, if the business is an established business, I will ask, "Do you have financial statements?" Again, I ask these questions not because I am great at numbers; I ask these questions as a test of the want-to-be entrepreneur's knowledge of what it takes to be an entrepreneur.

If the want-to-be entrepreneur does have actual numbers or projections, I will ask someone like my partner Sharon, a trained CPA and a great entrepreneur, to come with me to interpret the numbers. The numbers tell a story, and I need someone who can read the numbers and interpret them to tell me the story. As an entrepreneur, I believe it is very important to tell your story in the numbers.

Before You Quit Your Job

If you are serious about becoming an entrepreneur, an interesting exercise is to hire an experienced accountant to help you with a proposed budget and cash flow analysis. The reason this is an important exercise, even if you do not go through with the product or the business, is that the exercise will give you a better idea of what it costs to start and run a business. Once you know your budget, you will have an idea of how much you will have to sell, the communications level, to support the business. The experienced accountant may also point out expenses you may not know about. I wish I had done this exercise before starting my nylon surfer wallet business. I might not have lost as much money as I did. The cost of hiring a trained accountant for guidance would be a drop in the bucket when compared to the money I lost. More important, the money you spend for an accountant will be priceless in your educational development as an entrepreneur.

If you ask most accountants, I am certain they will tell you that most entrepreneurs lack knowledge of accounting laws and practices and are horrible at recordkeeping. Their lack of accuracy with numbers may eventually get them in trouble. It is this lack of knowledge that eventually costs them even more money. In other words, pay them a little early rather than pay them a lot more, later.

Why I Created the Board Game

One of the primary reasons I created the CASHFLOW board game is the reprimand my rich dad gave me back in the 1970s. For most of my life, rich dad had been emphasizing the importance of the numbers, and I sincerely thought I understood them. It was not until he chewed me out when I lost so much money that I began to understand why he put such emphasis on the numbers. Today I understand.

The game serves as a communication bridge between you and your accountant. It will not make you an accountant. The game will give you the advantage of being more familiar with the T-Thinking and A-Thinking logic of the accounting profession.

If you are like me, weak at the subject of accounting and numbers, I strongly suggest you use the CASHFLOW games as an educational tool. Please go to our website www.richdad.com and find out more about the CASHFLOW Game products and the CASHFLOW clubs throughout the world.

Again, before quitting your job to start your business, I strongly recommend that you sit down with an *experienced* accountant and go over a budget on what it may cost to start and operate your business. If the numbers shock you, simply take a deep breath and sleep on it for a night or two. Give yourself time to expand your mind around the costs. The cost of starting, building, or growing a business is often more than originally imagined.

Keep Your Job

If your costs frighten you off, then maybe being an entrepreneur is not for you. High expenses are an everyday challenge in business. Taking on that challenge is one of the most important jobs of an entrepreneur. It requires a lot of A-, T-, P-, and C-Thinking power to solve these challenges. Personally, I do not like the challenges, but every time I have taken them on, I have become a better, wiser, and more confident entrepreneur.

Show Me the Numbers

When want-to-be entrepreneurs call looking for money, they fall into two categories. They are:

1. Those with a business plan and financial projections
2. Those with nothing

If a person comes with empty hands, it either means they are very early in the process or they don't have a clue what they are doing, or both. Talking only about the product without financial projections indicates these people have not really thought through the process. If I am interested, I may suggest they go back to the drawing board, follow the B-I Triangle as an outline, and then hire an accountant and come up with a business plan, which includes a set of numbers.

(For those who want to learn more about how to write a business plan, Garrett Sutton has written the perfect book for you. It is the Rich Dad Advisor book *The ABC's of Writing Winning Business Plans,* Warner Books.)

One Step to Raising Money

Whenever someone asks, "How do I raise money for my business?" I respond by asking, "Do you have a business plan?" A good business plan with a great presentation can raise the money you need. A bad business plan with a poor presentation can lose you money.

This does not mean that the numbers of the business plan are cast in stone. The financial results of most startup businesses do not typically follow the plan or precisely meet the projections. The process of creating a business plan with numbers is an A-Thinking and T-Thinking process that causes the entrepreneur to think through the venture in more detail and then put it down on paper. As stated in Chapter One, a successful business is created before there is a business. This is the creation process put down on paper.

The plan does not have to be elaborate. It can be very simple. A plan simply lets the potential investor see the thoughts inside the mind of the entrepreneur. Also, it allows the investor to know that the person is serious about the proposed business.

Again, even if the business does not take shape, the process of thinking through the creation of a business, putting it down on paper, and matching it with numbers that tell the same story is an excellent educational process and reality check. It begins to balance school smarts and street smarts.

Tell Me a Story

A number of years ago, a young man called me and asked for an appointment. When I asked for what purpose, he said, "I have a business proposal I would like to present to you."

"Are you looking for investment money?" I asked directly.

He stumbled and haltingly said, "Yes. I am."

Normally I do not look at businesses at this early stage, yet I was curious and agreed to meet him for lunch.

A week later, I met him at a local restaurant. He was very well-dressed and had an impressive-looking business plan. As I said, I am not good at reading the numbers, yet I do my best to listen to the story the numbers and the plan are telling me. The first thing I look at is the salary and wages line of the financial projections. For me, that is where the story begins.

This young man had himself down for a $120,000-a-year salary. My first question was, "Why do you need such a high salary from a business that does not exist?"

"Well, that is what I am being paid at my job today," he replied, a little indignantly. "Besides, I have a wife and three kids in school. It's the bare minimum I can live on."

"Okay," I said and continued looking at the business plan. As I said, the business plan and the financial projections tell a story. The salary requirement line was introducing me to the lead character, the hero of the story. I was gaining a glimpse into his brain, how he thought, how he spent money, and the priorities of his personal life.

In my mind, seeing his salary requirements and getting into his head, I felt he was still thinking like an employee, looking for a high-paying job. As far as I was concerned, the lunch was over. I had seen enough just by getting to know the hero of the story to know that I did not want to invest in his business.

The Relationship Between a Financial Statement and the B-I Triangle

Since we had not yet ordered lunch, and I still had to be polite, I looked next at the other expenses of the business and how they related to the B-I Triangle. In other words, my first step was to call on my P-Thinking mind. I needed to get a sense of who this person was in front of me. My second step was to call on the C-Thinking, A-Thinking, and T-Thinking minds and create a relationship between the financial statement and the five job levels of the B-I Triangle. The diagram in my mind looked like this.

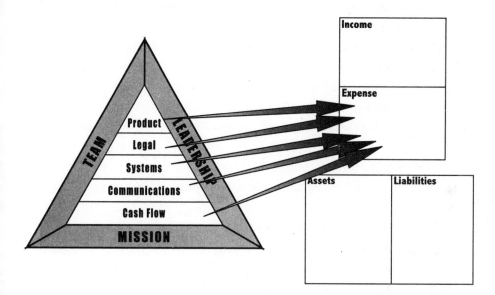

My next question was, "What do you do for your current employer? What is your job?"

"I am a mechanical engineer by training," he replied. "I work in customer service—tracking customer orders through our system. That is where I developed my product. Let me tell you about it."

"Just a moment," I said. "I just have a few questions about your projections." Pointing at the line entitled Advertising and Promotion, I asked, "What is this expense for $10,000 a month? What is your marketing plan?"

"Oh, I haven't given that much thought yet. My plan is to hire an agency and let them handle our marketing."

"Have you had much experience in sales or marketing?" I asked.

"No, I haven't," he said. "I've spent most of my career working on the internal systems of a business. That is where I got my idea for my new product. It will revolutionize order tracking."

"Have you talked to an intellectual property attorney to protect your idea?"

"Well, I have looked but I really have not found one yet."

"In your plan, you only have $4,000 for attorneys' fees. Why is that?"

"Well, I wanted to keep my expenses down. Later on, when money comes in, then I'll hire more attorneys. For now, I think $4,000 is adequate to get me off the ground."

"And who helped you with these projections?" I asked. "I do not see a line for accounting expenses."

"Oh, you're right. I forgot that expense. How much do you think should be allocated to accounting fees?"

"I don't know," I said. "I'm not an accountant. If you *really* want to know you should ask one."

"How do I find a good one?"

"You can call my accountant, but he is very expensive and may be more than you need at this stage."

"Oh," said the entrepreneur. "I am trying to keep my expenses down. I'll look for a cheaper accountant."

Heard Enough of the Story

Although this was hardly an in-depth look at the business, I had heard enough of the story. Eventually I did get a look at his product, which never should have happened if he had an intellectual property attorney's advice. He did not have me sign any document saying I would keep the product a secret—a big and clear indicator of this want-to-be entrepreneur's lack of real world experience.

My Own Lesson Learned

If I had liked the product I could have simply taken his idea and taken it to market. How do I know this? Painfully, I know this lesson because I had made the same mistake he was making. In 1977, I should have patented my nylon shoe-pocket wallet for runners, but I decided to save a few dollars so I did not hire a patent attorney.

This is why after coming up with the idea for the CASHFLOW 101 board game, I did not tell anyone about the game except for Kim and my engineer behind the game. The first person I went to find was an intellectual property attorney. The person I hired was Michael Lechter, one of the most respected intellectual property attorneys in the world. Also he is the husband of Sharon Lechter, who, as you know, became my coauthor on all the Rich Dad books and Kim's and my partner in The Rich Dad Company.

This is one more example of turning bad luck into good luck. My bad luck, caused by inexperience and cheapness in not patenting my nylon wallet, and subsequently losing millions of dollars, was turned into good luck when I learned from that mistake. It also turned the mistake into a lesson. Kim and I were rewarded by first meeting Mike and then meeting Sharon and having her join Kim and me to start the next business. If not for that horrible mistake in 1977, the partnership between Kim, Sharon, and me would never have happened in 1997.

Michael Lechter is a great attorney but he is also very expensive. He is proof positive that you get what you pay for. That is why he was asked to write the Rich Dad's Advisor book entitled *Protecting Your #1 Asset* (Warner Books). In his book you will learn how you can protect your ideas, products, trademarks, and logos from the pirates lurking in the real world of business. You will still need to find your own intellectual property attorney. But by using Michael's book to educate yourself and to prepare for your meeting with your own attorney, you can save yourself thousands of dollars. His second Rich Dad Advisor book, *OPM, Other People's Money* (Warner Books), shares the strategies of starting and growing your business using other people's money and resources. If not for Michael's brilliance and years of experience, our business would not be as valuable as it is today.

One reason why the legal level lies just below the product level of the B-I triangle is that the entrepreneur's ideas are often the company's most important assets. The attorney's job is to protect the company, its products, and its intellectual property—*before* there is a product or a business. If you are a C-Thinker, you need to get Michael Lechter's books and protect your ideas, your most important asset. His books should be part of the library of every entrepreneur. Any time you have a new idea, check with an attorney or check with Michael's books before you share it or talk about it with anyone else.

Saying "No"

The young engineer looked good. He had the look of a successful business leader. His new product looked promising. Yet, I said, "No, I don't think I will invest in your business." The cash flow level of the B-I Triangle had revealed his strengths and weaknesses as an entrepreneur. In the end, I was not saying "no" to his product or ideas. I was saying "no" to him. He still had a lot of homework to do.

Although the product looked promising, the entrepreneur's story did not. He might succeed, but I had my doubts. If he did succeed, I doubted if he had the ability to grow the business to a point where, as an investor, I could get my money back. So I passed on the opportunity to invest with him.

There Are No Bad Investments

My rich dad often said, "There are no bad investments, but there are many bad investors." He also said, "There are no bad business opportunities, but there are many bad entrepreneurs." In my opinion, this young engineer had a great idea for a great new product. However, his ideas about business were not so great.

What rich dad wanted to pound into our heads was that the world was filled with mega-million-dollar opportunities. The problem is that there are more mega-million-dollar opportunities than there are mega-million-dollar entrepreneurs. That is why the cash flow level of the B-I Triangle is so important. It tells the story not of the opportunity, but of the entrepreneur. This is especially true in the creation phase of the business, when the business is not yet a business.

Red Flags

One reason why your banker does not ask you for your school report card, or your grade point average, or what subject you majored in, is that a banker is not looking for a measure of your academic intelligence. Your banker is looking for your level of financial intelligence, which indicates your level of financial responsibility, how much you earn, what you spend your money on, and how much you keep. When looking at financial projections, or better yet, the actual financial numbers from an existing business, I have learned to look for similar indicators. When looking at the numbers, forecast or actual, there are certain items that are red flags for me. They are:

Red flag: Salaries more than a paycheck. You may have already noticed that I looked at that line first. It tells me a lot about the entrepreneur. One thing it tells me is what is more important to the entrepreneurs—the business or their personal lives. Many, many times, I have met entrepreneurs who rape, starve, and torture their business rather than feed and nurture the business. A friend of mine consulted with a building maintenance company that was having cash flow problems, in Denver. The business had great contracts with offices and apartment houses to keep the parking areas swept in summer and free of snow in winter. With low overhead and high margins, the company should have been doing well. Instead, the business was always in financial trouble.

Upon further inspection my friend found that the owner had expensive ski chalets in Vail and Aspen with the accoutrements (doo-dads) to match. On top of that the company had flashy cars and threw lavish parties, all at company expense. To make matters even worse, he had been lying to the IRS, and the state tax department, and his actions were starting to border on tax *evasion* rather than tax *avoidance*.

When my friend recommended that he sell his houses and his cars, cut back on his spending, and hire a high-powered accounting firm to beg for mercy, my friend was fired. The owner still thought there was something wrong with the business. This is an extreme example of an entrepreneur putting his needs before the needs of the business. The numbers of the business told the story of both the business and the entrepreneur.

Red Flag: Good expenses and bad expenses. This is one of rich dad's most important lessons. He said, "The reason so many people are *poor* is that they are *poor* spenders. In other words, there are good expenses and bad expenses." He also said, "The rich are rich because they have expenses that make them rich. The poor are poor because they have expenses that make them poor." Regarding the subject of entrepreneurship, he said, "Most people are not good entrepreneurs because they are savers rather than smart spenders."

One of the downfalls of my nylon surfer wallet business was my desire to *save* money and not *spend* $7,000 on patent attorney fees. That saving of a few thousand dollars cost me a multimillion-dollar business. My lesson was to learn to spend money that made me money.

A friend of a friend has always had a tough time in her business. Over lunch with her, she told me she was spending $50,000 redecorating her apartment. When I asked her if she owned the apartment, she said, "No. I don't have enough money for a down payment so I just rent." When I quizzed her as to why she would spend so much money on a property she didn't own she got angry. "Well I need to have a nice place to live." At that moment, I believe I got a glimpse of what caused her business struggles. She simply spends money foolishly.

One of the reasons the B-I Triangle is named after the B and I quadrants of the CASHFLOW quadrant is that, on the right side of the quadrant, an individual must know how to spend money, and get that money back with a respectable return. One of the reasons why people on the E and S side of the quadrant have a tough time as entrepreneurs is simply that they know how to work for money, but they do not know how to spend money and then have the money come back with more money. This ability to spend money and have your money come back with more money is essential to entrepreneurs and investors on the B and I side of the quadrant.

Between 1997 and 2005, the real estate market boomed. Even though the market boomed, I met many individuals who invested in real estate and failed to make any money, any passive income. To me, this is a signal that this person does not know how to spend money and have the money return with more money. These people may not make good entrepreneurs or they need to work on their business skills. When I look at the numbers of a business, I am looking for this ability, the ability to spend money and have the money return with more money. This is an essential skill.

Red flag: Money talks. Rich dad said, "There is a big difference between a *business* and *busyness.* The reason most people do not make good entrepreneurs is that they are busy, they work hard, but they do not make any money. An entrepreneur must make money and that money shows up at the cash flow level of the B-I Triangle.

A few years ago, I read an article about a couple who were both laid off after September 11. Both were highly paid marketing executives, making over

$250,000 combined income, with a major New York firm. After a year in their own business as marketing experts, their business earned less than $26,000. Why? I suspect one reason was that as high-paid corporate employees, they were never held accountable to the bottom line of the company they worked for. As entrepreneurs, owners of their own business, they had to be very accountable. They found out that their marketing skills in the corporate world did not translate to financial success on the streets.

Suddenly they found out that owning a business does not mean simply working hard and being busy. Owning a business means your activities show up directly to the bottom line as money made and money lost. Rich dad would say, "An employee can be paid for being busy. An entrepreneur is paid for results." The results are often known as the bottom line. That is why the cash flow level is the base of the B-I Triangle. As rich dad said, "You do not need a safe deposit box for excuses."

To me, certain red flags indicate the entrepreneur is stuck in a part of the developmental process. Will the entrepreneur learn from the process and move on or keep raising the same red flags?

Red flags occur in life as well as in business. Whenever someone gets stuck in their process, I have noticed that life will send up red flags of its own. They can be warnings such as bad health, bad luck, or bad relationships. Rich dad said, "Red flags are warnings. We can choose to heed the warning and learn, or ignore the warning. If you do not heed the warning the process may change directions on you and a new process may begin."

My real dad smoked two to three packs of cigarettes a day. The red flags were flying for most of his life. He did not heed the warnings and was eventually diagnosed with lung cancer. He finally quit smoking, but it was too late. One process ended and a new one began. His next process was a battle for life, a battle he lost a year later.

Before You Quit Your Job

There is an overused statement that goes, "Money talks and BS walks." Where money talks the loudest is in a financial statement, at the bottom line. As an entrepreneur, you do not have to be an *accountant,* but you do need to be *accountable*. Before you quit your job, please remember two things:

1. Employees and advisors are not responsible for the bottom line. Entrepreneurs are.
2. When you look at the CASHFLOW quadrant,

people on the E and S side of the quadrant are *not* required to have financial statements. However, financial statements are required by people on the B and I side. Why? Because money talks and the story it tells is of the financial acumen of the individual in the B or I quadrant. These individuals are measured by their financial successes in the B or I quadrants.

Think Like a CFO

If you would like to improve your financial skills at the cash flow level of the B-I Triangle, I strongly recommend you get the CASHFLOW game and play it often. The game teaches you to think like a CFO, a chief financial officer, who is an important member of any entrepreneurial team.

Entrepreneurs Passing the Buck

A CEO or entrepreneur cannot pass the buck. Making excuses or blaming subordinates is never attractive. The buck stops with the entrepreneur or CEO. That is why the cash flow level is the base level of the B-I Triangle. That is where the bucks stop. As an entrepreneur, you are the person responsible for the entire B-I Triangle. So before you quit your job, always remember where the buck stops and that *money talks.*

SHARON'S INSIGHTS

Lesson #5: The Process Is More Important than the Goal.

WHERE ARE YOU TODAY?

My own father once told me that you can have a great map with your destination clearly marked on it, but if you don't know where you are starting from, the map is not going to help you reach your destination.

In becoming an entrepreneur, you need to be honest with yourself when assessing where you are. As I mentioned in an earlier chapter, determine where you are in skill level at each of the five levels of the B-I Triangle and surround yourself with a team that complements your weaknesses.

CASH IS KING

Understanding cash flow and cash management is an absolute necessity for any entrepreneur or business owner. Ultimately the entrepreneur is responsible for the bottom line. Starting a business almost *always* costs more than an entrepreneur expects.

LEARN THE CASH CYCLE TYPICAL IN THE INDUSTRY OF YOUR BUSINESS

What Are Your Sources of Cash?

- *How much money are you investing?*
- *How much investor money are you intending to raise?*
- *Are you borrowing money to start the business?*
- *Do you have a joint venture partner willing to produce the product with their dollars and resources for a share of the profit?*
- *Will your customer pay at the time of sale? Or do you need to extend credit?*

- *If you need to extend credit to your customer, how long will it take to collect on your receivables?*
- *What level of bad debts should you expect from your customers?*
- *How many production cycles will it take before you start seeing positive cash flow?*
- *Can you license your product to other companies that are in different industries, so they don't compete with you, and collect royalty payments?*
- *Can you license your product to other companies that are in different geographical territories, so they don't compete with you, and collect royalty payments?*

What Are Your Uses of Cash?

- *Do you have an idea for a product?*
- *Do you protect your product?*
- *Do you plan the business around the idea or product?*
- *Do you need to pay your advisors for their consultation?*
- *Do you need to build a prototype?*
- *Do you need to find your source of goods, your suppliers?*
- *Can you negotiate payment terms with your suppliers?*
- *Do you need an office? A warehouse? A vehicle?*
- *What kind of office supplies do you need?*
- *What kind of office equipment do you need? Computers? Copiers?*
- *How long will it take for you to produce your goods?*
- *How many employees will you need, at what pay levels, at what stage of development?*
- *How much salary do you and your team require during the initial stage of the business?*
- *How much money will you need, and when will you need it, to produce the goods?*
- *How will you package your product?*
- *How much will it cost?*
- *How will you promote your product?*
- *Will you create a website?*

- *Do you have credit-card-processing set up for your customer orders?*
- *How much will your marketing materials cost?*
- *Where will you store your inventory?*
- *How much will it cost to get the inventory to your warehouse?*
- *How long is the production cycle to replenish your inventory?*
- *How will you take orders?*
- *How will you ship orders?*
- *What types of insurance do you need? How much will the insurance cost?*
- *How will you process returns of your product?*
- *How will you handle customer service related to your products?*
- *If you have debt, how much interest or debt service will you owe?*
- *How many production cycles will you go through before you start seeing collections on your sales cycles?*

Plan the Cash Cycle

I know these questions can appear overwhelming, but they are necessary for any serious entrepreneur to consider. A potential investor will want to see the answers to these questions thoroughly examined and planned for in determining the cash needs of the business as an integral part of the business plan. This is where the skill of an excellent accountant will be invaluable in helping you create the plan for your cash requirements.

I have seen many successful businesses enter crisis mode because they did not properly plan for the time lag between the production expenses of their product and the collection of the receivables from their customers.

In one of the electronic children's book companies I ran, this time lag was over fourteen months, because we had to pay for the production of an electronic component that took six months to build. It took another two months to ship the product from Asia to the United States and six more months to sell and collect on the sales. Having a fourteen- to sixteen-month cash cycle was extremely challenging and the cash cycle had to be monitored constantly. A delay in any one of the cycles could result in a cash crisis. We worked diligently with our suppliers and to shorten the cycle wherever possible.

Entire industries can change in less than the time it took to build, sell, and collect on the sales of our product.

When Cash Becomes Tight

When cash becomes tight the entrepreneur loses focus on building the business and starts focusing on survival.

1. "It's Friday, and I can't make payroll."
2. "I have to pay my supplier before he will ship my goods and I don't have enough cash."
3. "I have large accounts receivable, but no cash in the bank."
4. "The bank just put a hold on our credit card deposits."
5. Or your spouse calls and says, "We *need* a paycheck."

When I start hearing these statements in a company, they are the red flags that rich dad spoke to Robert about. The entrepreneur enters a critical time in his or her business if he or she cannot stop these types of cash emergencies from taking his or her focus away from building the business.

Time Is Money

As an entrepreneur, ask yourself how you are spending your time. In the beginning, all your time is spent on the future—developing the product and the systems to create and launch the business. It is a very exciting time that energizes most entrepreneurs.

As the business grows its demand on the entrepreneur's time will automatically change. But should it? Day-to-day operations become important. Legal and accounting issues must be addressed. One day the entrepreneur may find that he or she has lost focus on the future of his or her company. It is critical to surround yourself with the right team of people who can support you in these various needs of the company.

I have included a wonderful exercise I learned from a friend who learned it at a seminar. I would love to give credit to the source, but I don't know where it originated. Ask yourself the following questions:

As It Relates to Your Business

How much time are you spending on the future?	_ _%
How much time are you spending on the present?	_ _%
How much time are you spending on the past?	_ _%
Total time	100%

In analyzing your time, I would identify the following tasks and how they might be categorized:

Future—marketing, public relations, research and development, strategic partnerships, licensing, new deals, cash projections and requirements, good legal issues. (See box: Good Legal Fees versus Bad Legal Fees.)

Present—sales order taking, shipping and receiving, customer service, cash requirements.

Past—accounting, bad legal issues, compliance requirements with federal, state, or local governments, or regulatory agencies, employee reviews.

What Is the Right Answer?

As an A student, I recognize the immediate desire to get the "right" answer. Unfortunately, the right answer for your business may not be the same as the right answer for my business. Typically, I encourage entrepreneurs to spend more than half of their time working on the future of their business and build a strong team to concentrate on the present and past issues of the business. In some cases, the entrepreneur may need to spend more than 80% of his or her time focusing on the future. When an issue arises that requires the entrepreneur to focus attention on present or past issues, have a process planned that will allow other people on your team to increase their focus on the future.

Good Legal Fees versus Bad Legal Fees

Robert mentioned that few things are a bigger waste of money than a lawsuit. However, a distinction must be drawn between legal fees wasted on unnecessary litigation and fees paid to implement the legal element of the B-I Triangle.

Just as there is a difference between "good debt" and "bad debt," there's a difference between types of legal bills.

A loan that lets you acquire an asset that generates cash flow in excess of the loan payments is good debt. By analogy, legal bills that allow you to build a business foundation, form an entity, create precise, unambiguous, thoughtful contracts, establish or maintain intellectual property rights, and create strong business partnerships are "good" legal bills. Spending that money will save money, or perhaps make you money in the future.

Taking a loan merely to permit instant gratification with respect to purchase of some doo-dad is bad debt. By analogy, bills for legal services that will not save you money or make you money in the future are "bad" legal bills. For example, bills for litigation, in a business context, are typically not "good" legal bills in the sense that litigation per se will rarely make you money.

Of course, there may be circumstances where spending money on litigation makes absolute sense, and, in fact, may be absolutely necessary for the survival of a business. For example, there are times when litigation will be necessary to keep from losing valuable rights (and losing the income generated through those rights), and in that sense these are "good" legal bills. However, litigation is not something to enter into lightly, particularly when you recognize that it is often pure expense that will add nothing to the bottom line. Litigation is extremely expensive, and is not something that you can initiate and then simply walk away from if the going gets tough. After spending years as a litigating attorney, I can attest that "litigation is the sport of kings" and "litigation is like an airplane flight; once it gets off the ground you had better be prepared to pay the fare all the way to the end of the flight."

Let's go back to our analogy between debt and legal bills. There are circumstances where taking on "debt" to acquire or maintain a nonincome-producing asset—"bad debt" under our definition—makes perfect sense. For example, taking on a mortgage in order to purchase a home for you and your family to live in can make perfect sense, even though the mortgage is "bad debt" under our definition. The same is true with respect to taking a short-term loan in order to buy needed medicine or medical treatment that you could not otherwise afford for a sick family member. Or let's assume you have young children, and you take a loan in order to pay for putting a fence around your yard to prevent the children from wandering into the street or prevent rabid skunks (or other bad guys) from getting into the yard with your children. While the loan does not meet our definition of "good debt," it certainly makes sense to spend what it takes to protect your children. It is important to recognize and know what type of debt you are acquiring.

The same is true with respect to some legal bills that do not meet our definition of "good" legal bills. There may be times when you have to enforce your rights out of principle or as a strategic necessity. For example, sometimes the only way to deal with a bully is to fight. If you do not meet the bully head-on, the bullying will continue. Sometimes initiating litigation is the only way to stop a "pirate" competitor.

> Michael Lechter, Esq.
> Rich Dad Advisor, author of *Protecting Your
> #1 Asset* and *OPM: Other People's Money*

WHAT IS THE PROCESS?

Going back to rich dad's Lesson #5: The process is more important than the goal: The process I have addressed in this section is the process of your cash management and the process of your time management. Keep them under control and focused on the future, and your business will continue moving toward your goal.

Are You Serious?

If you are serious about becoming a successful entrepreneur, we recommend you carefully study the B-I Triangle. In **Rich Dad's You Can Choose to Be Rich™**, we provide a more in-depth analysis of the B-I Triangle.

We provide distinctions between how the rich, the poor and the middle class think... and then leave the choice up to you as to which path you want to follow. **Rich Dad's You Can Choose to Be Rich** is a must for anyone serious about becoming a successful entrepreneur. For more information about this product, please visit:

www.richdad.com/choosetoberich

The Best Answers Are Found in Your Heart . . . Not Your Head.

Chapter 6

The Three Kinds of Money

"What did you learn in Vietnam?" asked rich dad.

"I learned the importance of mission, leadership, and the team," I replied.

"Which was the most important?"

"The mission."

"Good." Rich dad smiled. "You'll make a good entrepreneur."

A Green Marine

In early 1972, my job was to pilot a UH-1 Huey helicopter gunship in Vietnam. After two months in the war zone, my copilot and I had flown several missions but had not yet encountered enemy fire. This was soon to change.

On the day I finally met the enemy, things were already very tense for me. We flew with our doors open, and the wind chattered through the aircraft. Looking back at the aircraft carrier, our home, I once again reminded myself that this was a war zone and my school days were over. For two years I had trained for this mission.

I knew that each time we crossed the beach and flew over land, there were real live enemy soldiers with real guns and real bullets waiting for us. Turning to look back at my crew of three, two machine gunners and a crew chief, I asked on the intercom, "Are you guys ready?" Not saying anything, they simply gave me a thumbs-up.

My crew knew I was green and untested. They knew I could fly but they did not know how I would perform under the pressure of combat.

Initially there were two helicopters in our flight. About twenty minutes into the flight, the lead aircraft had to turn back. Apparently there were electrical problems with the aircraft. We were told by the powers that be on the aircraft carrier to continue and to remain on call in the area. You could feel the tension mount in our aircraft because the lead aircraft had the more experienced pilots. They had been in combat for over eight months. On top of that, their aircraft carried air to ground rockets. My aircraft only had machine guns. As the lead aircraft turned and headed back toward the ship, the anxiety in my aircraft was very real. None of us liked being out there alone.

We passed over some of the most beautiful beaches in the world and headed north. We had dark green rice paddies to our left, blue green ocean to our right, and white sand beaches below us. Suddenly over the radio, two Army helicopters broadcast that they needed help. They were in a battle with a fifty-caliber machine gun in the hills beyond the rice paddies. Being close by, we responded and began flying toward their location. Flying just below the clouds, we soon saw the Army helicopters in a firefight with the machine gun on the ground. There was also a lot of small-arms fire coming from enemy troops in the area. It was easy to tell the difference between the rounds from the thirty-caliber guns that the troops carried and the heavier fifty-caliber rounds from the machine gun. The tracers from the thirty-caliber small-arms fire looked like hot red-orange specks zipping up against the dark green sky. The fifty-caliber tracer rounds looked like flying ketchup bottles. I took a very deep breath and kept flying.

Watching the battle as we flew closer, I kept hoping the Army helicopters would destroy the machine gun and not need our help. But no luck. When one of the Army helicopters was hit and fell from the sky, I knew we were going to be part of the fight. As the smoking helicopter spiraled to the ground, the tension climbed even more in our aircraft. Looking back at my crew I simply said, "Clear the decks. Make the guns hot. We're going in." I did not know what we were going to do. I simply knew we had to be prepared for the worst.

The second Army helicopter broke off from the fight and went down to pick up the crew of the first helicopter. That left us—a single aircraft with only thirty-caliber machine guns, about to face an estimated fifteen troops with guns and a fifty-caliber machine gun. I wanted to turn and run. I knew that it was the smart thing to do. Yet, not wanting to appear like a wimp to my men, I kept flying toward the location of the fifty-caliber machine gun. I was now flying on pure bravado and hoping for the best.

With the two Army helicopters out of the way, the ground fire turned on us. Although it was far away, seeing real live rounds being fired at me was a sight and feeling I will never forget. School days were definitely over.

My crew had been in this situation before. Their silence told me that this was a particularly bad situation to be in. As the first fifty-caliber rounds came up short of our aircraft, my crew chief tapped me on the helmet, pulled and turned my helmet so we were face to face and said, "Hey, Lieutenant, do you know what is bad about this job?"

Shaking my head I feebly said, "No."

Smiling his broad toothy grin, the crew chief, on his second tour in Vietnam, said, "The problem with this job is there is no second best. If you decide to fight, either we are going home today or those guys on the ground are going home. But both of us aren't going home. One of us is about to die. It's up to you to decide which one of us that is—them or us."

Looking back at my gunners, young men of nineteen and twenty, I spoke into the intercom again and said, "You guys ready?" Both young men gave me a thumbs-up, as all good Marines are trained to do. They were ready. They were trained to follow orders, regardless of whether their leader was competent or not. Realizing their lives were in my hands did not make me feel any better. At that moment I stopped thinking only about myself and began thinking about all of us.

Silently I shouted to myself, "Think. Should we turn and run or should we fight?" Then my mind began feeding me excuses as to why we should turn and run. "You're a single aircraft. There should be at least two aircraft. Isn't there a rule saying you cannot fight unless there are two aircraft? The lead pilots are gone. They had the rockets. No one will blame us if we turn and run. Maybe we can go down and help the Army pilots. Yeah, let's go help them. Then we don't have to do our job. Then we have an excuse for not fighting. We were on a rescue mission. We saved some Army fliers. Yeah, that sounds good."

Then I asked myself, "What if we miraculously win? What if we beat that fifty-cal and live? What will we get?"

The answer came back, "We all might receive some medal for bravery. We'll be heroes."

"And what if we lose?"

The answer came back, "We'll be dead or captured."

Glancing back at the two young gunners, I decided their lives were worth more than a medal on a ribbon. So was mine, I admitted to myself. Being brave and stupid was ruled out.

The fifty-caliber rounds were flying closer to us. The gunner on the ground was increasing his accuracy with every shot. Back at flight school, we learned that a fifty-caliber round had a greater range than a thirty-caliber round. We had thirty-caliber machine guns. That meant he was going to be able to hit us long before we could get to him. Suddenly, a burst of fifty-caliber rounds zoomed just past my window. Without thinking, I banked to the left and dove toward the ground to increase the distance between the enemy gunner and us. Since I had no idea what I was doing, I decided it was time to think. Flying straight into the machine gunner was certain death. As my aircraft was diving toward the ground in a sharp left bank, I used my radio and broadcast to anyone in the area, "This is Marine helicopter, Yankee-Tango-96, fifty-cal located. Need help."

Out of the blue, a loud clear confident voice crackled through my headset, "Yankee-Tango 96, flight of four Marine A-4s RTB [returning to base] have extra ordinance and fuel on board. Give us your position, and we'll give you a hand."

Relief ran through our crew as I radioed our position to the Marine Corps pilots of the jets. In a few minutes, I could see four specks flying low to the ground coming to our assistance. Seeing us, the flight leader radioed, "Before we get too close, fly back toward Charlie and see if you can draw his fire. Once we see his tracers, we'll take care of the rest." With that, we turned and once again flew toward the fifty-caliber machine gun. Once his tracers began flying at us again, the wing leader of the four jets radioed, "Target in sight." In less than five minutes the fifty-caliber machine gun was no longer a problem. My crew and I were the ones who went home that night.

Different Teams, Same Mission

There have been many times I sit quietly and reflect on that day. Although I said, "Thank you," over the air, once the fight was over, I still wish I had had the chance to meet those guys in person, shake their hands and say, "Thank you." We were on different teams, from different ships, but we all shared the same mission.

All wars are horrible. War is simply humanity at its worst. War is a time when we use our best technology and our bravest people to kill our fellow human beings. During my year in Vietnam, I saw the worst of humanity. I saw sights I wish I had never seen. I also caught glimpses of a spiritual power, a dedication to a higher calling, I would never have witnessed if I had not gone to war. When the term *A Band of Brothers* is used to describe the bond between soldiers, I wonder if someone who has never fought in a war can ever know what that bond feels like. For me, it is a spiritual bond dedicated to a higher calling—something known as a mission.

Mission Statements

In business today, it is very fashionable to tout one's *mission statement* . . . the sole driving purpose for forming the business. After my Marine Corps and Vietnam experience, I have remained skeptical each time someone says, "The mission of our business is . . ." My skepticism causes me to wonder how much the word *mission* is just that—only a word.

The Stronger Mission Wins

One day, I was flying near the DMZ, the Demilitarized Zone that used to separate North Vietnam from South Vietnam. Looking down upon the carnage raging below me, I noticed something that deeply disturbed me. Returning to the aircraft carrier that night, I raised my hand during the debriefing and asked, "Why do their Vietnamese fight harder than our Vietnamese? Are we fighting for the wrong side? Are we fighting for the wrong cause?"

Needless to say, I was threatened with a court-martial for such treasonous-sounding words. To me, I was not being treasonous. I was only asking a question. I was simply expressing an observation, something I had noticed since arriving in Vietnam. It seemed to me that the Viet Cong and the North Vietnamese soldiers fought harder, tougher, and with more tenacity than our Vietnamese soldiers. From my perspective, the Vietnamese soldiers on our side did not seem to fight as hard. Personally, I did not feel we could count on them. I often wondered if we stopped paying them, would they keep fighting?

To be fair, there were many U.S. soldiers who were not there to fight either. Many were draftees who were unlucky enough to be drafted. If they were offered a choice of a plane ticket home or to stay and fight, many would have been on the plane.

Halfway through my tour, I realized we were not going to win. We were not going to win, even though we were better equipped, had the best technology, overwhelming firepower, the highest pay, and well-trained men and women. I knew we were not going to win simply because our side, the South Vietnamese as well as the Americans, lacked a strong enough mission, a higher calling, a reason to fight. We had lost our hearts. At least, I had lost mine. I did not want to kill anymore. I was no longer a good Marine.

My experience in Vietnam proved to me that the stronger mission wins. The same thing happens in business.

A Vow of Poverty

Most of us know that men and women of religious faith have taken vows of poverty in support of their spiritual mission. When I was a little boy, my dad explained to me that his friend, a Catholic priest, had taken a vow of poverty. Asking him what that meant, he said, "He has dedicated his life to God and God's work. That means money is not to be a part of his life. He lives an austere life in the service of God."

"What does *austere* mean?" I asked.

Tiring of the thousand questions a child asks, my dad's answer was, "Never mind what austere means. You'll find out later on."

A number of years later, I found out what austere meant. Sitting in a classroom for new Marine Corps officers, the instructor explained to the class that throughout history, men and women of war have also taken vows of poverty. The instructor said, "In the feudal times, many knights took a vow of poverty in order to be true to their calling. They did not want money or desire of worldly goods to interfere with their dedication to God and king."

Before joining the Marine Corps, I was a ship's officer on an oil tanker for Standard Oil of California, being paid over $4,000 a month, which was a lot of money in 1969. Even though I was draft-exempt because I was sailing for the oil industry, a classification known as *nondefense vital industry,* both my dads encouraged me to serve my country in time of war. As a Marine Corps officer my pay dropped to less than $300 a month. Sitting in that classroom, listening to the instructor remind us that throughout history, men and women of war took vows of poverty, I finally found my definition of the word *austere,* the definition my dad did not give me some years before.

The Three Kinds of Money versus Income

In earlier books I wrote about the three kinds of income. They are:

1. Earned income
2. Portfolio income
3. Passive income

My poor dad worked for earned income, the highest-taxed income there is. My rich dad worked primarily for passive income, the lowest-taxed income.

These terms for the three types of income actually come from the Internal Revenue Service. The tax department taxes the three incomes at different rates. An entrepreneur has the opportunity to work for all three types of income and needs to know the differences because the different tax rates can make a huge difference to the bottom line. I mention these incomes now not to confuse you but to distinguish them from the discussion on the three different types of money I am about to discuss.

While we were in high school, rich dad taught his son and me that people work for three different types of money. They are:

1. Competitive money
2. Cooperative money
3. Spiritual money

Competitive Money

To explain *competitive money* he said, "We learn to compete early in life. We compete in school for grades, we compete in sports, and we compete for the person we love. At work, we learn to compete for jobs, for raises, for promotions, for recognition, and for survival. In business, companies compete for customers, market share, contracts, and good employees. Competition is survival of the fittest dog or the dog that eats the other dogs. Most people work for *competitive money*."

Cooperative Money

To explain *cooperative money* he said, "In sports and in business, cooperation is known as *teamwork*. The richest, most powerful entrepreneurs have built the biggest businesses in the world via cooperation. They become more competitive due to the cooperation of their team. Most entrepreneurs of large businesses are great team leaders."

Spiritual Money

Explaining *spiritual money* was a little bit more difficult. He said, "Spiritual money is created by doing God's work—work that God wants done. It's work being done in response to a higher calling."

Not understanding what rich dad meant, I asked him, "You mean like forming a church?"

His reply was, "There are entrepreneurs who do form churches, just as there are entrepreneurs who form charities. Both could be examples of working for spiritual money, but spiritual money is not restricted to simply a church or charity."

For years, this category puzzled me, and I often had discussions with him on this subject. During one of these discussions he said, "Most people go to work for money—nothing else. They do not care if it is competitive, cooperative, or spiritual. For many people, work and money are just a means to an end. If you paid them twice as much to *not* work, many would take your offer."

"You mean they would not work for free?" I asked with a smirk.

"No, definitely not. If you did not pay most people, they would move on looking for another job. They may want to help you and your business but they have bills to pay and families to feed. They need money, any kind of money. They would choose their job depending upon which one paid the most and had the best benefits."

"So is spiritual money like loving your work and doing what you love?"

"No," smiled rich dad. "Doing what you love is not what I mean by spiritual money."

"So what is spiritual money?" I asked. "Is it working for free?"

"No, that is not it either. It's not about working for free because spiritual money is not really about money."

"Spiritual money is not about money? If it is not about money then what is it about?" I asked.

"It's about doing a job *not* because you want to do it but because it must be done and you know deep down in your soul you're the one that is supposed to do it."

"How do you know you're supposed to do it?" I asked.

"Because it disturbs you that no one else is doing it. You may say to yourself, 'Why isn't someone doing something about this?'"

"Could it anger you?" I asked.

"Oh, yes," said rich dad softly. "It can also sadden you or even break your heart. It may seem like an injustice or a crime to you. It probably disturbs your sense of decency. It seems unfair—an injustice."

"Don't most people have these feelings about something in their life?" I asked.

"Yes, but most people don't do anything about it. They go to work and say things such as, 'Why doesn't the government do something about it?' or they write letters to the editor and complain."

"But they don't do anything about it," I added.

Quietly, rich dad said, "In most cases, no. They may talk about it, they may complain about it, but they do little about it. After all, they are too busy at their job, earning enough money to pay the rent and saving enough money to take the kids to Disneyland."

"What would happen if they did do something about it?" I asked. "What might happen?"

"If they were truly committed to solving the problem, I would say that the invisible forces of this universe, of God, might come to their support. Magic might happen in their lives. This is when spiritual money comes into play. But it is more than money. People you never met before come to join forces with you, not for the money, but for the mission."

"Why do they join you?" I asked.

"Because they are on the same mission."

That was about all I could handle that day. I had a test the next day and my mission at the time was to get out of high school.

Giving Your Gift

About a year went by and once again I brought up the subject of spiritual money. "If I simply work on a problem I know needs to be worked on, will that bring in the invisible forces, the spiritual money?"

Rich dad laughed and said, "Maybe and maybe not. I'm not the one who makes those decisions. I will say this. One of the keys to attracting the invisible magical forces is to be dedicated to giving your gift."

"What?" I responded with a jolt. "Giving my gift? What do you mean by a gift?"

"A special God-given talent," rich dad replied. "Something you are the best at. A talent God gave especially to you."

"And what would that be?" I asked. "There is nothing I know of that I am the best at."

"Well, you have to find it."

"Does everybody have one?"

"I'd like to think so," smiled rich dad.

"If everyone has a gift, why are so many people below average?" I asked.

Rich dad roared with laughter at that question. Finally composing himself he said, "Because finding your gift, developing your gift, and giving your gift is very hard work. Most people do not want to work that hard."

Now I was puzzled. It seemed to me that if God had given us a gift it should be apparent; it should be easily accessible. When I asked rich dad to clarify this, he said, "Great doctors spend years in school and then practice for years developing their gift. Great golfers have practiced for years, developing their gift. While there are the exceptions such as child prodigies, most people have to dedicate their life to finding and developing their gift. Unfortunately, the world is filled with gifted people who never develop their gift. Finding one's gift can be hard work, and then developing one's gift can be even harder work. And that is why so many people appear to be below average."

"So that is why most professional athletes practice harder than amateurs?" I asked. "They dedicate their life to developing their strength and skills in order to develop their gift."

Rich dad nodded.

Once again, I had heard more than I could handle. The discussion was over but I remembered the lesson.

Good to Great

There are two books I recommend to friends who are dedicated to becoming the best they can be in life. The first one is *Good to Great* (HarperCollins, 2001) by Jim Collins. We have read and held study groups on this book five times and each time our group studied the book in depth, it seemed like we were reading a different book. The other book, *The War of Art* (Rugged Land, 2002) by Steven Pressfield, is another one of those books for anyone who wants to make the best of their lives. *The War of Art* is about the self-saboteur in all of us. I strongly recommend both books for anyone dedicated to becoming a great entrepreneur.

The opening line of *Good to Great* says it all. Collins begins by stating, *"Good is the enemy of great."*

Keeping with the subject of finding one's gift, we all know the world is filled with *good* business people, good athletes, good parents, good workers, and good governments. But the world has a shortage of *great* business people, great athletes, great parents, great workers, great governments, and so on. Why? Because for many of us, good is good enough. If my rich dad were here today, he would say, "Bringing out your gift is about bringing out your greatness, not just what you are good enough at."

Good to Great is filled with lessons essential for big and small businesses. In our study groups, each person seemed to find a lesson that was written just for him or her. For me, the lesson that hit me the hardest was the lesson that *greatness is a choice.* It is not about being gifted, or talented, or more fortunate than others. *It's about a choice we all can make.*

Being a person who has been average and below average for most of my life, the idea that I had the choice to change all that was a message from the book that went straight to my heart and my soul.

Resistance

In *The War of Art*, Steven Pressfield identifies *resistance* as that force inside each of us that holds us back. I know this character named resistance well. Except in my case, my resistance comes in different characters with different names. In the morning, my resistance goes by the name of Fat Boy. As I awake, look at my clock, and say, "Time to go to the gym," immediately Fat Boy says, "Oh, no, not this morning. You're not feeling well. Besides, it's chilly outside. Go to the gym tomorrow." Fat Boy is the guy inside me that would rather eat than exercise.

My *resistance* comes disguised in many different characters. I have lots of them. In addition to Fat Boy another character is *Lazy Husband*. This character often says things such as, "Why didn't Kim do this or do that?" Another resistance character that runs my life is *Financial Slob*, who is always saying, "Why check the numbers?" After *Financial Slob* has his say, then Lazy Husband says, "Kim, will you check these numbers?" As you can tell, Fat Boy, Financial Slob, and Lazy Husband are close friends of mine. We are together every day. Pressfield calls it *resistance*, I call them my *buddies*.

Steven Pressfield's book is about overcoming your resistance by tapping into your creative power, your spiritual allies, your angels or muses. I would say this book is essential for entrepreneurs. It is not a book for people who simply want to get rich quick. Like *Good to Great*, *The War of Art* contains many priceless lessons, yet there is one lesson that pertains directly to this subject on giving one's gift. It comes from a chapter entitled Professionals and Amateurs and says:

> Aspiring artists defeated by Resistance share one trait. They all act like amateurs. They have not yet turned pro.
>
> To be clear: When I say professional, I don't mean doctors and lawyers, those of "the professions." I mean the Professional as an ideal. The professional in contrast to the amateur. Consider the differences.
>
> The amateur plays for fun. The professional plays for keeps
>
> To the amateur, the game is his avocation. To the pro it's his vocation.
>
> The amateur plays part-time, the professional full-time.
>
> The amateur is a weekend warrior. The professional is there seven days a week.
>
> The word amateur comes from the Latin root meaning "to love." The conventional interpretation is that the amateur pursues his calling out of love, while the pro does it for money. Not the way I see it. In my view, the amateur does not love the game enough. If he did, he would not pursue it as a sideline, distinct from his "real" vocation.
>
> The professional loves it so much he dedicates his life to it. He commits full time.
>
> That's what I mean when I say turning pro.
>
> Resistance hates it when we turn pro.

An Overnight Success

A news journalist, writing about the success of the Rich Dad series of books, said, "This author is an overnight success. Only three other books in the history of the *New York Times* bestseller list have been on the list longer than Kiyosaki's *Rich Dad Poor Dad*. Most authors write for years and write many books and never make the *New York Times* list."

The words "overnight success" and "author" always cause me to chuckle. While I do write my books, with Sharon Lechter's assistance, I do not consider myself an author and I am certainly not an overnight success. I am simply someone who found my mission. I have been working on this mission for years and have partners who share that mission, and being an author is just one of the jobs I perform in order to fulfill that mission. I really wish I did not have to write. Ever since failing English because I could not write in high school, at the age of fifteen, I have had a deep aversion to writing. For years I hated writing. It was the hardest thing I had to do. There are many other ways to communicate that are easier for me and I would rather do, like audio or video recordings or live appearances. In spite of this, *Rich Dad Poor Dad* has been the number-one business book in America for two years in a row, according to *USA Today*.

Lance Armstrong, perhaps one of the greatest cyclists in history, has won six Tour De France races, but his biggest battle was conquering cancer at the peak of his career. In comparison, if it's cold outside, I won't go to the gym. Armstrong has cancer and continues to be the best in the world. His level of professionalism and love of his sport are an inspiration to us all, regardless of what our game is. As he said in his book, *It's Not About the Bike* (G. P. Putnam's Sons, 2000):

> I was beginning to see cancer as something that I was given for the good of others.
>
> All I knew was that I felt I had a mission to serve others that I'd never had before, and I took it more seriously than anything in the world. (p. 150)

It's Not about the Money

Another question I am asked by journalists is, "Why do you keep working? If you have all this money, why don't you just go on permanent vacation?" Just as Lance Armstrong states, "It's not about the bike." For me, "It's not about the money." It's about the mission.

In 1974, seeing my poor dad, sitting at home, watching TV a broken and broke man, I found my mission. Watching my dad sitting there, I could see the future. Not just for him but for millions, maybe billions of people worldwide.

In the next few years, by 2015, it will become more apparent that, throughout the world, there are millions, maybe billions, of people just like my dad. These are smart, educated, hard-working people who will need government support for food, shelter, and medicine. This is a worldwide phenomenon, affecting every country in the world, even the richest of countries such as the United States, England, Japan, Germany, France, and Italy.

In 1974, I realized the problem was that too many people, like my dad, were depending upon the government for life support. My rich dad had seen the problem growing and that Social Security and Medicare were going to be massive financial problems for the United States and the world. I could see that the richest country in the world could become a country filled with poor people, expecting the government to take care of them.

In 1974, when my poor dad recommended, "Go back to school, get your Ph.D., so you can find a job with good benefits," I found my mission. At the time, I did not know that I had found my mission. All I knew was that my dad's advice—advice I used to listen to—now disturbed me deeply. In 1974, seeing my dad sitting on the couch, watching TV, unemployed, smoking and collecting his government benefits, I knew there was something terribly flawed in his advice. Times had changed but his advice had not.

There is a saying that goes, "As General Motors goes, so does the U.S." In March 2005, General Motors announced it was cutting pension and medical benefits for employees. In 2005, parents and schools are still saying to their kids, "Go to school, get good grades, so you can find a good job with benefits." I believe seeing my father in 1974 was seeing the future.

Why Doing What You Love Is Not Enough

Very often I hear people say, "I'm doing what I love." Also I hear people say, "Do what you love and the money will follow." While this is good advice, there are also some flaws in the advice. The most obvious flaw is the use of the word "I." One's true mission is about *who you love.* It is not about *you.* A mission is about *who you do your work for.* It's not about working for yourself.

In his book, Lance Armstrong goes on to say:

I had a new sense of purpose, and it had nothing to do with my recognition and exploits on a bike. Some people won't understand this, but I no longer felt that it was my role in life to be a cyclist. Maybe my role was to be a cancer survivor. My strongest connections and feelings were with people who were fighting cancer and asking the same question I was: "Am I going to die?"

It's Not about You

Recently, a friend asked me to talk to his sister, an office manager who had just joined a network marketing company. He said, "She read your books and has decided to take a leap into starting her own business with a network marketing company."

"That's good," I said.

"Would you mind talking to her?"

What could I say? He was a friend, so I agreed.

During her lunch break she came by to meet with me. "So why did you join this company and decide to build your own business?" I asked.

"Oh, I'm tired of the rat race. I'm not getting ahead at my job. So after reading your book on the advantages of starting a network marketing business, *The Business School for People Who Like Helping People* (Warner Books), I decided to take the plunge. So I gave notice at work and will be out on my own in a month."

"That's courageous," I said, acknowledging her. "Tell me how you came to choose the network marketing company you're going to build your business with?"

"Oh, I really like their products. Their training seems good. But I really liked their compensation plan. I can make a lot of money quickly."

"Okay," I said, reserving my comments about doing it primarily for the money. "What are your plans?"

The conversation went on for about another half hour. There was not much to discuss since she had not yet started. To be fair to my friend, I suggested she call me in six months and let me know how she was doing. At that point, I thought she would have more real world questions to ask.

Six Months of Failing

During the sixth month, she called and wanted to continue our meeting. This next meeting was not as pleasant.

"I'm not doing very well," she started. "Nobody wants to listen to me. Nobody gets it. They just close their minds the moment I mention network marketing. How can I make any money if they don't listen?"

"Have you attended the training sessions the company puts on?" I asked.

"No. I don't want to," she said angrily. "All they do is pressure me to practice selling. I don't want to be pressured. They want me to bring my friends to meetings and my friends won't come."

"Okay," I said quietly. "Have you read any books on selling or how to influence people?"

"No. I don't like to read."

"Okay, if you don't like to read, have you looked into a sales training course?"

"No. All those guys want is my money so I refuse to give them any."

"Okay," I said. "So what do you want?"

"All I want is to work a few hours a week, make a lot of money, without hassles, and have the time and money to enjoy life."

"All right," I said, now beginning to chuckle to myself.

"So tell me what I should do," she said, flashing her frustration at me.

"Go see if you can get your job back," I suggested.

"Are you saying I can't build a business?" she demanded.

"No, I am not saying that."

"So what are you saying?" she demanded. "You're supposed to be the smart guy, the guy who writes all these bestselling books. Tell me what you see in me. I'm strong. I can take it."

"Okay," I said in a more serious tone. "Have you noticed how many times you have used the word 'I'?"

"No," she replied. "Tell me how many times I have used the word 'I' and what the use of it means to you."

"Well, I heard you say, 'I'm not doing well.' 'I don't want to attend training classes.' 'I don't want to read.' 'I refuse to give any money.'"

"So I say 'I' a lot. So what?"

As gently as I could, I said, "Because building a business is not about you. It's about other people. It's about your team, your customers, your teachers, and how well you can serve them. You sound very self-centered, very *me, myself,* and *I* oriented."

Obviously, she did not like what I had to say, yet she sat back, kept quiet, and listened. I could tell she had heard what I had said and was processing it. Composing herself, she replied, "But I really do not like to read. I really do not like going to training classes. I really hate rejection. I hate closed-minded people who do not get what I am offering them. I hate this emotional pain I am going through. I hate not having a paycheck."

Nodding slowly, I softly said, "I understand. I have had to go through similar feelings. I too hate to read, hate to study, hate to train, hate to pay for advice, hate the long hours without pay. But I do it."

"Why?" she asked.

"Because I don't do it for me. My work is not about me. It's about them."

"So you study because you want to do better for them, your customers."

"Yes," I replied. "Not just my customers. I study, train, and practice hard for their families, for their community, and for a better world. It's not about me or about the money. It's about being of service."

"Well, I want to be of service, too," she blurted out. "I'm trying to help people."

"Yes, I can tell you are. You have a good heart. The problem is you must first qualify to serve."

"Qualify? What do you mean by qualify?"

"Well, medical doctors spend years in medical school qualifying to serve their patients. I do not know of anyone who has quit a job as an office manager and the next day is in the operating room, performing eye surgery. Do you?"

"No," she said, shaking her head. "So that is why I need to read, train, and practice? It's not about me, it's about being better able to serve other people."

Our discussion went on for about an hour more. She did have a very good heart and sincerely did want to serve people. She simply needed to take time to gain the skills required to be better at serving people. Explaining to her the differences between P-Thinking, A-Thinking, T-Thinking, and C-Thinking people, I told her I thought she was gaining invaluable P-Thinking people skills from her network marketing company. As she left I said to her, "Dealing with people is the hardest part of any business."

The conversation went to the book *Good to Great,* and we discussed how greatness was a choice, not luck or chance. To encourage her to continue I said, "Your company is not training you to be *good* but to be *great* at dealing with people. That is a priceless skill and a skill essential to be of service to your fellow human beings. But you and only you can make that choice to be great. Most people are happy just to be good because being good is all they need to serve themselves."

As she left she asked, "So not all people are in business to serve other people?"

"That is my experience. Too many people go to work simply to make money. A few people go to work to be of service. Different people, different missions."

In the next chapter we will go into how to build a team and how to deal with different people with different missions. It is a very important chapter because people come to work for different reasons. If their reasons are not aligned to the mission of the business, the results are often chaos and losses of time and money. Many businesses fail simply because in business there are different people with different missions.

The Power of a Mission

In Vietnam, I witnessed firsthand a third world nation beat the most powerful nation in the world, simply because its fighting forces had a stronger sense of mission. I see the same thing in business today. Today, we have all seen smaller entrepreneurial companies, such as Microsoft, Dell, Google, and Yahoo, blast past big stodgy blue-chip companies, making the young entrepreneurs far richer than older corporate executives climbing the corporate ladders. Today, while blue-chip corporate executives are becoming millionaires, youthful entrepreneurs are becoming billionaires. As in Vietnam, it's not a matter of the size of the business, it's a matter of the size of the mission. That is why I have dedicated so much time to this subject.

Earlier in this book, I wrote about the three ten-year phases of my development. Once again they are:

1. 1974 to 1984—The Learning Years
2. 1984 to 1994—The Earning Years
3. 1994 to 2004—The Giving Back Years

In 1974, my mission was simply to master the B-I Triangle. My mission was to learn. It was a dark period of life. I was often broke and often depressed, and it was the mission that kept me going. There were periods of months on end that nothing seemed to work. Yet the memory of my dad sitting on his couch watching TV kept me going. I was not learning for me, I was learning for my dad and people like my dad throughout the world.

Around 1980, my world became brighter. Money was once again rolling in. I had learned many lessons on the B-I Triangle, especially the five levels from cash flow to product. In 1980, we shipped our factories offshore because it was cheaper to manufacture in Korea and Taiwan. On one of those trips, I saw first-hand what a real world sweatshop was. I saw kids stacked above kids on mezzanines, manufacturing my products, products that were making me rich.

At the time, I was manufacturing nylon wallets, bags, and hats for rock bands. We were selling our legally licensed products at rock concerts and through record stores throughout the world. I was back on top again, but the sight of those kids in sweatshops haunted me.

I knew my days as a manufacturing entrepreneur were over. Besides, I realized my mission to learn was changing. I knew it was time to move on.

In December 1984, Kim and I moved to California. That began the worst year of our life, 1985. I wrote about this period of time in the book *Rich Dad's CASHFLOW Quadrant* (Warner Books). My mission was similar but it had evolved. Now my mission was to find my gift and develop it. It was also to earn money and create wealth from my gift.

Passion is different from love. Passion is a combination of love and anger. At that time, I was in love with learning and still angry at the school system. Taking my passion, Kim and I became students of education and how people learned. We spent 1985 traveling with different great teachers, such as Tony Robbins, and studying the way they taught. Once a week, we were helping

Tony teach people to walk across two-thousand-degree hot coals. It was a great education on getting people to go beyond their fears and limiting thoughts.

After a year with Tony and other teachers, Kim and I went on our own and began teaching entrepreneurial skills, along with Blair Singer, author of the Rich Dad Advisor books *SalesDogs* and *The ABCs of Building a Business Team That Wins.*

Blair and I still laugh to this day about our first workshop. He and I flew to the island of Maui to do the workshop and only two people showed up. Even though it was a dismal start for our new business, we went on to form the Business School for Entrepreneurs and Business School for Investors. By 1990, five years later, we were filling rooms with hundreds of people, teaching the business and investing principles of my rich dad. By 1994, Kim and I were financially free. Blair went on to form his own corporate training business. Most important, I had found my gift, which is to teach, but not in the same way my poor dad was trained to teach.

In 1994, I retired and began to work on developing CASHFLOW 101 and writing *Rich Dad Poor Dad.* In 1997, Sharon joined Kim and me and the rest is history. Sharon's mission was totally aligned with ours. Our third mission had begun to give back what we had been given in the form of financial and business education. *Our mission was to serve more people* . . . and once we did that, the money poured in like magic, almost from day one.

Sharon still chuckles about the credit card company calling us because we had too much business. After doing one talk over a weekend, the phones in Sharon's garage, where the business initially started, began to ring off the hook. Orders were pouring in. The credit card company tried to shut us down because they were certain we were selling drugs or weapons because we had processed so much business after one event. The president of the bank said to Sharon, "I cannot believe a new business can generate so much cash so quickly." Little did he know that it was the power of the mission and the three types of money—competitive, cooperative, and spiritual money—that was causing the phone to ring.

At the risk of sounding arrogant or "holier-than-thou," I sincerely believe the worldwide success of The Rich Dad Company is not due to Kim, Sharon, and me as individuals, but rather as people dedicated to our missions in life. When the three of us founded The Rich Dad Company, none of us needed to work. It was not about needing a job. It was not about needing money. It was about answering a higher calling. It was about doing a job that needed to be done. If it had been just about the money, there are easier things the three of us could have done.

If our success was luck, then it was spiritual luck. There is no other way to explain it. There simply has been too much magic and too much good fortune to be attributed to merely the combined business skills of the three of us. Steven Pressfield, in his book *The War of Art*, says, "A process is set in motion by which inevitably and infallibly, heaven comes to our aid. Unseen forces enlist in our cause; serendipity reinforces our purpose." Lance Armstrong says, "It's not about the bike."

Before You Quit Your Job

Before you quit your job, remember the three kinds of money and that one type of money is not better than the other. For example, competitive money is not better or worse than cooperative or spiritual money.

Competition has its place in business. Competition keeps prices down and quality up. It keeps us as business people sharp, and keeps us on our toes. Without competition there would be fewer new products or life-changing innovations. Without competition we would be approaching a communist, centrally controlled type of economy. Without competition, there would be less need or incentive for entrepreneurs.

If you are about to become an entrepreneur, your first mission is to master the B-I Triangle, especially the levels from cash flow up through product. If you do not learn the B-I Triangle, and continually work on mastering the levels, and if you are not competitive, you might not survive.

If you are not competitive, you will find it difficult to be cooperative and to work for cooperative money. In the game of business, it is tough being cooperative with poor people or poor companies. It's like playing football with a teammate who has a broken leg.

As stated in an earlier chapter, the B-I Triangle actually applies to all four quadrants of the cash flow quadrant. For example, people in the E quadrant also have a B-I Triangle. If they are having financial challenges, it makes it easier to diagnose their financial challenge by simply looking at their private lives through the B-I Triangle. For example, many employees struggle financially simply because they are weak at the cash flow level. Even if you give them a raise, their weakness at that level will keep them financially poor.

One of the reasons The Rich Dad Company shuts down the office for half a day each month is to have our employees play CASHFLOW 101 and 202 as a company activity, to keep them financially strong at this level of the B-I Triangle. By doing this, when raises are awarded, they are able to use the extra money to get ahead financially, rather than end up deeper in debt with consumer credit.

The Marine Corps did teach me that the mission of the organization starts at the core, in the soul of the organization. Without integrity to a mission, an organization does not have a soul. That is why we take a half-day to play the game or talk about investments, business, and money management. We practice what we preach and live our company mission as a company. All employees are encouraged to start their own business or investment portfolios so that one day they can leave the company for good. We do not want loyal employees. We want loyal employees who have a plan to become financially free and leave the company.

As a side note: Several Rich Dad employees have achieved financial independence. They choose not to leave the company because they do not want to leave, which is another blessing of being true to the mission.

We do not want our good workers to leave. We celebrate their becoming financially free, because that is the mission of The Rich Dad Company.

So before you quit your job remember that your mission starts at your core, in your soul, felt in your heart, and spoken through your actions—not just your words.

SHARON'S INSIGHTS

Lesson #6: The Best Answers Are Found in Your Heart . . . Not Your Head.

We have talked about the five job levels of the B-I Triangle that are intregal to the success of any business. But let's take a step back and look at what holds those jobs together—the framework of a successful business, the three sides of the B-I Triangle: Mission, Team, and Leadership.

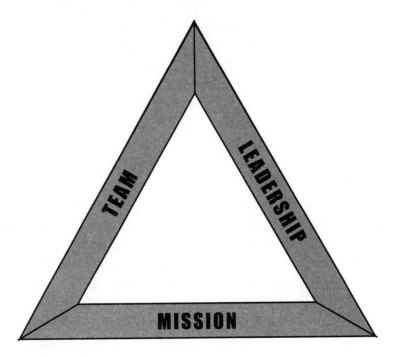

The mission is the true purpose of the business. From the moment we became partners, Robert, Kim, and I agreed the mission for The Rich Dad Company would be "to elevate the financial well-being of humanity."

When we discuss the mission of a company, we talk about two missions, one the business mission and the other the spiritual mission. Can a business be started with only a business mission, to make a profit, and succeed? Absolutely. But the businesses that adopt a spiritual mission create a higher purpose that allows others to align themselves with that spiritual mission.

We have many partners and individuals who have aligned with our spiritual mission, working to elevate the financial well-being of humanity. With the spiritual mission as the driving force of our company, the spiritual money has appeared. If our focus had been on making competitive money by selling financial education products, these same partners might not have aligned with us. Are we competitive? Absolutely. Are we cooperative? Absolutely. Are we spiritual? We make every effort to focus our efforts on the spiritual mission.

We are often presented with ideas and opportunities that would have been financially successful for The Rich Dad Company. For instance, we have been approached to start a Rich Dad hedge fund, or a syndicated real estate investment, both of which could have been very profitable. But when we really looked at the proposals, the missions of the teams behind these proposals were more profit-motivated, and therefore not aligned with our company's spiritual mission, "to elevate the financial well-being of humanity." These initiatives would probably have elevated our personal financial well-being, but that is not our true mission.

In fact, we often confuse potential partners because we give them more than they ask for, or have them recoup their investment more quickly than they originally propose. Why do we do this? We know that if we make our partners successful first, they will be more anxious to support our company's mission and efforts. In our hearts, and in our experience, we have learned that if you put the partner and the mission first, the financial reward will follow.

Have we made mistakes along the way? Absolutely. But when you have partners or advisors who are not aligned with your mission, discord will appear in the relationship. In fact, we have had advisors who could not tell you what The Rich Dad Company mission statement was. This highlighted that they were not aligned with our spiritual mission. They are no longer our advisors.

We are getting better at spotting individuals who are not aligned with our mission. We listen to their words and look behind them. If they say, "We're here to help you," we know to run the other way. More often than not, their true purpose is to "benefit themselves" by associating themselves with the popularity of the Rich Dad brand. On the other hand, if they say, "We want to be part of educating people about money," we are eager to listen to more.

As rich dad said, "The more people you serve, the richer you become."

In planning your business, what is your mission? Do you have both a business mission and a spiritual mission? Your mission is the foundation of the B-I Triangle.

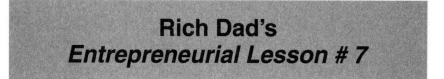

The Scope of the Mission Determines the Product.

Chapter 7

How to Go from Small Business to Big Business

"Why do most small businesses remain small?" I asked.

"Good question. They remain small because there are weaknesses in their B-I Triangle," answered rich dad. "It's tough going from the S quadrant to the B quadrant if the B-I Triangle is not strong."

America: A Nation of Small Businesses

America in 2005 has approximately 16 million businesses. Eighty percent are small businesses with nine employees or fewer. Eighty-five percent of the employment in America is found in small businesses. These small companies compose 53% of the nation's GDP, Gross Domestic Product. Approximately 150,000 new businesses are formed every month and another 150,000 disappear every month.

After the Wreckage

There is a saying that goes, "Hindsight is 20/20." While that is true, there is some hindsight that is clearer than others. Visual aids such as the B-I Triangle

and the CASHFLOW Quadrant not only helped me see forward when designing a business, they have also assisted me in seeing backward. After the crash
of my nylon surfer wallet business, having the quadrant and the triangle as visual aids was like having eyeglasses or a magnifying glass when combing
through the wreckage of the business.

It was obvious that success and incompetence wiped us out. Yet, behind
the success lay deeper, darker factors that caused us to crash. Being honest
with myself, and looking at the CASHFLOW Quadrant, it became crystal clear
why we crashed. The real cause was youthful arrogance. Having a successful
business early in life was like giving a kid a Corvette and a six-pack of beer
and then saying, "Drive safely."

Looking at the quadrant shown below it is easy to see my arrogance.

In 1976, my best friend Larry Clark and I were in the E quadrant, working
for Xerox as salespeople. Because we were tops in sales, we thought we
knew all the answers. In our business plan, we thought we could pull an Evel
Knievel, and jump the Grand Canyon on a motorcycle. That means we
thought we would take a shortcut to the B quadrant. Instead of going from
E to S, our plan was to rev up our motorcycles and jump from E to B. Instead
of climbing down the canyon from E to S, and then climbing up the other
side, from S to B, we decided to leap the canyon. Even Evel Knievel was
smart enough to make the leap with a parachute attached to his motorcycle.
We didn't.

Instead of being Evel Knievel, we looked like Wile E. Coyote chasing the Road Runner over the edge of a cliff and out into space before realizing there is nothing but air below his feet. Somewhere between 1978 and 1979, we realized we had nothing but air below us. We almost made it to the B quadrant. In fact we touched the edge of it, but it was the weakness of our B-I Triangle that sent us crashing into the valley. It was not pretty and it was painful. Today, every time I see a Road Runner and Wile E. Coyote cartoon, I know how the coyote feels. Beep! Beep!

Crashes Are Good If You Survive

Between 1979 and 1981, I felt like I was the NTSB, the National Transportation Safety Board, inspecting the wreckage of an airplane. My partners had moved on to other businesses and two new partners took their place. One of them was my brother Jon, who was a strong business partner as well as a tremendous moral support. Together, we went through the wreckage and rebuilt a new but smaller business. We went from B back to S.

In 1981, our downsized company entered a joint venture with a local radio station and created what is to this day reportedly the most successful merchandising program in the history of radio. Together with the radio station, we created a merchandising brand named 98 Rock. The star product was a black T-shirt with a splashed paint logo of red and white, screaming 98 Rock FM Honolulu. In Honolulu, our 98 Rock Shops had thousands of kids lining up to buy tens of thousands of T-shirts and other accessories.

The product line soon went worldwide, doing especially well in Japan. Seeing a little 98 Rock Shop in Tokyo, with thousands of Japanese kids in line to buy the products, brought smiles back to our faces, smiles that had not been there for a number of years. When I told rich dad about our worldwide success, he reminded me, "The *process* will give a glimpse of your future, but you must be faithful to the process." Although I was not out of the woods, I knew I was getting closer to my goal. The *process,* although tough, was working.

The 98 Rock craze lasted about eighteen months. It made a lot of money. It was through this one marketing campaign that I was able to pay back over $700,000 to my creditors and pay off my back taxes. At the end of the fad, I was financially back to zero. Although still without money, my B-I Triangle skills were stronger, my confidence was back, I had turned bad luck into good luck, I did not have to declare bankruptcy, and once again I had caught a glimpse of the good life—my future at the end of the process.

In 1981, an agent for the rock band Pink Floyd called. He had heard of our success with 98 Rock merchandise and wanted us to work with them on the rerelease of their album *The Wall*. Obviously, we jumped at the opportunity. Once again, our small company was growing into a big company. With this growth, once again the strength of our company's B-I Triangle was being tested.

Our joint venture with Pink Floyd's merchandise was successful. Soon, other bands came to us and without really planning it, our little company in Honolulu was solidly in rock and roll merchandising. When Duran Duran and Van Halen joined our list of rock bands, the business exploded. Simultaneously, around 1982, MTV was launched. That meant rock and roll was back, disco was dead, and once again our systems were overstressed. We were in the right place at the right time in the right business. The problem was, we could no longer keep up with demand. We also knew we could no longer produce products in America. The costs of government regulations, labor, labor laws, and factory space were too much for a little company. In order to expand, it was much more economical to move our manufacturing to Asia.

The three partners worked day and night expanding into Asia. It was about six months of hard work—not 24/7 but at least 20/7. I was virtually living in New York or San Francisco; Dave, our other partner, was in Taiwan and Korea; and my brother kept the Honolulu operations going. Operating in time zones that spanned half the globe, we were constantly on the phone (before cell phones and e-mail) staying in touch, building a bigger B-I Triangle. With an expanded B-I Triangle, the money once again poured in.

Occasionally I would stop in and see rich dad. During this period of time, we were not on the best of terms. He was still angry because he thought I had not listened to his advice just before the crash of the original wallet business. Although not happy with me, he was still very giving with his time and advice. Even when I reported that our new wallet business had been rebuilt and I had learned a lot from the process, he remained a little grumpy.

In hindsight, rebuilding the business was a priceless experience. My two new partners and I had all learned a lot and had grown up a lot. We were less flaky. We were smarter business people and our cash flow was the proof. Our new B-I Triangle was not leaking, it was not collapsing—it was holding its own.

One day, my partner Dave suggested I go with him to Korea and Taiwan to see our operations. Since I had been only in San Francisco and New York during the expansion period, I had not gone to Asia to see our factories. As stated in an earlier chapter, it was on this trip to Asia that I saw the kids in sweatshops and my career as a manufacturer ended.

Mission Accomplished

On the plane ride back from Asia to Hawaii, I realized that my mission was accomplished. Sitting in my seat, I began looking back at the *process.* As if it was only yesterday, I remembered deciding to join the Xerox Corporation to learn how to sell in 1974. My mind also brought back memories of the day in 1976 when my friend Larry and I decided to start the nylon surfer wallet business part-time. In 1978, once I was number one in sales at Xerox and our surfer wallet business was being written up in *GQ, Runners World,* and *Playboy.*

Larry and I left Xerox to run our tiny business full-time. I recalled all the high times and then the crash. My emotions sank as I remembered how badly I felt when I told my family, my creditors, and the tax department that we were shutting the business down. I remembered the lessons from rich dad during this period. A smile crossed my face when I thought of my brother, Dave, and I agreeing to rebuild the business and our success with 98 Rock, and then MTV and rock and roll. Now the business was strong and it was time to move on. My mind kept saying, "Stay, it's now time to make a lot of money. You're back on top again. Why leave now? You're just about to get rich. The hard work is done. Your dreams will come true." Yet in my heart, I knew it was time to move on.

Deciding to move on was tough, especially with the money beginning to pour in. I struggled with the conflict between my head and my heart for months. Many times, when I received my paycheck and bonus check, I definitely wanted to stay. Yet, I knew my mission to learn the fundamentals of the B-I Triangle had been accomplished. I could now be competitive in the business world. The problem was I did not like what I had to do to stay competitive. I did not want to employ kids in horrible conditions, conditions that would probably scar many of them for life. In late 1983, I let Dave and my brother, Jon, know that I was leaving the business. I asked for no financial compensation. I had gotten more than I wanted.

Meeting Kim

Just as I was preparing to make these changes in my life, I met Kim. Still the disco duck of Waikiki, I had met her months earlier, but she would not have anything to do with me. It must have been the long-collared shirts and disco boots. It did not bother me, since Waikiki was full of beautiful young women.

For some reason, after I returned from Asia, Kim came back into my thoughts. I asked her out again and she turned me down again. This went on for six months. I would run into her, talk to her, ask her out, and she would turn me down. I would call her and she would turn me down. I sent flowers and she turned me down. Again and again she turned me down. I tried every sales tactic I learned in sales training on her. I tried the *puppy-dog* close, the *Colombo* close, the "*assume the sale and close*" close but none of them worked.

Finally, out of tricks from my sales bag, I stopped being a disco-duck salesperson and applied what I had learned from the marketing classes I had been taking at night. In marketing, a rule of thumb is to do your market research first. With my marketing cap on instead of my sales cap, I began asking around to find out who this woman named Kim really was. In marketing it is called, "Know your customer."

The first person I asked was a guy who knew her from work. When I began asking questions all he did was laugh. "You don't have a prayer," he said. "Do you know how many guys are after her? She has cards, flowers, and phone calls from guys like you all day. She probably does not know who you are."

He was not helpful so I kept digging. Finally, I was having lunch with a female friend of mine and I mentioned I was not getting far on my market research project, codename Kim. Phyllis cracked up after she heard my story. "Don't you know who her best girlfriend is?"

"No. I don't."

Laughing hysterically, Phyllis said, "Her best friend is Karen, your old girlfriend."

"What?" I said. "You're kidding me."

"No I am not," laughed Phyllis.

Giving Phyllis a big hug and kiss, I ran out the door and back to the office. I had a phone call to make—to Karen.

The split between Karen and me had not been the most pleasant, so I had some patching up to do. After I had made a few belated apologies, Karen listened to the story of my six-month pursuit of Kim. She, too, laughed her head off.

Finally composing herself, she asked, "So what do you want me to do?"

Taking off my marketing cap and putting on my salesperson's cap, I asked for what every salesperson is trained to ask for from a satisfied customer, I asked for a *referral.*

"You want what?" screamed Karen. "You want a referral from me? You want me to recommend to her that she go out with you? You've got your nerve."

"Well, that is why I was number one in sales," I said as a joke.

Karen did not laugh. "Okay," she said, "I'll talk to her. But I warn you, that is all I am going to do. No more favors."

Karen did talk to Kim and gave me an excellent referral. About six weeks later, our calendars finally cleared and we finally had our first date on February 19, 1984.

A New Process Begins

Our date was a table overlooking the beach and a simple walk along a white sand beach with a bottle of champagne. I did not have much money, so that was about as romantic a date as I could think of for a good price. Sitting on the beach at the foot of Diamond Head, Kim and I talked until the sun came up. We had a lot of catching up to do.

That night she told me about her life and I talked about mine. When the subject of work came up, I told her about rich dad and his lessons. As she had been a business major in college she was very interested in rich dad's B-I Triangle and the process of becoming an entrepreneur. Sitting on the sand at the water's edge, in the moonlight, talking to the most beautiful woman I had ever known about business, was like being in heaven. Most of the women the disco duck had dated up to this point were not into business. Kim was. She was very interested.

She shook her head when I told her the story of the nylon wallet business. I told her about flying high and then the crash that followed. When I told her about the kids in Asia, one stacked on top of another, four tiers of workers when there should only be one tier, inhaling toxic fumes from the paints we used, she nearly cried. Then I told her about resigning from my company because the mission was over.

With that she took over the conversation, saying, "I'm glad you're moving on. But what are you going to do?"

Shaking my head, I replied, "I don't know. All I know is that sometimes you have to stop before you can begin again. So right now all I am doing is stopping."

At that point I told her about my dad who was still unemployed, taking odd jobs when he could find them. I told her about how I thought education was inadequate and not preparing kids for the real world—it was preparing kids to be employees not entrepreneurs, teaching kids to expect a company or the government to take care of them once their working days were over. We then discussed the future, how rich dad envisioned a coming Social Security crisis, a medical crisis, and a financial crisis in the stock market, growing bigger and bigger as the baby-boom generation aged.

"Why are you concerned?" she asked. "Why do you think the coming financial crisis is your problem?"

"I can't really say," I said. "I know that the world has a lot of problems, such as problems with the environment, diseases, enough food, shelter, and so on. But for me, this problem of money, poverty, and the gap between rich and poor interests me the most. I feel it in my stomach and in my heart."

The conversation shifted to Dr. Buckminster Fuller and my studies with him and how he shared the same concerns about the financial system as my rich dad. I did my best to explain to her how Dr. Fuller said the rich and powerful were *playing games with money*, keeping the poor and middle class constantly at the edge of financial crisis. I also told Kim about Fuller's saying that each of us had a purpose to our lives. That each of us held a vital piece of the puzzle and our job was to not just make money, but to also make this world a better place.

"It sounds like you're looking for a way to help people like your dad and people like those kids in the factory," said Kim.

I said, "That is pretty accurate. While I was in that factory I decided it was time for me to work for the kids, instead of having the kids working for me. It is time for me to make the kids rich, rather than just myself rich."

The sun was breaking over the ocean. The young surfers were out testing the smooth glassy waves. It was time to get ready for work. We had been up all night but were full of energy. We have been together ever since.

Finding My Passion

In December 1984, Kim and I moved to California. As I have stated many times in my writings, this began the hardest period of both of our lives. The business opportunity we thought we were part of did not pan out. That left us without money, sleeping in our car for a few nights. It was a time that tested our commitment to our new business and to each other.

California was the hotbed for new models of education. Many of the hippies had grown older and were teaching seminars on some very strange and interesting subjects. The common themes were: open your mind; change your paradigms; break through your limiting realities. Kim and I attended as many seminars as we could, gaining new ideas and observing different teaching techniques.

Earlier in this book, I wrote about attending Bob Bondurant's School of High-Performance Driving, and also about working with Tony Robbins and teaching people about walking across two-thousand-degree coals. As you may already know, I did not like the traditional system of education. I didn't like being taught by the fear of failing, learning to memorize all the right answers, and being afraid of making mistakes. In school I always felt I was being programmed to do only the right things and to live in fear of living life. In school, I often felt like a butterfly caught on a spider's web, with the spider wrapping its web around and around me until I could no longer fly.

The kind of education I was looking for was an education that taught people how to break through their fears. Education that would help them discover their own power within, so they could walk on fire or drive a high-speed Formula One racer. The more I studied these techniques, finding out how we all learn, how the mind works in conjunction with our emotions and its effects upon our physical abilities, the more I wanted to learn. I became fascinated by the subject of how we as humans learn.

I discovered why I loved the Marine Corps so much. I loved Marine Corps training and flight school because it, too, was about going beyond fears and limiting thoughts. The Marine Corps was the perfect learning environment for me. The learning environment was tough and rigorous, requiring my body, mind, emotions, and soul to get through the programs. In the Marine Corps memorizing the right answers is not enough. Just as in the world of business, the Marine Corps was about results not reasons. It was about actions not words. It was a learning environment that insisted the mission be first, team second, individual last. It was a learning environment that taught me to fly rather than a learning environment that clipped my wings.

Breakthrough Learning

It was dawning on me that what we were studying was what I came to call Breakthrough Learning, the type of learning that is powerful enough to cause a transformation, a paradigm shift of reality, much like how a chick must feel when it finally breaks through the shell of the egg it is in.

During one of the seminars on learning I attended, I learned about Ilya Prigogine, a person who was awarded the Nobel Prize for his findings.

The Nobel Prize was awarded to him for his research on dissipative structures. To put it into as simple an example as possible, his research proved why a child will climb on a bike, fall off, climb on, fall off, and then suddenly be able to ride. Again in the simplest of terms, under the extreme stress of falling down and getting up again and again, the stress of the process causes the brain of the child to reorder. It goes from not knowing how to ride a bicycle to being able to ride a bicycle forever.

To me, his research verified why people who do well in school may not do well in the real world. There are many people who know what to do but cannot do what they know. Like my dad, once they fall down, they stay down, often saying, "I'll never do that again." Instead of pressing on with increasing stress and frustration, they back off to reduce the stress. In many ways, it is like the chick remaining in its protective shell.

As Prigogine summarized, "Stress is the way intelligence grows." Or as rich dad would say, "Stay with the process."

How Fast Can We Learn?

Another person whose work I researched was Georgi Lozanov of Bulgaria, the pioneer of what is now called Super-Learning. Although I never took one of his classes, it is reported that he was able to teach people a complete language in one or two days. Obviously, traditional academics discredit him and his work. I began experimenting with his techniques and found out that they really did work.

One reason I disliked school so much was simply that the pace was too slow. It took too long to learn too little. Combining different teaching techniques increased the speed of learning, reduced boredom, and resulted in greater long-term retention. I began to become excited about education—and a new category of education. What I liked most about what I was discovering was that it did not matter if you were an A student or an F student. With this method of teaching, all it took to learn was the desire to learn.

Finding My Passion

Rich dad had said to me years earlier that once you complete a process, you take the best with you and leave the rest behind. You then move on to the next process. Once again, once the process is over, you take the best of the process with you and leave the rest behind.

As Kim and I were going through this learning period, rich dad's words began to make sense. Suddenly, it dawned on me that I was beginning the best of several processes in my life. I had my experience from the process of going to school, which I really hated. Next were my experiences from the process of being a Marine pilot. Then I had my experiences from learning to be an entrepreneur with my nylon wallet business. As tough as that nylon wallet process was, I did have many great experiences to take with me. And now, actually becoming a student of how people learn, all my past experiences were coming together. My often disorderly life was beginning to make sense.

Around August 1985, I found my passion. My next business was forming in my mind. From 1986 to 1994, Kim and I ran an organization that put on the Business School for Entrepreneurs and the Business School for Investors. Instead of being your traditional business school, this business school had no prerequisites. We did not require scholastic records. All that was required was the will to learn and the time and the money for the courses.

Employing the techniques we had learned, we were able to teach people the basics of accounting and investing—normally a six-month course—in one day. Instead of talking about business, the class actually built a business touching on all parts of the B-I Triangle. Instead of talking about team building, each business team also had to train for a triathlon. Instead of one person finishing first, it was the team that finished first that won. I do not know if you know how hard it is to get fifteen people, of different ages, different genders, different levels of fitness, and different mind-sets, to compete in a swim, bike, and run contest as a team. Some of the contests reminded me of scenes from Vietnam where team members were carrying other team members across the finish line. Of course, to be a real business school, we bet money. Every participant put money into the pot and it was winner take all. A winning team of fifteen could walk away with as much as $50,000 in prize money.

At our Business School for Investors, instead of talking about investing, we actually would build a stock market trading floor. The different teams would represent different mutual funds and money managers. As market conditions changed, the teams had to adjust their investment strategies. Again, at the end of the school, the winning team walked away with the money.

In 1993, although the business was successful and profitable, I knew it was once again time to move on. In the summer of 1994, Kim and I sold our share of the business to our partner and retired. The passive income generated from our investments was now greater than our expenses. We were finally out of the rat race. We weren't rich but we were financially free. If you can find a copy of *Rich Dad's Retire Young Retire Rich* (Warner Books), you will see on the back cover a picture of Kim and me sitting on horses, on a hill overlooking a crystal blue ocean. That vacation on a private island in Fiji was our reward for retiring early. Kim was thirty-seven and I was forty-seven.

Know When to Stop

In his book *Good to Great*, Jim Collins does a whole piece on knowing when to stop. Reading his book in 2004 took me back to the times when I also stopped in 1984 and 1994. There was no clear signal, no sign from God saying, "It's time to stop." Each time, there was simply a moment when I knew the process I was in had come to an end. It was time to stop and wait for the beginning of the next process.

Many times I meet business people who want to stop but can't stop. They cannot stop for different reasons. One common reason is that their B-I Triangle is weak. To cover up for the weaknesses the owner often has to work harder or longer to make up for the weaknesses. Another reason is that the owner cannot afford to stop. Again, this is a symptom of a weakness in the B-I Triangle. Another common reason is that the owner, although successful, continues to work because he or she does not know what to do next. According to Jim Collins, a person may need to stop first, take some time off, and then look for the next thing. In my situation, this is what I did. I simply stopped, let the dust settle, waited a few years to see what would happen next.

Going from S to B

From 1984 to 1994, I was firmly entrenched in the S quadrant. I was not going to make any premature moves toward the B quadrant. As expected, as our success grew so did our exhaustion. Exhaustion is what often occurs with successful people in the S quadrant. Since an S individual often works himself, more success means more work. An S often works for a dollar per hour compensation plan, and as we all know, there are only so many hours in a day.

When Kim and I stopped, it was not the hard work or long hours that caused us to stop. What was disturbing me was how few people our work was reaching. After all, only a few people actually pay money to attend seminars. And our seminars were not only expensive, they were tough like the Marine Corps. We asked people to devote ten or more days to attend one of our business schools.

Dr. Buckminister Fuller, the teacher who has had a tremendous influence on my life, often said, "The more people you serve, the more effective you become." He was not into money but he was into being of service. Rich dad said, "One of the big differences between an S and a B quadrant person is the number of customers they can handle." He also said, "If you want to be rich, simply serve more people."

By 1994, the last business school I was part of had over 350 people in the class paying $5,000 each to attend. So, do the math; the money was good. What was not good was that there were only 350 people. I knew that if I truly wanted to help those kids in Asia, I was not going to be able to do it doing things the way I was doing them. In other words, I knew it was time to stop and figure out how to go from the S quadrant to the B quadrant. Instead of trying to leap across the Grand Canyon, Kim and I were now ready to climb up the other side. It was time to go through what rich dad called "the eye of the needle."

Going through the Eye of the Needle

As most of you know, one of the problems with being self-employed in the S quadrant is the word *self*. In many cases, the self-employed person is the product, the person who is hired to do the work. When you look at the B-I Triangle, starting from the cash flow level on up to product, the self-employed person is in charge of everything, all the levels. In most cases, being self-employed makes it very difficult to get to the B quadrant. It can be difficult to get your *self* out of the way of the process.

Between 1984 and 1994, I was that person. I was the *self* in self-employed. Although I did it intentionally, the reality disturbed me. A question I often asked myself was, "How do I teach people what I had been teaching in our business schools without my personally teaching them?" We tried training other instructors, but that process was a long, hard, tedious process. It was difficult to find people like Blair Singer and another friend, Wayne Morgan, to go through the training process to become instructors. Although they were already entrepreneurs, it was hard to teach them to teach the way we taught. It takes a lot of talent to get a class of over three hundred people to learn accounting and investing in one day. It was almost as tough as teaching them to walk across fire.

After selling the business in 1994, I had time to go back to my question, "How do I teach people what I had been teaching in our business schools without my teaching them?" Moving into the mountains near Bisbee, Arizona, I was secluded enough to begin working on the answer to my question. For two years I worked on the question, and when I left Bisbee, I had the rough draft for *Rich Dad Poor Dad* in my Macintosh computer and a rough sketch with computations for the CASHFLOW 101 board game. I was going through the eye of the needle and moving from the S to the B quadrant.

Rich dad had learned about the eye of the needle from Sunday school. He said, "A popular saying in church goes something like, 'It is easier for a camel to pass through the eye of a needle than for a rich man to pass into heaven.'" Rich dad continued, modifying the saying to, "Forget the camel. If a man can pass through the eye of the needle he will enter the world of tremendous wealth."

Now rich dad was a very religious man and was not making fun of the religious lesson. He was simply using the lesson and modifying it to create his own lesson. In business terms, what he meant was that for an entrepreneur to pass through the eye of the needle, the entrepreneur had to leave him- or herself behind. What passed through the eye of the needle was the intellectual property of the entrepreneur. Looking at the diagram below, you may better understand what rich dad meant.

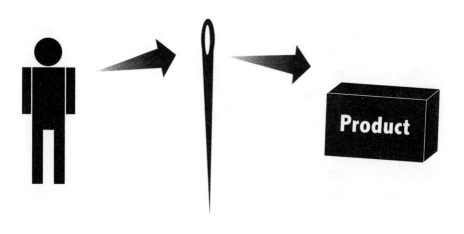

There are many examples of entrepreneurs going through the eye of the needle throughout history. A few are:

1. When Henry Ford designed his automobile to be mass-produced he passed through the eye of the needle. Up until then, most cars were custom-ordered and hand-made.

2. When Steven Jobs and his team at Apple Computers created the iPod, they went through the eye of the needle.

3. When someone like Steven Spielberg or George Lucas creates a movie, they, too, go through the eye of the needle.

4. McDonald's went through the eye of the needle by franchising their hamburger business worldwide.

5. When a network marketer builds a *down line* of other business owners, it goes through the eye of the needle.

6. When investors buy an asset, such as an apartment house that cash flows money into their pocket each and every month, they have gone through the eye of the needle.

7. A politician who uses television to campaign is going through the eye of the needle. A politician who goes door to door is not.

8. When inventors or authors sell their invention or their book to a large company, which in return pays them royalties, they have gone through the eye of the needle.

9. By taking what I had learned from rich dad and my research into learning, and creating the board game and starting the book, I was going through the eye of the needle. I was getting myself out of the equation.

10. When I created my nylon shoe pocket wallet for runners, and *did not* first have my idea protected by an intellectual property attorney, I was *not going* through the eye of the needle. I was simply giving my idea to my competition and making them rich. They went through the eye of the needle and I fell into the Grand Canyon. I had a great new product, but without the legal level to protect my product, the B-I Triangle was not complete.

The Chick Breaks through Its Shell

When I returned from Phoenix with a draft of the book and the CASHFLOW board game in hand, I knew that in order to move to the B quadrant, the first thing I needed to do was find a great team. Having a great team is essential for moving from the S quadrant to the B quadrant. And rich dad always said, "If you are the smartest person on your team, you are in trouble." With the right mission and the right team, our B business began to flourish.

Once I found Michael Lechter and the products were protected, and Michael introduced me to Sharon, I knew we had a great team. Sharon, Kim, and I began to design and build a company according to the B-I Triangle. The moment we put our products in the marketplace, the heavens of abundance opened up. The product line was officially unveiled on my fiftieth birthday, April 8, 1997, at Sharon and Michael's home. From the start of The Rich Dad Company, we had no struggles, no working hard to breathe life into the business. The only struggles we had were keeping up with demand, traveling the world to open new markets, and counting the money. In June 2000, the call from the Oprah show came and the heavens really opened. The three of us were leaping from S to B.

At this point I began to better understand what rich dad meant by:

1. Being true to the process
2. That the process will give you glimpses of a better future, just to keep you going
3. The power of mastering the B-I Triangle
4. Harnessing the power of the three types of money, competitive, co-operative, and spiritual money
5. Going through the eye of the needle

After the Oprah show, I truly felt like the chick that had finally cracked through its shell. Before Oprah, no one knew me. After Oprah, regardless of where I go in the world, people stop me on the street to let me know they have read *Rich Dad Poor Dad* or played the CASHFLOW games.

In 2002, I was in an antique store in Stockholm, Sweden. The owner, a very blond Swede, was an expert in Chinese antiques. Recognizing me, he said, "I was on a buying trip to China a few months ago. While floating down the Yangtze River, I glanced into a houseboat and saw a Chinese family playing the Chinese version of your board game CASHFLOW."

At that moment, I realized that I had kept my promise to those kids in the sweatshop, kids who were working to make me rich. Now my products were working for kids just like them, teaching families, people young and old how to have money work for them, rather than working all their lives and then hoping to have the government take care of them.

In February 2004, the *New York Times* did a full-page feature story about the CASHFLOW game and about the hundreds of clubs forming throughout the world. They were forming just to play the game and to learn what my rich dad had taught me. When I saw that article, I could not believe my eyes. I could not believe the magic. To me, having the *New York Times* doing this article was as big as being on Oprah.

When I saw the article, I knew that what I had learned from teaching my Business School for Entrepreneurs and Business School for Investors had been successfully transformed into a product, CASHFLOW, that could teach what I used to teach. People were now learning the fundamentals of accounting and investing in less than a day. On top of that, many of the players have had significant breakthroughs in how they see the world. For them, the game delivered the paradigm shift, the shift from seeing the world of money as a frightening place to seeing it as an exciting place. Instead of looking for experts and blindly turning their money over to these so-called experts, after playing the game many people realized that they could become their own financial experts—they could take control of their own financial future. And many of them have.

Best of all, instead of teaching only 350 people at a time, having them come to me and charging them thousands of dollars, the CASHFLOW game was now going to them and teaching many thousands more people, many of them for free. Instead of my teaching them, they were teaching themselves and then teaching and sharing with others.

When I saw the *New York Times* article, I knew the ten-year period from 1994 to 2004 was coming to an end. However, while this ten-year process is complete, we know the mission continues.

Before You Quit Your Job

Before you quit your job, you may want to remember the lesson of this chapter. The lesson is that the scope of the mission determines the product. It is very tough making a lot of money or serving a lot of people simply by working harder physically. If you want to serve a lot of people and/or make a lot of money, you may need to get yourself out of the way and pass through the eye of the needle.

Before you quit your job, you may also want to determine if you would be happiest in the S quadrant or the B quadrant. If you want to grow into the B quadrant, remember that it takes much stronger fundamentals in the B-I Triangle and an even stronger team to allow you to go through the eye of the needle.

And before you quit your job, you may want to have a moment of silence in memory of the dot.com companies that failed. I believe the reason so many failed was that many of the entrepreneurs were attempting to leap from the E quadrant to the B quadrant. When the bust came, they, too, looked like Wile E. Coyote with only air beneath their feet. They *did not* make it through the eye of the needle.

SHARON'S INSIGHTS

Lesson #7: The Scope of the Mission Determines the Product.

PICKING YOUR MISSION

The most successful businesses usually do one of two things:

- *Solve a problem*
- *Fill a need*

Having a mission that relates to the solution of a problem or filling a need, combined with a desire to serve as many people as possible, are fundamental building blocks of the most successful businesses.

As Robert learned in the Marines, it was mission first, team second, and self last. Wouldn't the world be a better place if we all lived with that core set of beliefs?

In this book we share a lot about The Rich Dad Company and our core mission "to elevate the financial well-being of humanity." When we sat down to start the company, and Robert shared this mission with me, I must admit I felt overwhelmed.

I also felt gratified that my own personal mission and philosophy was absolutely consistent with that lofty goal. Now, eight years later, each phone call, e-mail, or fax that we receive from someone who sees light at the end of the tunnel, or is finally out of debt, or has purchased his or her first investment property—all the way to those people who are financially free and out of the rat race—I realize that our mission is being accomplished and is continuing to be accomplished. It is being accomplished, not by us, but by each of you who takes action to improve your financial lives.

I am involved with The Rich Dad Company because of its mission. The events leading to the formation of The Rich Dad Company are described in the next chapter, but my initial introduction to Robert and the CASHFLOW game illustrate this point. I first heard about Robert and the CASHFLOW game in a phone call from my husband. I distinctly remember the call.

"Honey," he said, "I've found the man who has what you've been looking for!"

I choked. What was my husband saying? He found the man who has what I've been looking for? He obviously didn't mean it the way that it sounded. He continued before I was able to ask him to explain what he meant.

"One of my clients—his name is Robert Kiyosaki—has come up with a game that teaches basic finance, the fundamentals of both accounting and investing. I think it's something that you might want to look at."

Michael was fully aware of my passion for financial education, and was apparently very enthused with this game. I was intrigued, and said so.

"I'm intrigued. Does it really work?"

"I think so. The logic is certainly there. What they've done makes sense. They're getting ready to test it."

"I'd love to check it out. Let me know," I replied. A few weeks later my daughter Shelly and I went to the beta test to test the prototype of the game before it went into production, and were introduced to Robert, Kim, and the CASHFLOW game.

We will talk more about what happened at the beta test, and how The Rich Dad Company was formed, in the next chapter. For now, let's just say that the beta test made it clear to me that the game was a means to further my personal mission of making sure that financial education was available to as many people as possible—making sure that our kids had a fighting chance, and didn't, through ignorance, start their adult life already deep in debt. Knowing about money is a life skill that needs to be taught to our children to prepare them for the world they will face.

Conversations with Robert and Kim made it very clear that my personal mission was consistent with theirs. Our shared mission would be achieved by making the CASHFLOW teachings available to as many people as possible. What was the best way to do that? The answer is simple in concept—to build a successful business around the CASHFLOW game. My experience in starting and building companies in the publishing and game industries could be very helpful in the process. Initially I began sharing my experience with Robert and Kim and discussing business issues with them, such as outsourcing the manufacturing of the game, and then I began working with Robert on the book *Rich Dad Poor Dad*. Ultimately Robert, Kim, and I formed The Rich Dad Company as partners, and I became its CEO.

The motivation for my involvement was not money. I was willing to work for free. My focus was strictly on the achievement of the mission. Frankly, Michael and I didn't need the money. Michael was a very successful attorney, and we had made a number of excellent investments. We were already financially free. The compensation that I sought was spiritual in nature. Of course, after we formed The Rich Dad Company and we stayed true to our mission, the money followed.

YOU DON'T NEED TO SAVE THE WORLD

It is important to note that a business may be successful without a mission of such a global nature as The Rich Dad Company's. Once again, a successful business usually solves a problem or fills a need. The mission of those businesses is to make the solution to the problem or need available to those who need it. For instance, I have a friend who owns a cardboard company that makes specialty boxes. It is an incredibly successful business that both solves a problem and fills a need. Its mission is significant in its own right—to provide specific types of boxes to those who need them.

Another perfect example of someone solving a problem, or turning a problem into a viable business, was Rob, a friend of my son's who worked in a Chinese restaurant. He heard the owners complain that they could not get their supply of a particular kind of rice at a reasonable price or in sufficient quantities. He had an idea. He checked with other restaurants in the area and found they had the same difficulties. So he called the importer in San Francisco and arranged to buy this particular rice in large quantities at a much-reduced price. Within just a few months he had a successful business. Rob had solved a problem and filled a need. The mission of his business was to provide the restaurants in Wisconsin and other markets in the Midwest with a stable supply of rice at a lower price than they had been paying before. Rob started in Wisconsin, and had enough margin left between the price he paid and the price he sold the rice for to grow his business all over the Midwest. He has since expanded into importing many other items.

In reviewing the B-I Triangle, there is a reason that the mission is the base of the triangle, and the product is the tip of the inside of the triangle. This is why we smile when someone comes to us and says, "I have a great idea for a product—do you want to buy it from me, or invest in it?"

Does this mean a business can't be built around a product? No, it does not. Sometimes the "product" is really a solution to a problem, a manifestation of a mission, and the promoter simply doesn't communicate that fact. Sometimes the mission is there, but the promoter just doesn't know it (although the fact that the primary promoter doesn't recognize and "preach" the mission is a telling fact). Sometimes, a product (such as an improvement on an existing product) is in support of someone else's mission. However, a product by itself without the supporting foundation of a mission is rarely a viable basis for building a business. The mission need not be earthshaking, but the more people who are served by accomplishment of the mission, the greater the potential for the growth of your business.

Typically, a company whose mission is "to make money first" or to be the "biggest and best provider of a certain product or service" instead of solving a problem or filling a need will not have the fundamental strength to build a strong B-I Triangle. Obviously, there is nothing wrong with making money, or wanting to be the "biggest and best." However, that type of mission provides no real direction or focus for the company, nor does it provide the proper mind-set for building. Accomplishment of that mission serves only that company, not the many. Perhaps that company should redefine itself in terms of the benefits it provides to its customers.

We believe that if you focus on fulfilling a mission that solves a problem or fills a need, the money will come. As rich dad said, "The more people you serve, the richer you will become."

So as you plan your business, start with your mission. What is your goal? What problem will your business be solving? What need will your business be filling? Once you have your mission established, look to building the other parts of the B-I Triangle. But most important, take action and get started with your new business.

A Winning Team

Success or failure in business has to do with work ethic, determination, and desire. Most people who make that jump have tons of all three. Yet the biggest determining factor has even more to do with learning three critical skills that will turn any business into a success.

First, in order to build a business, you have to be able to *sell*. Because "Sales = Income." When income is lacking, it's usually because the owner doesn't like to, doesn't know how to, or is simply reluctant to sell. Without sales, however, you have no income. There is a myth that you have to be an attack dog to sell. Not true.

Second, in order to build a real business or network, and move out of the "S" quadrant, you have to be able to *attract, build, and motivate a great team*. And in the world of small business, everyone on that team has to be willing to sell, regardless of their position in the company.

In order to make that happen, the third element becomes critical. That is your ability to *teach* others in the business how to sell, how to be great team players, and how to succeed. It is this skill that ensures growth, profit, and longevity.

The sad fact is that most business owners are never taught how to do any of those things. As a matter of fact, most of us are conditioned to believe that (1) sales is a nasty task; (2) that if you want things done right you have to do them yourself; and (3) that teaching is what you experienced in school.

When we work in business, the very first thing we do to increase income is to help people establish what we call the Code of Honor. The Code is a simple set of rules that turns even ordinary people into a championship team—a team that not only sells, but is hungry to learn and enforces an incredible level of accountability for personal conduct, performance, and numbers. It articulates the behaviors that are critical for success, and it demands the agreement of all team members to play that way.

Most people would like to be the best that they can be. As a business owner, you have to create the environment or context that will make that happen. It's not only something that you can learn, but it's something that will make you extremely successful. Many times in business, it's not what you deliver but *how* you deliver it that makes the biggest difference. It's the strength and commitment of your team and their passion to promote and serve others that determines your reputation, your success, and your cash flow.

Blair Singer
Rich Dad Advisor and author of
SalesDogs and
The ABCs of Building a Business Team That Wins

Choosing the Right Entity

Few people appreciate it, but choosing the right entity structure for your business ranks up there with choosing the right partner for your business.

If you go into business with the wrong person, your efforts may be doomed from the start. The wrong person may too freely spend your money, may obligate the company to contracts it cannot fulfill, and may alienate coworkers before the first product or service is ever delivered. The wrong partner can leave you unprotected and waste all of your efforts and energy.

Likewise, choosing the wrong legal structure can also lead directly to failure. Starting out, you want to have as much asset and legal protection as possible. But by choosing a sole proprietorship or a general partnership, bad entities that offer no protection whatsoever, you stand to lose everything you have built in your business, along with all of your personal assets as well. Plaintiffs and their attorneys love to see businesses operated as sole proprietorships and general partnerships, because they can reach both business and personal assets when they bring a claim. They have free rein to reach all of your assets.

Instead, use a good entity, such as a C-Corporation, S-Corporation, limited liability company, or limited partnership. These entities protect your personal assets from attack against the business. And like the right partner, the right entity will help you advance your protection and prospects in the future.

Garrett Sutton, Esq.
Rich Dad Advisor, author of
Own Your Own Corporation,
How to Buy and Sell a Business,
The ABCs of Getting Out of Debt, and
The ABCs of Writing Winning Business Plans

Design a Business That Can Do Something That No Other Business Can Do.

Chapter 8

What Is the Job of a Business Leader?

The Business Leader

"What is the business leader's most important job?" I asked rich dad.

"Well, there are many jobs that are very important. It would be hard to say if any one job is more important than the other. Instead of just one job I can tell you what I think my eight most important jobs are."

The following is rich dad's list.

1. Clearly define the mission, goals, and vision of the company.
2. Find the best people and forge them into a team.
3. Strengthen the company on the inside.
4. Expand the company on the outside.
5. Improve the bottom line.
6. Invest in research and development.
7. Invest in tangible assets.
8. Be a good corporate citizen.

"What happens if the leader cannot perform those jobs?" I asked.

"You need to change leaders," said rich dad. "Besides, if the leader cannot do these things, the company will probably disappear anyway. That is why most new companies are gone within ten years."

Only a Mission

Over the years, I have met many people with an extremely strong sense of mission. I have had people come up to me and say things such as:

1. "I want to save the environment."
2. "My invention will eliminate the need for fossil fuels."
3. "I want to start a charity that provides shelter for runaway kids."
4. "My technology is what the world has been waiting for."
5. "I want to find a cure for that disease."

While their care and concern may be genuine, many of these good-hearted people fail to fulfill their mission simply because all they have is a mission. If you were to look at their life skills through the context of the B-I Triangle, it would look like this.

A Lack of Business Skills

Earlier in this book, I mentioned that many people spend years in school or at work developing skills that are not relevant or important to the B-I Triangle. I mention the example of a schoolteacher, who may have years of education and teaching experience, yet those years of education may not transfer to the B-I Triangle if that person decides to become an entrepreneur. That person simply lacks business skills.

When I left the Marine Corps in 1974, I, too, was in that predicament. By 1974, I had two professions. My first profession was as a licensed ship's officer, licensed to sail any ship of unlimited tonnage throughout the world. I could have made a lot of money with this profession; the problem was I did not want to be a ship's officer anymore. My second profession was that of a military pilot with great training and years of experience. Many of my friends went to work for the airlines or with police and fire departments as pilots. I could have done the same thing, except that I no longer wanted to fly.

In 1974, when I returned home to see my dad struggling financially, I suspected that I had found my new mission, or at least a problem worth solving. The problem was, all I had was a mission. When you look at the B-I Triangle, there are levels for people specially trained in accounting, law, design, marketing, and systems. There are not levels that say *ship's officer* or *pilot*. So, I was just like the many people I mentioned above—people with a mission but with a lack of real business skills.

What I did have going for me was that I had years of apprenticeship to rich dad. I had worked in all aspects of the B-I Triangle through his businesses. So I did have some business experience, but only as a kid. At least I knew that a business was a system of systems and the importance of the B-I Triangle as a business structure.

Complaining to Rich Dad

One day I complained to rich dad that I had almost no marketable skills that applied to the B-I Triangle. Pointing to the *Team* side of the B-I Triangle, I complained that no major corporation would hire me to be on their team. I whined on about not having a formal education at any of the levels. After I was through complaining, I looked up at rich dad for what I hoped would be a sympathetic answer. All he said was, "Neither do I."

All rich dad started with was a *mission*.

What a Leader Does

A leader's job is to change the company to allow it to grow and serve more people. If the leader cannot change the company, the leader keeps the company small and the company may begin to shrink.

Once again, I use the B-I Triangle to further clarify this point.

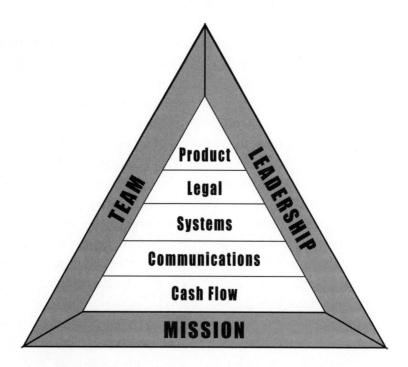

When I was in the S quadrant, our products were the Business School for Entrepreneurs and the Business School for Investors. The problem with the business was that I was too much a part of the product as well as the rest of the B-I Triangle. If I was going to be a leader, I needed to stop and completely redesign the business. Trying to fix a poorly designed business while the business is running is like trying to change a flat tire while the car is still moving. That is why Kim and I stopped and took two years off before starting a new business.

Building a New B-I Triangle

In 1996, when I came out of the mountains around Bisbee, Arizona, all I had were pencil sketches of the CASHFLOW game board, a rough draft of *Rich Dad Poor Dad* in my computer, and a simple two-page business plan. As the sole employee of my yet to be formed company, I knew my next step was to find the right people and put a team together.

Sketching the game board was the easy part. Finding someone who could engineer the information systems required to make the game work was the first step. The game had to be engineered to literally change the way people think about money. At that time there was only one person I knew who had such a mind and that was an old friend named Rolf Parta, fondly known as *Spock*. We call him *Spock* because he looks like Leonard Nimoy of *Star Trek* fame. He also happens to be as smart as the character Nimoy plays.

This is where the four types of thinking are important. For this phase of the business, I brought the C-Thinking and P-Thinking to the project. I was creative enough to sketch a crude game board design and I understood how people learned from my ten years of teaching. Spock brought the T-Thinking and A-Thinking to the project. As a trained CPA with an MBA, and a former banker with an extremely high IQ, Spock lives in a world of his own. Very few people can carry on a conversation with him. He speaks a dialect of English I doubt anyone else understands.

Arriving at his home, I spread my crude sketches and diagrams on his dining room table. Doing my best to communicate by words, gestures, and pointing at my sketches, Spock and I finally began to converse. It is tough being the *creative* and *people* side of the project speaking to what I hoped would be the *technical* and *analytical* side.

Finally, about an hour into the discussion, Spock's eyes lit up. He was beginning to understand the *people* and *creative* side. "Why do people need this game?" he asked. "This is common sense."

Chuckling, I replied, "To you it's common sense. You have an MBA. You're a CPA, and a former banker. So to you, this is common sense. But to the average person, this is a foreign language. For many people, this is a radically new way of thinking."

Spock grinned. The points on his ears grew a little longer. "Give me three months and I'll give you what you want." We agreed upon a price for his services, shook hands, and I left feeling confident I had found the right person for the task.

Three months later, and after much interaction with me, he had all the complex mathematical equations done. I had done my part and made better crude sketches. Together, Kim, Spock, and I played the game. Surprisingly, the game ran well. It was a tough game, but the numbers worked, the lessons were revealed, and we were happy.

The next person I went to see was Michael Lechter, the attorney on our team. As I said earlier, Michael is one of the most respected intellectual property attorneys in the world of technology, patents, and trademarks.

When the Browns football team tried to leave Cleveland, move to Baltimore, Maryland, and become the Baltimore Browns, it was Mike's firm, Squire Sanders and Dempsey, that the City of Cleveland called in to stop the loss of the name. The team did move and became the Baltimore Ravens, but only after Cleveland was promised an NFL expansion team, and most important, the team name, the Browns, remained in Cleveland. That would be like saying to me, "You can move but your name, Robert Kiyosaki, remains here. It belongs to the city of Phoenix, Arizona. Find a new name to use. How about Joe Smith?"

Once Mike had both my work and Spock's, Mike then began the process of filing for patents, trademarks, and other legal fences to protect my intellectual property. As I left his office, he said, "I'll call you when I hear back from the patent office."

"How long will that take?" I asked.

"It might take a while. It depends upon how many questions or challenges they have. The chances are good they will reject parts or all of our claims in the patent. That's when we dig in and go back to them again."

Spock went back to work with his A-Thinking cap on, using his analytical mind this time, and began back-testing the game on a computer. He ran the game through 150,000 different simulations, without a failure. When he handed me his pages of mathematical computations, he was grinning from ear to ear. The challenge of the project had made him very happy.

To this day, I have no idea what the math on those pages meant, but when I turned those same pages over to Michael Lechter, he grinned just like Spock. I felt like I was in school again. The two A students going over test papers and enjoying it and me, the C, D, and occasional F student wondering what they're so excited about.

As you may have already guessed, I was now building a new B-I Triangle. As entrepreneurs, Kim and I were clear on our mission. Now, as leaders of the project, and using the five levels inside the triangle as a guide, we were now putting together a team.

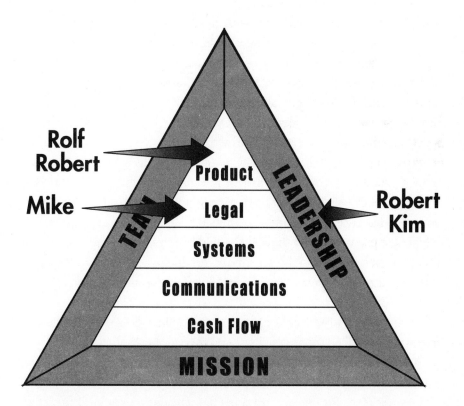

Meeting Sharon

After about a month, Mike Lechter called and said, "You can now move forward and show your game to other people. We do not have a patent yet, but I have filed the application and you've staked your claim. You still need to have people sign confidentiality agreements before they see your product."

As you may recall, this is the step I left out when I created the runner's shoe pocket wallet. Within weeks after inventing the product, I began selling the shoe pocket without protection. In less than three months, our competitors were selling my creation. It was a devastating mistake. But learning my lesson from that mistake was about to pay off in a very, very, big way.

"Before I hang up," said Mike, "you told me when you first came into my office that your mission was 'to improve the financial well-being of humanity.'"

"That's the mission," I replied.

"And you plan on doing that with this game?" From the inflection in Mike's voice, it was more a statement than a question.

"That's correct," I said.

"Teaching people to manage their own money, the fundamentals of accounting, and the fundamentals of investing, all by playing a game?" Again, more a statement than a question.

"That's what we are doing," I affirmed.

"Would you mind if I told my wife, Sharon, about your game? She's a trained CPA. She's worked for one of the big accounting firms and she's started several businesses. But the real reason I'd like to tell her about what you are doing is that she shares your mission. She's passionate about teaching people about money. I think she would be really interested. Would you mind if I tell her—just the broad strokes, not the details?"

"No, please do," I replied hesitantly. "But please remind her that I am not a CPA."

"You're not a CPA? Who'd have guessed," Mike kidded me, laughing at his own joke. "I'll be sure to tell her." And then we hung up.

The reason I was hesitant goes back to what I said earlier in this chapter. Just like rich dad, I am one of those people who have no formal training in any of the levels of the B-I Triangle. As I spent time creating the game, the idea that

I, a person with no formal accounting training, was creating a game that taught the basics of accounting was a little daunting. Mike thought he was just kidding with his wisecrack about my not being a CPA, but he actually hit a nerve. Now he was going to talk to his wife, a CPA. I felt like I was about to be busted, exposed as a fraud.

The Big Test

For the next few weeks, Kim, Spock, and I worked to get our prototype games ready. We had played the game with a number of our friends and the game worked well. The reason the game worked well is that all of our friends are professional investors. Now we were about to beta test the game. A beta test is a trial run to see if the game works on normal people.

The game at that stage was just rough sketches on heavy butcher paper, and we used different-caliber bullets as game pieces. The bullets worked well because their weight helped keep the paper down.

We reserved a hotel conference room, enough for about twenty people, and then began calling people, mostly strangers, to come and play. You have no idea how hard that was. When people found out the game was an educational game about investing and accounting, most people found an excuse to not be there.

"Does it require math?" asked one person.

When I said, "Yes," he hung up.

Just when we thought we were going to be short of people, Mike called and said, "Hey, would you mind if I brought my wife and daughter to the beta test?"

"Your wife?" I gulped. "The CPA?"

"Yeah. I think she'd get a kick out of it."

"Okay," I said weakly. "And how old is your daughter?"

"She's nineteen. In fact, she's on her way to college that day. I think it would be great if she were there, too."

"Okay," I said feebly again. Silently, to myself, I was saying, "Oh, great . . . an accountant and a teenager. Probably a teenager with an attitude."

When I told Kim about Mike bringing his wife and daughter, Kim said, "That's perfect. No wonder we had two extra seats. It was meant to be."

"Oh, God," I said as I shook my head at the idea that divine intervention was the reason for so many people backing out of the beta test and leaving exactly two seats open. But then, that is the way Kim thinks.

The Game Is Played

One bright Saturday morning, in walked nine people; one who agreed to be there simply did not show up. Sharon, Mike, and their daughter Shelly were prompt. As I shook Sharon's hand, the fear of being exposed once again flooded my body.

After a few niceties, the game was on, and it went on and on and on. There were two tables—one table with four people and one with five. After about three hours, Sharon raised her hand to signal she had won her game. The game had worked—for one person—and the game went on and on and on.

As the two tables ground on and on, Sharon stood and left, taking her daughter with her. She had told us ahead of time that she needed to get on the road to take Shelly to Tucson, where she was a student at the University of Arizona. Not having the opportunity to talk to Sharon, I did not know what she thought of the game. My mind immediately began to wonder about all the horrible things a CPA could say about me, and my game.

Finally at about 1:00 P.M., we shut the game down—frustration was *so* high, I thought fights were about to break out. No one else had gotten out of the rat race. No one else had won the game. As people left, many politely shook my hands but no one said much. Most just gave me a strange look and left. Even Michael did not get out of the game. I could tell that he was also very frustrated. Shaking his head, all he said was, "Tough game. I never made it out of the rat race." From the way he growled when he said it, I thought he was going to bite me.

To Go Ahead or to Shut It Down

After packing up our boxes, Kim, Spock, and I had a debriefing session. "Maybe it's too hard," I said. Kim and Spock nodded.

"But Sharon, Mike's wife, got out of the rat race. She won the game," said my perpetually optimistic wife, Kim.

"Yeah, but she's an accountant," I moaned. "She doesn't need the game. The people who really need the game didn't win . . . they didn't get out of the rat race . . . they didn't learn anything. All they did was get frustrated."

"I did my best to make it simple," said Spock. "I don't know if I can make it any easier without losing the objectives for playing the game."

"Well, let's get the boxes into the car and go home. Kim and I leave for Hawaii tomorrow. We'll have to decide if we go forward with this project or shut it down."

On the Beach

For the next week, Kim and I would get up, have our coffee, and walk on the beach. One morning I would be overly enthusiastic, ready to continue with the project. The next morning, I would awake depressed, ready to shut the project down. This went on for a week. It was a horrible vacation. As we packed and headed for the airport, Kim said, "Why don't you call Sharon? Instead of guessing about what she thinks, why not just call her and ask for her feedback?"

"But she's an accountant," I said. "She has to hate the game. She knows I'm a fraud and the game has no merit."

"She didn't say that," said Kim. "That's you saying that about yourself."

The reason I spend so much time writing about this period is that it was a very tough time for me. When people say they have fears about taking risks and going forward on a project, well so do I. Kim and I were in turmoil during this period of time. It was *go or no go*. It was *put up or shut up*. It was live our mission or just go back to making money.

A New Partner

Upon landing in Phoenix, we called Sharon and set up a meeting. Standing in front of the door to her massive home in an expensive neighborhood, I pressed the doorbell. Expecting the worst, Kim and I sat down to listen to her thoughts, her feedback on our game.

"I loved the game," said Sharon. "It's better than I expected. When I saw the components of the game, jobs, financial statements, and the amount of math to do, I was concerned that it would be boring. But it brings everything together."

"Thanks," I said. "I know you are a CPA. You have no idea how nervous that made me."

"There are a lot of CPAs who need this game. But I am even more excited about the game because my daughter Shelly loved it," smiled Sharon, beaming like a proud parent. "Do you know what she said to me as we left your beta test?"

"No, please tell us. She was the youngest person in the room and we would like to know what a teenager thought of the game."

"Well, as we left the conference room, I thought she was going to blast me. You know how teenagers are—and we were at the beta test much longer than I had told her we would be You know we were moving her into her very first apartment that day. And on top of that, she had as tough a time with the game as the others did," said Sharon. "As we were leaving the room I thought she was going to complain about how late we were, but instead she said, 'Mom that game was *awesome*. I learned more in the last three hours than I learned in the last three years of high school.' At that moment I knew you had a great product that could really make a difference in people's lives."

Kim smiled and chatted away with Sharon. I zoned out. I was in another world. I couldn't believe my ears. I could not believe that many of the important lessons that rich dad had taught me had now been transferred into a game that someone like Sharon, with her credentials, agreed with. Spock, Kim, and I had gone through the eye of the needle. We had transferred this knowledge I had learned from rich dad and placed it in a tangible product.

This took place in the summer of 1996. Kim and I then went forward and hired Kevin Stock, a fabulous graphic artist, to bring the game to life. Kevin then shipped his work to a game-manufacturing company in Canada. In November 1996, the commercial version of the game was played at a friend's investment seminar in Las Vegas, Nevada. The game worked. Participants loved the game. The paradigm shifts we wanted were happening. Immediately, we flew to Singapore to another friend's investment workshop and once again the game did its magic.

While Kim and I were showing the game off to the world, Sharon volunteered to look at the rough draft of the book sitting in my computer. She asked for nothing. She simply wanted to support the mission. She transformed a hodgepodge of stories about lessons that I learned from my rich dad into *Rich Dad Poor Dad*. On April 8, 1997, the book was launched at Sharon and Mike's home on my 50th birthday. Soon thereafter, Sharon, Kim, and I formed The Rich Dad Company. Sharon agreed to be the CEO. Looking at the B-I Triangle, you will see how the pieces had been put together.

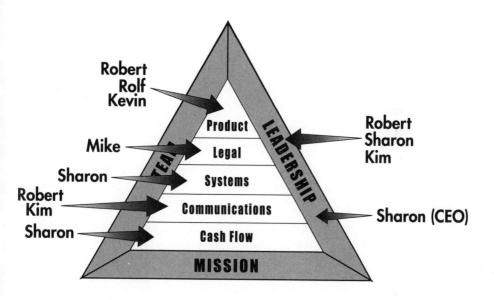

Me, Rolf, and Kevin Stock on product. Mike on legal. Sharon covering systems and cash flow, Kim and Robert, on communications. As the team.

As leadership, Kim, Robert, and Sharon, with Sharon as CEO.

Trademarks and Trade Dress

Kevin Stock also worked with Michael Lechter on what is known as trade dress, the graphics that help identify the Rich Dad brand. You may notice that all of our products have a similar theme, look, and feel. The colors we use are specific shades of purple, yellow, and black. People recognize that color scheme on a product as indicating that the product comes from The Rich Dad Company. As Michael says, "That isn't by accident." If people infringe upon our trade dress or trademarks, which people often do, Michael Lechter's legal team begins talking to them. Our trademarks and trade dress are assets called intellectual property that have great value all over the world. In China, they call Rich Dad the "Purple Storm."

The Business Takes Off

Once the business was put together, almost immediately, the business began to take off. Orders started flying through the door. Cash flowed in. All debts were immediately paid off and soon the company was bursting at the seams. Starting in a big closet in Sharon and Mike's house, we soon expanded into their garage, and then into every spare room in the house. We were forced to go and buy an office building to house a growing company. *Rich Dad Poor Dad* made the *Wall Street Journal* and the *New York Times* bestseller list, one of the few books on the lists not published by the big book companies (we were originally published by TechPress, Inc., a company owned by Sharon and Mike—and were therefore essentially self-published).

Book companies started calling, offering us a lot of money to sign with them. Oprah's show called and in summer 2000, after I was on her program, the company exploded. Almost overnight we became an international success.

How to Expand a Business

There are many ways a business can expand, including:

1. **Replicating the entire B-I Triangle.** Basically, once you work the bugs out of the business, you open more of them. Many retailers and restaurants expand this way. In many cities, there are restaurants that have three or four successful stores located throughout the city. In order to grow bigger, the leader may need to change leaders. Often, the owner will sell to a bigger company and start over again.
2. **Franchising.** McDonald's is the most famous example of expansion via franchising.

3. **Taking the company public through an IPO.** With the funds from places like Wall Street, the company can tap into virtually an unlimited supply of money as long as the company keeps on expanding.

4. **Licensing and joint ventures.** This is the way we designed the company to expand. Licensing is basically allowing another business to produce your products. For example, The Rich Dad Company partners with Warner Books with respect to the English version of the Rich Dad and Rich Dad Advisor series of books. Instead of us using our capital to produce, store, ship, and collect the money for our books, via the agreement, Warner Books, a great company, by the way, takes care of production, distribution, and collections, and sends us a quarterly check. As our success grew, our licensing, which is the legal level of the business, expanded to over forty-four different languages in over eighty countries. Once again, it costs us no money to produce or store the books. We do not need a giant warehouse, hire an extensive sales force, or deal with inventory or shipping product around the world.

The Single Tactic-Multiple Strategy Plan

My training as a military officer required we know the difference between a tactic and a strategy. In very simple terms, a tactic is what you do. A strategy is the plan on how to get the tactic done. One of my military science instructors was adamant about the importance of using a single tactic, multiple strategy of warfare to win. He would say, "A military leader must focus on one objective or tactic. He must only want to do one thing. Everything else is a strategy on how to get that one tactic done." He would then use examples of military conflict after military conflict that was won by the leader that had the best strategies focused on a single tactic.

When I entered the business world, I carried his lessons with me. Soon I began to see companies that used the single tactic—multiple strategy type of planning were companies that won in business. For example, Domino's Pizza started with a single tactic to beat its competition. To distinguish itself in the pizza wars, Domino's designed a company around a single tactic, and that tactic was to promise "pizza in thirty minutes or less." An entire business was designed around that single promise—a single tactic. To make that single tactic a reality, the company then had multiple strategic plans. Once Domino's entered the marketplace, it immediately began taking market share from its competitors. Competitors such as Pizza Hut could not compete because the business was not designed to meet such a promise. To combat Domino's, Pizza Hut increased advertising, the communications level, to announce new and different types of pizza, the product level. The pizza wars were on. Pizza Hut was fighting with a better product and Domino's with a guaranteed faster delivery.

If you have read Jim Collins's book, *Good to Great*, you will notice that many of the great companies have single tactics. Jim Collins does not call it *a single tactic–multiple strategy* way of winning, instead he calls it the *hedgehog* principle. In his book his uses Wal-Mart's single tactic—the lowest price for good products—as the reason it beats its competitors who have multiple tactics and even more strategies. In other words, Wal-Mart's competitors simply have not clearly defined their own single winning tactic.

Wal-Mart's entire business is focused on one promise, a promise customers clearly like. That means Wal-Mart does not win in the product category. Like Domino's, it wins in the system level of the B-I Triangle.

You may recall from earlier that Thomas Edison also won the electric light battle at the system level, not at the product level. Henry Ford also won at the system level. He simply mass-produced low-priced cars for the working family. He never promised the best-made cars. He just promised the best-priced cars and then designed a business around his promise. McDonald's does not produce the best hamburger. Ray Kroc built a business around the idea of selling the best franchise to people who wanted to own a franchise.

When I was in the Arizona mountains the very simple business plan I came up with was based upon one single tactic and three strategies. The first page of the simple two-page plan looked like this.

TACTIC: PLAY THE CASHFLOW GAME
STRATEGIES:

1. WRITE A BOOK
2. DO AN INFOMERCIAL
3. TEACH INVESTMENT SEMINARS USING THE GAME

On the second page, I wrote a brief plan on how I thought I could accomplish the three strategies.

The single tactic was to get as many people as possible to play the game. I knew that if I created a great game and people played it, their lives would change. They would be able to see another world of opportunity. They would be less inclined to blindly turn their money over to people they thought were experts, such as mutual fund managers, and might become inspired to become their own financial experts.

That was it. I knew, if successful, I would make money from the strategies as well as the single tactic.

A Low-Risk Idea

The first lesson: Always have a low-risk idea or strategy to fall back on.

Rich dad taught me that whenever you start a business or invest in something, you need to have a low-risk idea. For example, when investing in real estate, if the investment paid me something each and every month, that was a low-risk investment. Even if the property did not go up in value, I was still receiving some compensation for my investment dollars.

The strategy of teaching investment seminars using the game was my low-risk idea. Since I came from the seminar business, I knew that if the other two strategies did not work and no one wanted my game, I could recoup my investment in the product development of the game simply by putting on investment seminars.

Simply put, a low-risk idea is something you know you can do.

Design A Business That Can Do Something That No Other Business Can Do

The second lesson: Design the business around a *unique* tactical advantage.

In my plan, by having the tactic be to play the game, I virtually eliminated all competition. I eliminated all competition because if the legal work was strong, no one else could do what our business did. No one else has our CASHFLOW games. As rich dad said, "Design a business that can do something that no other business can do."

Simply put, focus all your efforts on your core strength, your unique product.

The plan worked. Once we had built the books to a certain level of success on our own, we partnered with Warner Books to publish and distribute the English-language version of our books. We licensed other publishers around the world to publish versions in other languages. We licensed the rights to sell certain of our products through television infomercials. We went on the road to do investment seminars across the United States, in Australia, and in Singapore. Cash flowed in from all three strategies, as well as from the sales of the game.

When I talked about spiritual money, I really did not think we would have made as much money as we did from just our strategies. It was like magic.

More Strategies Today

Today, the tactic is the same. All of our strategies are focused on getting people to play the CASHFLOW games.

Today, in 2005, the number of strategies has increased. Today our business looks like this:

1. Books in forty-four different languages
2. Games in fifteen different languages
3. Network marketing companies using our products
4. A coaching company
5. Learning Annex, a seminar company that puts on megaevents with me on stage with people such as Donald Trump
6. Radio promotions, including seminars produced and promoted by Infinity Broadcasting
7. PBS (public television) broadcasting our program
8. CASHFLOW clubs throughout the world
9. Maricopa Community Colleges, the largest community college system in America, offers a two-credit Rich Dad course that uses our books and games as the curriculum. This curriculum is spreading to other colleges around the world.

10. The website www.richkidsmartkid.com offering free curriculum for kindergarten through twelfth grade around the world; schools can also receive free downloadable copies of our game CASHFLOW for KIDS.

Our company grows by adding partners who can add to our strategies. Via licensing or coventuring, we do not have to grow the size or number of employees of The Rich Dad Company. Our company remains small, but has big partners. Worldwide, we estimate we have over fifteen thousand people working for us, in one way or another.

Forbes defines a big business as one with five thousand or more employees. The Rich Dad Company qualifies because it has thousands of people working for us via licensing. It was all part of the plan before there was a business.

Grew Big Yet Remained Small

At the start of this chapter I listed a set of jobs rich dad thought were important for a leader. Once the product was developed and protected legally via patents and trademarks, Kim, Sharon, and I focused on the following three jobs of leaders. We:

1. Strengthened the company on the inside
2. Expanded the company on the outside
3. Improved the bottom line

Working for Cooperative Money

Through all this very rapid growth the company handled the expansion without a hitch. Instead of success destroying us as it did with the nylon wallet company, The Rich Dad Company grew stronger with the growth. The company grew because we were cooperative, working for cooperative money. Every dollar that came in from our licensed strategic partners was a *cooperative dollar*. By cooperating instead of competing, our strategic partners get richer and so do we. If I may say so myself, I believe this little company was pretty well designed. It was designed to grow. We leveraged the talents of our team to build and protect intellectual property and then leveraged the intellectual property through licensing all over the world. We found the right team to guide us in this process. (In Michael Lechter's Rich Dad Advisor book *Other People's Money* he describes how we accomplished this and how you can use the same strategy in your own business.)

As we grew The Rich Dad Company, we did not have the growing pains many small companies go through. We did not have cash flow problems, space problems, adding-employee problems. The company remained basically the same size even as we grew exponentially. What expanded was the number of strategic partners. As we grew, more and more money flowed in and very few dollars flowed out. All my years of screwing up, correcting, and learning are paying off.

No More Glimpses

Today, instead of just a glimpse of the world I want to live in, Kim and I live in a world better than we ever dreamed of. It seems like magic and it is magic. Obviously the money and lifestyle are great but it is the sense of making a difference in so many lives that is the true magic. When I think back on my dad sitting unemployed in front of the TV set, the kids in the sweatshops in Asia from my wallet business, and then to the families playing CASHFLOW on the Yangtze River, that is the real magic. As Dr. Buckminster Fuller would say, "The work of the great spirit." As Lance Armstrong says, "It's not about the bike."

The Entrepreneur's Job Is Done

Once I saw the article about the CASHFLOW game in the *New York Times*, I knew my job as an entrepreneur was over. We had done our job. Sharon, Kim, and I had taken the business as far as the three of us could take it. We knew it was time for a new team. In summer 2004, our new team took over. The team has changed but their jobs are the same. Their jobs as leaders are:

1. Clearly define the mission, goals, and vision of the company.
2. Find the best people and forge them into a team.

3. Strengthen the company on the inside.
4. Expand the company on the outside.
5. Improve the bottom line.
6. Invest in research and development.
7. Invest in tangible assets.
8. Be a good corporate citizen.

SHARON'S INSIGHTS

Lesson #8: Design a Business That Can Do Something That No Other Business Can Do.

When someone asks my husband, Michael, the patent attorney, what he does for a living, he would tell them that he "helps create assets out of people's ideas." With these assets a business can do something that its competition can't do—and can keep them from doing it. He refers to it as "maintaining a sustainable competitive advantage."

The subject of "sustainable competitive advantage" came up when I first discussed the B-I Triangle with Michael. Robert and I were in the process of writing *Rich Dad's Guide to Investing* (Warner Books), and I wanted to get his perspective. As usual, I found him glued to his computer, working on something or other.

He grudgingly looked up from his work and smiled, so I had my opportunity to interrupt him (which he claims I do all the time). I showed him the graphic, and explained, "We are working with a graphic that represents the essential elements of a successful business. The outer border represents the framework of three foundational elements for a business: mission, team, and leadership.

"The 'mission' defines the purpose and direction of the business. The 'leadership' makes the decisions and keeps the business focused on the mission. The 'team' provides the business with all the different types of special expertise and skills necessary to operate."

"What skills are those?" Mike asked.

"Things like legal and accounting expertise, and the stuff used in day-to-day operations and management—sourcing, manufacturing, order-taking, fulfillment, human resources, marketing, customer service, warehousing, and the like."

"Are you saying you need all those skills in-house? A lot of companies . . ."

I anticipated his comment. "No. The 'team' we refer to includes not only the owners and employees of the business, but also its outside advisors—and its virtual employees through strategic relationships with other businesses, like licensing or joint venture arrangements."

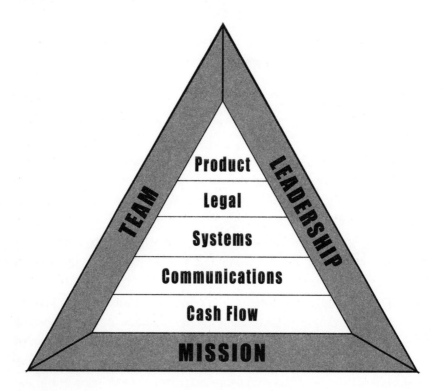

"Okay. Go on."

"Inside the framework are the five components essential for a business to operate," I said

"Cash flow, communications, systems, legal, and product or service." He read off the elements. "All right. Is the order in the pyramid supposed to be significant?"

"Somewhat. The business has to provide some type of product or service. But merely having a product or service isn't enough for success. It has to be supported by a foundation formed by the other components of the B-I Triangle.

"Think about it. Cash flow provides the base of the foundation for any healthy business. Timing of when cash comes in and when it is needed to go back out—alone—can make or break a business. The business needs enough cash or capital to cover operating expenses and to execute its business plan. We are really talking about cash flow management. All of the orders for product in the world will do a business no good if it can't get hold of the materials needed to produce the products."

I stopped for a breath, then continued.

"'Communications' represents the interaction and relationships between the leadership and the team, and between the business and the outside world—things like public relations, marketing, and sales. The best product in the world is essentially worthless in the marketplace if no one knows about it."

"What about reputation and goodwill? And the trademarks that connect products to the company—that identify the company's products as coming from the company. Are those part of the 'communications' that you are referring to?" he asked.

I thought about it for a moment, and replied, "Yes, trademarks, reputation, and goodwill would be part of the 'communications' element. Getting the protection is part of the 'legal' level, but once you have the protection it does 'communicate' who you are to the public. Even with the best product in the world you'd have a real problem if your reputation for service is so bad that potential customers are reluctant to do business with you. And on the flip side, even if your product wasn't the best, you could get by very well just on the basis of a good reputation for integrity and service."

Moving my finger up the list, I pointed to the "systems" component. "This refers to the business processes and procedures used to run the business," I said.

"You are talking about things like customer service, taking and processing orders, delivery and fulfillment, sourcing and inventory control, manufacturing, assembly, quality control? Stuff like that?" he asked.

"That's right," I replied. "Any business system. Things like processes for billing and accounts receivable, and accounts payable, and human resources, and marketing, and product development, and record keeping . . . I guess even procedures for working with attorneys and accountants would be covered by 'systems.'

"Systems represent the biggest difference between a small business and a large one. Systems are the way that a large business leverages the expertise of the owner or other skilled workers without losing quality control. You leverage the expertise to define processes or standard procedures followed by less skilled—less expensive—workers."

"Okay," Michael acknowledged. "I assume 'legal' covers things like forming the right type of business entity, intellectual property protection, and having the right type of agreements."

"That's right. So what do you think?"

He looked down at the diagram and thought for a moment. "What about leverage?" he asked.

The "leverage" that Michael referred to is the mechanism to take maximum advantage of—expand or magnify—a resource. The ability to leverage resources is one of the defining characteristics of an entrepreneur. "Leverage" is also one of the most significant distinguishing features between a small business and a big business. I should have expected Michael to bring up the issue of leverage. "Leverage" is an area where we have particular expertise. I guess you could consider it one of our specialties. Over the years Michael and I had helped build a number of businesses using the tool of leverage.

There are a number of forms of leverage that can be applied by a business. Buckminster Fuller refers to one type of leverage as "ephemeralization"—building a physical tool or artifact that embodies intangible ideas, so that those ideas can be taught merely by making the artifact available, without requiring the physical presence of a person to teach. The CASH-FLOW game is an example of an artifact—it is a tangible embodiment of and teaches the Rich Dad principles.

There are also other forms of leverage. For example, a business can leverage its intellectual assets internally—apply the expertise of the owner or other skilled workers through less skilled (less expensive) workers without losing quality control, by establishing "systems" in the form of standard business processes and procedures. It can leverage its intellectual property into the outside world through strategic relationships such as licensing agreements and joint ventures. It can leverage its financial resources through use of other people's money and resources.

Michael was asking if and how "leverage" was represented in the B-I Triangle.

"The B-I Triangle is intended to apply to both large and small businesses. Some form of leverage is essential to be a big business," I started to answer.

There are a lot of small businesses that do well financially based solely on the efforts of their resident "S." Professionals like doctors and lawyers are perfect examples. In fact, Michael himself, for years the quintessential "S," did extremely well in the practice of law, and he would be the first to admit (or, more accurately, complain about) the fact that market pressures had squeezed essentially all of the leverage that partners in law firms used to apply when they had a pyramid of associate lawyers working under them. In any event, the professionals and other Ss might work themselves to death, but they can be quite comfortable financially. They just don't have the benefit of leverage found in big businesses.

"Anyway," I said, "a business's leverage can be in the product, legal, or systems levels—in one or more of them."

"Okay," he said, and turned his eyes back to the diagram. I could see the wheels turning. From the way he was concentrating on the graphic, I could tell that he was entering into what he refers to as a "constructive contrarian" mode. I like to call it something else, but he's going to read this, so we won't get into that.

"You're still missing something. 'Sustainable competitive advantage.' In order for a business to be successful it must have some sort of competitive advantage. And if it's going to stay successful it has to be able to sustain that competitive advantage."

By "competitive advantage," Michael was referring to the aspects or features of a business that gives it an advantage over its competitors—the reasons why the business's customers come to it instead of its competitors, the things about the business that are perceived as "unique," "better," or "distinctive." An aspect of the business is "unique" if competitors don't have it or provide it. It's "distinctive" if it differentiates your business from the competition and brings

your business to mind. "Better" can mean many things—things like more efficient, more cost-effective, more powerful, more accurate, faster, more
durable, more versatile, better looking, less expensive to produce, and so
forth. You can find a competitive advantage in any one or more of the components of the business.

What happens when you achieve an advantage over competitors? What
happens when you add a unique feature to your products, or find a way to distinguish yourself in the marketplace? The competition will analyze the situation—how and why you are beating them in the marketplace—and they will
adapt and to the extent that they can do so without legal repercussions,
adopt. In other words, unless you have the proper legal protections in
place—intellectual property protection, agreements, and the like—they will
appropriate or copy whatever it is that gives you your competitive advantage.
So, in order to keep them from copying—in order to sustain your competitive advantage—you want to put as many legal protections in place as you
can. Competitive advantage and sources of competitive advantage as well as
the legal protections available are explained and discussed in Michael's Rich
Dad Advisor books.

How can you figure out what gives your business a competitive advantage? Dissect your business systems, products, services, and communications—customer and supplier relations and the like—and analyze each
component and feature to determine whether there is anything about it
that your customers would consider "unique," "better," or "distinctive."
Once you have identified the specific source of your competitive advantage, you then develop a strategy to secure exclusive rights by applying the
legal tools.

I started to respond, but he beat me to the punch. "Never mind," he said,
essentially thinking out loud.

"I guess you can find a competitive advantage in any one or more of the
components in the triangle. The product or service can be unique, better, or
distinctive.

"You can get a competitive advantage from favorable contracts—agreements that establish some exclusive right. That would be in the legal element.

"Business systems and procedures can give a competitive advantage if they're more efficient or effective than the competition's. Or if the processes are distinctive in the minds of potential customers they can create recognition and goodwill.

"A good reputation and goodwill in the marketplace are part and parcel of communications. They can provide a huge competitive advantage. Customers who have a good history with you, and referrals from those customers, will typically come to you instead of going to your competitors.

"I suppose that the big boys have an advantage with respect to cash flow—they may have cash on hand so that they can move more quickly to capitalize on opportunities that a smaller competitor cannot.

"Come to think of it, you could even get a competitive advantage from the framework—having the right leaders, team, or mission. The association with celebrity leaders or advisors can attract business. And wouldn't you rather do business with a company with a mission of helping people and making the world a better place, rather than one with a mission of merely making money or being the biggest and best?"

He paused for a moment, then shrugged his shoulders and started to turn back to his work.

"So the B-I Triangle makes sense to you?" I asked, insistently.

"It makes sense," he acknowledged. Turning to face his computer he said impatiently, "I've got to get back to work. I've got a brief that has to be filed."

At that point I knew the conversation was over and the S in my husband was taking over, so I just said "thanks" and left.

DO WHAT NO OTHER BUSINESS CAN DO

The easiest way for your business to set itself apart is through intellectual property and creating a competitive advantage. As in our example of the CASHFLOW game, our patent protection, trademarks, and trade dress prevent others from developing similar games.

So review your mission and the components of your B-I Triangle. Review each component from a standpoint of how your business will excel or be set apart from your competition. Then think of how you can leverage that competitive advantage to grow your business.

Don't Fight for the Bargain Basement.

Chapter 9

How to Find Good Customers

Be Choosy when Choosing Customers

One day during my junior year of high school, rich dad and I were walking past an entrance to a hotel when we heard a man's voice shouting loudly, "I will not pay you another dime. You have not kept your agreement."

Looking up I saw a family of five, with a very upset father, yelling at a local man in a Hawaiian print shirt. "But all you have paid is a deposit," the local man protested. "You still owe us the balance. I cannot let you check in until the balance is paid. You were to have paid your balance in full a month ago. You're lucky we even held your rooms for you. This is our peak season."

"It's a good thing you did hold our rooms for us," snarled the father. "You'd have heard from my attorney if you didn't."

"I still need to be paid," said the local man, holding his ground.

"I told you I will pay you. Don't you have ears? Just check us in and I will pay you," the father growled. "I have a check right here made out to you. Let us get into our room and we will settle this once and for all." (This was the era before credit cards.)

"You need to pay in cash. A check will not do. That is why we ask you to pay in full, in advance. It gives us time to clear a personal check."

"What is wrong with you?" asked the father, now shouting at the top of his lungs. "Don't you people understand English? I told you I would pay you. Now show us to our room. Do I have to call your boss to get things done?"

A crowd started to gather. Not wanting to make a scene, the man in the Hawaiian shirt picked up the mountain of suitcases, loaded them on a trolley and directed the family to their room.

"He'll never get paid," said rich dad as we continued.

"How do you know?" I asked.

"We dealt with the same guy three years ago. He did the same thing to us. He's going to go to the room, write the check, and then stop payment on it."

"What happened after he stopped payment?" I asked.

"By the time we found out his check was no good, he had already checked out. We called him once he was back on the mainland—I believe they live in California—and tried to collect."

"Then what happened?"

"When we threatened to take him to court, he agreed to pay us half of what he owed. He said our service was bad and he felt he had paid us what we deserved. He said he was being generous paying us 50% of what he owed us. Since it would have cost more to take him to court, we agreed. Even then, it was six months before he paid anything."

We walked for a while in silence. Disturbed, I finally had to ask, "Is this common in business?"

"Yes, unfortunately it is. You will always have good customers and bad customers. Fortunately, I have found about 80% of all customers are good customers, 5% are like him—just horrible—and the other 15% are in between," replied rich dad. "Oh, on top of that, this same guy had the nerve to call again last year and try to book a tour package with us. What nerve!"

"Did you do business with him?"

"Are you kidding?" laughed rich dad. "I had already fired him. Our reservation department had his picture and his name on our *Do not do business with again list*. The person taking the call remembered his name and told him we were full." (This was before computers, which can keep track of customers today.)

"You fire customers?" I asked in surprise.

"Absolutely," said rich dad. "You fire bad customers just as you would fire a bad employee. If you do not get rid of your bad employees the good employees will leave. If I do not fire bad customers, not only will my good customers leave, many of my good employees will leave as well."

"But aren't some of the complaints or upsets your fault, too?" I asked. "Could the complaints be legitimate?"

"Yes," replied rich dad. "Often it is our fault. Our staff does make mistakes or may offend the customers. Our systems can break down. That is why we look into every complaint and take it seriously. Just as you look both ways before you cross a street, when it comes to complaints, we have to look both ways—at the customer and at our operations."

"Is it hard firing people?" I asked. Being seventeen years old at the time, the thought of firing someone, especially an adult, frightened me. It was not something I wanted to do.

"It's never pleasant," said rich dad. "It's one of the more unpleasant yet important jobs of an entrepreneur. Your job is a people job. People are your biggest assets and biggest liabilities. One day you'll have to fire someone. I am sure it will be an experience you will never forget."

Rich dad and I entered a restaurant and found a table to have lunch. Once the waitress had filled our water glasses, handed us the menu, and explained the specials, rich dad continued with his lesson on people. "The same is true with advisors. You must be able to fire bad advisors. If you have accountants or attorneys who do a poor job, or if the job is too big for them, or if they are only interested in receiving their fees and not helping your business, your business will suffer. If you do not get rid of bad advisors, you are responsible. The ultimate price of bad advice is far more than what you pay your advisors in fees for good advice. I had one accountant give me bad tax advice, and it cost me nearly $60,000 in back taxes and penalties. On top of that it cost me another $12,000 to hire another accounting firm to straighten out the mess. In addition, this mistake upset me so much I was not effective for months and the business suffered as a result. So as an entrepreneur you must realize that you are responsible for your mistakes as well as the mistakes of others."

"Were you angry at your accountant?" I asked.

"Yes and no. I really could not blame him. At the time, my business was growing so fast I did not pay attention to the quality of my advisors. At the time, I did not realize that all accountants are not created equal. He should have told me he did not know what he was doing, but he didn't want to admit it and he was afraid I would fire him. Soon the size of my business was too big for his expertise. He was in over his head. I should have let him go earlier, but I was too busy. Besides, I liked the guy and I knew his family. I kept hoping he would grow with the company. Unfortunately, he didn't. Finally, I did let him go, but only after the losses from his bad advice were very high. So I don't blame him. I'm the only one ultimately responsible for the business. As the business grows your advisors need to grow with you or go. It was a valuable lesson I learned."

"Was it hard firing him?" I asked.

"It was extremely difficult. If you cannot hire and fire people, including yourself, you should not be an entrepreneur. Remember this: Your success or failure as an entrepreneur depends a lot on your people skills. If you have strong people skills, your business will grow. If you have poor people skills, your business will suffer. If you hire people simply because you like them, or because they are relatives, and you cannot fire them when they need to go, then you have poor people skills. Remember that people are different, and as an entrepreneur you need to be flexible enough to work with different types of people—people with different skills, ambitions, dreams, behavior, and experiences. If you cannot work with different types of people, once again your business will suffer."

"That is why you always said to Mike and me, 'A leader's job is to get people to work as a team.'"

"That could be your most important job. Remember that departments of a business attract different types of people. For example, salespeople are different from administrative staff people. They are very different people—almost opposites, and you need to treat them as opposites. For example, never ask an administrative staff person to hire a salesperson. Instead of hiring a hard-charging salesperson who loves busting down doors, the administrative staff person will prefer to hire a nice calm salesperson whose only sales experience was working as a checkout clerk at the supermarket. Also, the administrative staff person would want to make sure the person enjoyed filling out forms and doing paperwork."

"Why would they do that?" I asked.

"Because birds of a feather flock together. Administrative staff thinks that paperwork is the most important part of the sale. They have no experience in knowing how hard it is to get that sale. You'll see once you get into the real world. In general, salespeople don't like administrative people. Why? Because in general, salespeople hate paperwork and administrative staff people are terrified of selling. So don't try to make a top-flight salesperson into a file clerk or ask a file clerk to become a flamboyant salesperson."

"So is that where most of the friction lies?" I asked. "Between sales and administration?"

"Oh, no," said rich dad emphatically. "A business is one big ball of friction. It is a working model of human conflict. It is a melting pot of egos that is always boiling. When you look at the B-I Triangle you will understand why. A business is a blending of different people, different temperaments, different talents, different education, different ages, sexes, and races. Every day when you come to work, most of your problems will be people problems. A salesman made promises the company cannot keep. The customer is irate. Your attorney will not agree with your accountants. Assembly line workers will not agree with the engineers who designed the assembly line. Management is at war with labor. Technical people are fighting with creative people. Analytical people do not get along with people people. College-educated people feel they're smarter than people who did not go to college. Add to this interoffice politics, or worse, sexual affairs within the company, and you will never need to watch TV again. In most cases, a business does not need a competitor. A normal business has so many competitors *inside* the business it's amazing that anyone gets any work done at all."

"So that is why an entrepreneur needs to know when to fire someone. If one person upsets the balance, the whole business can boil over because the internal friction gets too great."

"Exactly," smiled rich dad. "I'm sure you see it in your classes at school every day. You can already see the different characters in your classmates."

I smiled and said, "And on my football team, my baseball team, and even in band class."

"That is why every team has a coach, a band has a conductor, and every business has a leader. A leader's job is to turn people into teams. One of the reasons so many people are self-employed or own businesses that stay small is that the leader is either not competent with dealing with people or simply does not want to learn to deal with so many different people. Business and making money would be easy if it were not for people."

The waitress returned to take our order. After she left, rich dad continued, "Let me give you three tips I learned about dealing with people in business. Tip number one is what I call the 'pain in the ass factor.' That means all people have skills and talents and are also pains in the ass. I do not care who they are, they have all three—including me. If their pain in the ass factor exceeds their skills and talents, it is time for them to go or to move them to another part of the business."

Chuckling, I said, "Maybe someday you'll earn a Nobel Prize for the pain in the ass factor."

"I should," said rich dad. "Every person in the world who deals with people will stand and applaud me."

"And what is tip number two?" I asked.

"Learn to hire slow and fire fast," said rich dad. "Take the hiring of people very seriously and slowly. Screen them carefully. And if it is time to let them go, do it quickly. Too many managers allow people too many chances. If you can't fire them for some reason, then move them and isolate them. Don't let them contaminate the rest of the people in the business. Maybe you can help them find jobs at a company where they might be happier and more productive. Or just pay them to leave. It will be less expensive in the long run. Remember to do it humanely and legally. All people need to be treated with the appropriate dignity. Many times, when I have let people go, they were happy to move on. I have found that if people are acting up or underperforming, it is not because they are lazy; many are simply unhappy for a number of reasons. If you as a leader can find a way to make them happy, find it."

"You mean a person can be a good employee but be working in the wrong job or department?"

"It happens all the time," said rich dad. "In fact, I have been the person who took a good employee and put him in the wrong job. I'm the person who made him unhappy."

"What did you do?"

"Well, years ago, I had this young man who was a great salesperson. He worked hard, treated his customers well, and made the company and himself a lot of money. So, after a few years, I rewarded him by promoting him to sales manager. I put him in charge of twelve other salespeople. He was fine for about a year, but then he began to come to work late, the sales numbers fell, the sales team was unhappy."

"Did you fire him?"

"No. I was going to, but I thought I should best reinterview him again. Once we sat down and had a heart-to-heart talk, I found the problem. By promoting him, I turned him into an administrative staff person doing exactly what he hated doing—paperwork. Oh, sure, he had a fancy title, VP of Sales, he made more money, had a company car, but he hated the mountains of paperwork and attending meeting after meeting. He simply wanted to be out on the street, talking to his customers."

"So did he go back to sales?"

"Absolutely! Good salespeople are hard to find. So I gave him a raise, a bigger territory, he kept the car, and he got richer and so did the company."

"And what is the third lesson?" I asked.

"The third lesson is that there are two kinds of communicators," said rich dad. "When upset or unhappy, one type of communicator will come talk to you face to face. They lay the cards on the table in front of you."

"And the second?" I asked.

"The second type stabs you in the back. They gossip, talk badly about you, spread rumors, or complain to everyone else but never to your face. Basically, these people are cowards. They lack the courage to confront you, to be forthright. Often they will blame you for their lack of courage, saying you are too mean or will not listen or they are afraid of being fired. Their perceptions about you could be true—but generally, these people will choose to talk behind a person's back, rather than face to face. It's just in their nature."

"So how do you handle that?" I asked.

"Well, one way is at every meeting I remind my staff of the two types of communicators and leave it at that. I say to them, 'There are people who speak to you face to face and there are others who speak behind your back. Which one are you?' Once the rest of the company is aware of the two types, they generally remind someone who is gossiping or stabbing someone in the back about the two types of people. It doesn't totally stop the gossiping, but it does keep it down and in general overall communication improves. I also tell them that I would prefer to be stabbed in the chest rather than stabbed in the back. So I don't tell them what to do, I simply give them a choice."

"Have you been stabbed in the chest?" I asked.

"Oh, a number of times—and I deserved it. I need to be corrected and reminded to be open-minded as much as anyone else. As much as it hurt, it was less destructive than a stab in the back."

"Aren't people afraid of being fired?"

"Oh, there is always that risk," smiled rich dad. "That is why it takes courage and excellent communication skills to be successful in business. In many instances, it is not what you say but how you say it. So if the communication is going to be unpleasant, put on your creative thinking cap and figure out the most humane and kind way of saying what needs to be said. And always remember that communication does not mean talking. Communication also includes listening. When two people are upset and both are talking, friction increases and communication decreases. The reason God gave us two ears and one mouth is to remind us to listen more than speak."

"So being an entrepreneur is a lot about people and the communication skills needed to communicate to them."

Rich dad agreed and continued, saying, "Leadership requires great communication skills. To become a better entrepreneur requires you to focus on improving your communication skills. One of your first steps in your leadership development is to develop the courage to be a face-to-face communicator and to work on developing your communication skills. If you are a stab-them-in-the-back type of communicator, I doubt your business will grow. Entrepreneurship is for people with courage, not cowards. If you will work on always improving your communication skills, your business will grow. Remember that just because you're talking you're not necessarily communicating. And in sales, telling is not selling. Communication is a far more complex affair than simply moving your lips and wagging your tongue."

Sitting quietly as rich dad enjoyed his meal, my mind went back to the angry father, the customer whom rich dad had fired. I asked, "And that is why you told that irate customer that you had no vacancies! It was better than telling him what you thought of him."

"Yes. As the entrepreneur, one of your jobs is to protect your company and employees from cheap customers—the customers who want more than they pay for, the customers who want something for nothing. I had to find a way of firing him without getting into an argument again. I know he would stab me in the back, if we got into it. That is why I make it a point to fire cheap customers—politely and discreetly."

"Isn't that cruel or discriminating against poor people?"

"I did not say poor people," said rich dad, raising his voice. "The word I used was cheap—cheap customers. Not poor people. There is a difference. There are rich cheap people and poor cheap people. Cheap has nothing to do with money. It has to do with a state of mind. In some cases, I would say it borders on a mental illness. Also, I would not classify cheap people in the same category as bargain hunters. We all love a bargain. Yet as much as we love value for our money, very few of us want value at the expense of someone else. But a cheap person does. A cheap person borders on being a thief—sometimes they are thieves. If it's not money they're stealing, they steal your time and your energy. They steal your peace of mind.

"For all the months of misery that one guy caused our company, it would have been better for us to let him just stay for free. He sucked the life out of our business for months. He seemed to enjoy messing with us. He always changed the deal, said we said things we did not say. He always wanted a better price even after he agreed to pay a set price. He seemed to enjoy having us come after him. Instead of spending time on our good customers, we spent time on him. Having a bad customer can cost us good customers. That is why I say you need to fire your cheap customers. They're too expensive. This is a very important lesson to learn, if you want to be an entrepreneur. Always remember, take very good care of your good customers and fire your cheap customers."

How to Find Good Customers

In business, a very important word is the word *margin*. It is as important a term as *cash flow*. In fact, both terms are intricately related. In overly simple terms, margin is the difference between what it costs to produce your product and the price you sell your product for. For example, let's say it costs you $2.00 to manufacture your widget and you sell your widget for $10.00. In this case, your *gross margin* is $8.00.

There are three reasons why a product's gross margin is so important. They are:

1. The gross margin finances the rest of the B-I Triangle. Looking at the diagram of the B-I Triangle below, you can see that a product's margin must provide enough cash flow to feed the rest of the triangle. Margin pays for the team's salaries, legal fees, operating the company's systems, marketing, and accounting, also known as operating expenses.

2. Margin determines the price of your product. Obviously, the more margin, the higher the price of your product.

3. Product and price determine your customer. To help clarify this, let's look at the automobile industry. A Rolls-Royce is known as a very expensive car. It attracts a certain type of customer. If Rolls-Royce suddenly announced it was going to produce a low-priced budget model, many of their rich customers would probably start looking for another brand of car.

Wrong Car–Wrong Price–Wrong Customer

Recently Jaguar announced it was dropping its lower-priced model, because it realized that offering a lower-priced model had hurt its sales. After losing $700 million in 2004, they finally realized that they should stay at the high end of the car market and not try to capture market share in the midprice market.

Today, many brands are made in the same factory. For example, a factory that produces blue jeans can produce jeans for a high-end brand and a low-end brand. It is basically the same product, but the high-end brand can command a higher price and is sold through a different distribution channel, let's say Saks Fifth Avenue. If the high-end brand wants to produce a low-end brand, they had best create another brand for a different distribution channel, let's say Kmart. In fact, that is what many big companies do. They produce the same product but under different brands representing different price points for different customers.

So to find good customers, you need to match the product and the price to fit the customer's needs, wants, and ego. In many cases, the customer's ego is far more important than wants and needs.

How Much Is Your Product Worth?

In 1996, after the CASHFLOW game was in its final production, ready for commercial use, the next question was, How much is this game worth? How much can we sell the game for? Those of you who have seen our game may recognize some of the challenges we faced. When Kim and I first saw our finished, commercial version of the game for the first time, both of us were as proud as new parents. We were also concerned. The packaging looked great but we thought it might have looked too much like a game for *entertainment* rather than *education*. We made it look bright and fun because we wanted learning to be fun. But as we looked at our finished product, we began to wonder, How much would someone pay for fun?

We wanted people to know the game was about education, but again, how much would someone pay for education? Looking at our finished product for the first time, Kim and I knew we had serious marketing challenges.

To find out what the market might think about our product, once again, we formed a group of people who did not know us, as we did with the beta test, and asked them what they thought of the packaging. The feedback was mixed, from, "It looks great," to, "It looks stupid." The people in the group did not know we were the creators of the game, so their opinions were pretty frank, often painful.

Next we asked them what they thought the price of the game should be. Again, not knowing us, or what went into creating a game, and not having played the game, the prices they suggested ranged from $19.95 to a high of $39.95. This was even more depressing. At that point in time, due to the small production runs, our cost just for the game, without freight, was $46.00 per game to produce, not counting the development costs. We were starting off with a product with a negative margin, before we added in the costs of the rest of the B-I Triangle. When I was manufacturing my nylon wallets, a joke amongst manufacturers was, "So what if I am losing $2.00 a unit. We're going to make it up on volume."

Calling In a Consultant

Sharon had experience in the publishing and game industries and had a friend who worked as a consultant to the toy industry. He had expertise with board games. After trying the game himself he discussed his opinion of CASHFLOW. His first comment was, "The game was too difficult." He said, "People have become less smart. If Monopoly were introduced today, it would be rejected because it, too, would be deemed too difficult. Today, games must be so simple that all the instructions on how to play the game can be understood within a couple of minutes."

We had also asked him how much we could sell the game for. He replied, "You might get $39.00 at retail. That means you would have to sell it to a retail store for $20.00, even less if you sell it to a major chain such as Wal-Mart. You might have to sell it for as low as $10.00 just to get it into a store."

Sharon added, "On top of that, if we did get it into a store, we'll have a bigger problem with customers' returning the product. They might buy the game for fun, because our packaging is fun, and place it with other games. But when they find out how hard it is to get started and that it is educational, many of them will return the game to the store and ask for their money back. We could find ourselves with huge losses from returns and damaged returned games."

Looking for New Answers

It was obvious that our game was not meant for the public market. We knew the game was not for everyone. We knew the game was intended for anyone who thought his or her financial education was important. The problem was to find that customer in the sea of people. The game was also hard to categorize by demographics. For example, if we had written a book for children, placing the book would be easy. We could place it anywhere parents shopped for kids. But this game could be played by anyone, from kids to adults, male or female.

It was also for people whether they were rich or poor, just as long as they valued their financial education. And we knew our customers wanted to be financially proactive. After teaching entrepreneurship and investing for years, I knew that most people wanted more money but very few people would actually take the time to learn about how to make more money. The challenge was to find the customer who would want the educational game and the information locked in it.

At a marketing seminar I learned a guideline known as the five Ps. These are the five things a marketer must know when selling a product. I believe they were identified by E. Jerome McCarthy. They are:

1. Product
2. Person
3. Price
4. Place
5. Position

A marketer must know what the *product* is, who the *person* who wants the product is, what *price* they are willing to pay, where the product will be *placed* so the customer can find it, and how to *position* it in the marketplace, that is, the biggest, the smallest, the first, the last, and so on.

Entrepreneurs should enjoy solving business problems and normally I do. But this problem had me stumped. All I had were the first two Ps. One day a friend called to say he was coming to Phoenix to go to a special seminar on marketing and wanted to know if I wanted to go along. I jumped at the chance.

The room was filled with approximately three hundred people, and by the look of them, most seemed to be entrepreneurs. Not too many had the corporate look. The instructor was a wild man talking about how ad agencies just wasted your money on expensive, good-looking ads or TV spots that sold nothing, a point of view I agreed with. He said, "The purpose of marketing is to get the phone to ring. With these ad agencies, the only phone that rings is them calling asking for more money to buy more advertising, so they can collect more fees. Ask them if they can guarantee your sales or measure your sales. In most cases they cannot or will not guarantee their work. All they want to do is win awards for creative advertising for their agency—with your advertising dollars."

SALES = INCOME

The seminar was exactly what I was looking for. It was marketing for entrepreneurs, not big corporations with millions in ad dollars to spend. The instructor had a great track record for success and told stories that came from real life experience. Some of the other points he made were:

1. The entrepreneur must be the best salesperson in his or her business.
2. The entrepreneur must be the best marketer in his or her business.
3. The marketing efforts must produce sales—not just good-looking ads or slick commercials.*

As obvious as these points are, you would be surprised how many entrepreneurs delegate those important roles to ad agencies. Ad agencies are generally for big corporations or established businesses. In a small startup business, the entrepreneur needs to be the best they can be at sales and marketing. With limited resources, every dollar spent must result in sales—because sales equal income.

Rich dad drummed into my head "Sales = Income." He would also say, the reason so many people have low incomes is that they are poor at selling. If he had been at this sales seminar, he would have loved it. The instructor was adamant about marketing that led to sales that could be proven and measured.

Toward the end of the day, I got the marketing answer I was looking for. When discussing how to price a product, the instructor said, "There are

---

*Author's note: One of the best books I have read on marketing for entrepreneurs is *Your Marketing Sucks* by Mark Stevens (Crown Business, 2003). It is blunt, to the point, and essential for entrepreneurs without much money at the start.

three price points for any product. The lowest-priced product, the highest-priced, and the middle-priced. The worst price to be is the middle price. Nobody knows who you are. The trouble with being the lowest-price product is that someone is always trying to beat you. Someone will find a way to sell the same product for less than you. To win the lowest-price competition, you have to make less and less money. On top of that you have to deal with cheap customers."

With that statement the pieces of the puzzle began to come together. Immediately, I remembered the conversation I had with rich dad years earlier, about cheap customers. Bringing my thoughts back into the seminar, the instructor roared on about why being the most expensive was the best position to fight for. He said, "When I was a struggling marketing consultant, I tried to keep my prices low. The problem was, the lower I made my prices, the cheaper my customers became. Soon, instead of selling my services, I was spending more time haggling about my fees with cheap customers. When I raised my fees a little, I joined the masses of other middle-of-the-road marketing consultants. Again, most of my time was spent discussing price rather than the value of my product, what I could do for the customer. Then one day, I decided to be ridiculous and simply raise my fees to the highest in my industry. Instead of charging $50 an hour for my services, I raised my rates to $25,000 per day. Today I work less, earn far more money, and work with a better class of client."

My mind raced when I heard his fee of $25,000 per day. I realized that I was the cheap client he did not want. Once I got over the shock of realizing I was the cheap one, I began to realize that it was my own cheapness that was causing me to struggle at pricing my board game. I was looking at price rather than the value of the game.

"Don't fight for the bargain basement," boomed the instructor. "The bargain basement attracts cheap customers."

Once again my mind drifted off, recalling how rich dad hated dealing with people who were cheap. Rich dad said, "Design your product and price it for a very special customer. Your marketing should then find ways of reaching that special customer. Be creative. Don't be cheap. The bargain basement is not a place to find good customers."

The Book Takes Priority

That evening, I went home and had a meeting with Kim and Sharon. The first thing I said was, "We should sell the board game for $200. We will *position* it as the most expensive game in the world. It's not just a game, it's a seminar in a box."

My two partners agreed. They did not flinch at the idea of selling a board game for that much money, even if our focus group said it should sell for $39.95.

"Our problem is we have been asking the opinion of people who will probably never be our customers. We have been asking for the opinion of people who shop in the bargain basement, not in the boardroom. We need to find customers who value education and are willing to pay for it."

"We'll need a way to find them," Sharon added.

"The book takes priority. Instead of focusing on marketing the game, we will begin to focus on marketing the book. The book will help us find our customers. The book will become our company brochure."

At the time, Sharon was working on *Rich Dad Poor Dad*. When she got my original notes for it, it was over 350 pages in length, full of grammatical errors, misspelled words, and illogical ramblings. "So we need to weave the game into the book," she said.

"And we go back on the road doing investment seminars," said Kim, "working with the same type of customer we have been working with for years."

"That's the idea. Sharon finishes the book and we get back on the road doing seminars for people who pay for financial education. We've been doing it for years. It's a low-risk idea. We know the business and we know how to reach those customers."

"In other words, the tactic remains the same. The sole tactic of the business is to get people to play the CASHFLOW game. The three of us now focus on the strategies. If the strategies work, people will play the game."

The three of us were in agreement. A few days ago we were heading in different directions and now we were a team again with a unified plan.

"So why $200?" asked Kim. "How did you come up with that number?"

"It took a while," I said. "But when the instructor said, 'A higher price can be perceived as more valuable,' the lights in my head went on. I realized I was

cheap and looking at my own product through cheap eyes, rather than looking at the value hidden in the game. So I went up to $59 a game, and that still
sounded cheap. I was now in the middle, not at the top. In my mind, I then
tested $99 a game. I was comfortable with that. I knew I could sell it at that
price so I knew I had not yet reached the top. When I tried $200 in my head,
I felt uncomfortable. Now I knew I had gone beyond my own comfort level. I
had found my price."

"Well, it certainly gives us a large margin. That will help us grow the business," said Sharon, putting on her CPA hat.

"And with that margin we can fund projects that make the game more accessible to people who really do not have much money. We can set up a tax-
exempt foundation that donates money to organizations that teach financial
literacy. Maybe someday we'll be able to fund a project that will deliver financial
education and our game electronically via the Internet to schools throughout
the world," she added.

"So we market the book through traditional distribution channels. That
handles the *place* category of the five Ps—where we *place* our product in
front of potential customers. Instead of trying to drop the price of the game to
fit into that distribution channel, let's use a conventionally priced book and
flow it through the book distribution system."

"So the book will sell the game, or at least help us find customers, and the
seminars will sell the game," Sharon summarized. "But there is still something
else behind charging $200 a game."

"Well," I began slowly, "if we compared games to games, the game is not
worth $200. But when compared as education to education, the game is really
inexpensive. Just look at how much a college education costs in both time and
money. On top of that, you don't learn much about money or investing in
school. Also look at how much it costs for people to lose money in the stock
market. That is even more expensive. But the biggest expense is the loss of opportunity. So many people want to invest, know they should invest, but fail to
invest simply because they lack the financial education. Not only can this game
help a person make millions of dollars, but it can also help a person become financially free."

"But what about the people who might feel ripped off at $200?" asked Kim.

"Many people will, and they may never buy the game," I replied. "If we make the game $200 people will have to think long and hard about the value of the game before they buy it. And that is what we want them to do. We want the price to make them think about value more than just entertainment."

"On top of that, just think of the number of people one game can reach. One $200 game can reach hundreds of people," said Sharon. "Not everyone has to buy the game."

"And that is why the sole tactic of our company is to have people *play* the game—not necessarily *buy* the game. People who are serious about their education and pay $200 for the game will be more likely to take the time to learn the game. The only way they can learn the game is to invite others to play. The game immediately begins to fulfill its mission. The more people who play the game and invite other people to play the game, the more the cost per play and player goes down—and the value of the game goes up. Our only job now is to find that person who values education and is willing to pay for it."

"We also make the game harder to get—harder for people to find. We will have to be smarter about letting people know how to find us through our website, richdad.com," said Sharon. "By keeping access to the game more restricted, instead of mass marketing it we will highlight its educational value. Our focus groups were looking at it as a mass-market 'game' not the educational tool it is."

"And what happens if it doesn't work?" asked Kim.

"Then we come up with more ideas," I replied. "Ideas are plentiful if you're creative. Our strategies are low-risk. Sharon can write and build the business, and we can do seminars. We should have cash flow from those two strategies so we do not need to sell as many games. In this way we give the game the opportunity to sell itself, to find its own fans and its own channels of distribution. If it is a valuable product, the plan will work. If our customers do not find the game valuable, we shut the business down. Only time will tell."

As stated earlier, the first time the game was played commercially was at an investment seminar in Las Vegas, Nevada, in November 1996. In February 2004, when I saw the nearly full-page article in the *New York Times,* I knew the game had found its rightful audience.

By February 2004, there were over 350,000 CASHFLOW games sold, primarily by customers finding us and coming to our website or through a handful of distributors. There are now CASHFLOW clubs all over the world meeting regularly to play the game. And we have very few complaints about its price. Our return factor is less than 1%. We found the right customers for the game.

Before You Quit Your Job

The five Ps are a simple guideline for your market plan. Before you quit your job remember these important points.

1. There are three price positions in any market. The highest price, the middle price, and the lowest price. Decide which price best fits you. Always remember that the middle price may be the most comfortable but it is also the most crowded. It's hard to be outstanding if you're average.

2. The lowest-price leaders do not just lower their price. The winners in the lowest-price category do something brilliant in business that their competitors cannot do. For example, Wal-Mart sells the same products many other retailers sell. Wal-Mart has a far better system of retailing that allows them to make a lot of money with smaller margins. Remember what rich dad said, "Any idiot can drop their price and go broke. It takes a brilliant business person to drop their prices, cut their margins, and get rich." He also said, "If you choose to compete at the low end of the market, you have to be a better businessman than those who compete at the top." Since I am not that good a business person, I find it easier to compete at the top.

3. If you are going to be the highest-price product in your market niche, then you have to give your customers something your competitors cannot give. If you are confused by what high-priced businesses do, then do your homework. Go to a high-priced auto dealer and then go to a low-priced auto dealer. Or go to a high-priced hotel and then go to a budget hotel. By taking notice of differences, you find ways of better defining your product and your customer. Know that the higher the price, the fewer the customers, and the more precise you

need to be in your marketing. Also, never ask people who shop in the bargain basements of the world what they think of a Rolls-Royce.

4. Don't try to be all things to all customers. If you want the high end and the low end, start two brands. As you know, Honda has its Acura brand and Toyota has its Lexus brand. To me, they look like the same cars, but what do I know? Obviously the marketers at Honda and Toyota have done a good job convincing the public they are selling two different cars. As stated earlier in this chapter, marketing needs to fill a customer's wants, needs, and ego. In many cases, ego has more buying power.

5. Instead of discounting down, bonus up. I know people look at the game and flinch at the price. Rather than drop the price, we prefer to add products to the mix and then increase the price of the package. As rich dad said, "Sales = Income." So rather than cut our price and reduce our margins, which anyone can do, we would rather find ways of keeping our prices while increasing the value to the customer and having the customer be happy.

6. Weak salespeople always want new products to sell. When I was at Xerox, it was always the weakest sales reps who said, "If we had new products I could sell more." Many businesses fall into this trap. When sales are down, they look for new products, which often leads to a phenomenon known as line extension. When line extension happens too much, the customer can become confused because there are too many products to choose from and your own products can become your competitors. Rich dad said, "Instead of looking for new products to sell, look for new customers." He also said, "A smart entrepreneur focuses on keeping existing customers happy and looking for new customers to sell existing products to."

7. Look for strategic partners who already sell to the customer you want to sell to. Earlier in this book, I wrote about the three kinds of money, competitive, cooperative, and spiritual. One of the ways to become richer faster with less risk is to be cooperative and earn cooperative money. An example of this is our relationship with Warner Books, through which we earn cooperative money.

8. Treat your best customers well. The Internet makes keeping in touch with your best customers easier than ever before. The rule of thumb is: Focus on keeping your best customers happy, because not only will they buy more from you, they will tell their friends about you, and that is the best kind of marketing of all. It's called *word of mouth*. When it comes to taking care of your best customers, be creative. One of the reasons small entrepreneurial companies beat the big corporations is simply that a small company can be more creative and be creative faster.

In Summary

Always remember the five Ps. Remember that *your very special product* is important to *a very special person*.

The *price* of your product must satisfy the person's needs, wants, and ego. When it comes to ego, we all like finding a bargain. Also, many of us like letting people know we spent a lot of money for a product only a few people can or will afford. So ego can work at the high end as well as the low end.

Where you *place* your product so your customer can find it is important. Always remember that a new Ferrari will look out of *place* in a used-car lot filled with cheap cars. If you *place* your product in the wrong *place*, your sales will suffer. When *Rich Dad Poor Dad* was first printed, we placed the book in our friend's car wash/gas station in Texas. Why that car wash? Because that was the *place* where the affluent people brought their cars for a wash and for gas. If we had put our book in a place were people came to buy cheap gas, I believe the books would still be there.

And the only *position* you want to be in is in first position. Always remember that most of us know that Lindbergh was the first human to fly solo nonstop across the Atlantic. Very few people know who was second. If you are not first in your category, then invent a new category you can be the first in. When the game was not known, we became the first game to claim the highest-priced-game category. If you have a hot dog stand, you could claim that this is the first hot dog stand owned by you. When Avis realized it was second to Hertz, it took first place by being first to claim to be proud of being in second place, which led to their WE TRY HARDER slogan. In conclusion, the most important place you want to be first in is in your customers' minds. For example, when you think of a soft drink do you first think of Coca-Cola or Pepsi? When your very special customers think of your product category, do they think of you first or your competitor first? Ultimately, the most important job of an entrepreneur is to be first in the mind of your customers.

SHARON'S INSIGHTS

Lesson #9: Don't Fight for the Bargain Basement.

FOCUS ON THE RIGHT TARGET

It is very important for you as a business owner to pick the right target customer. Are you going after a high-end customer or a low-end customer? A young customer or an old customer? Will you be competing for that customer based on price or quality? As rich dad said, when you compete based on price there is always someone else willing to offer a lower price. Creating a competitive advantage based on quality provides for better profit margins, and typically a higher-level customer.

In addition to determining your target pricing for your customer, it is also important to know which customers to focus your efforts on. Envision the typical bell curve and divide it into three sections. Imagine that one-third of your customers love you, one-third of your potential customers don't like you, and the remaining third in the middle don't care one way or the other about you or your products. A common mistake that I see with new business owners is that they concentrate on the one-third of their customers who don't like them instead of concentrating on the one-third who love them. In fact, many business consultants want to concentrate on your problem customers to help you grow your business. We couldn't disagree more.

As mentioned earlier in this chapter, it is difficult to be all things to all people. Instead of concentrating on the people who do not like you or your product, consider spending your energy on supporting the one-third of your customers who love you. Turn these customers, who are already fans, into testimonials for you and your products. The result is called *viral marketing*. With their help, you can more easily convert the one-third of potential customers in the middle. Plus it is a lot more fun spending time with people who love you, instead of worrying about those who don't. And there's something else—it takes much less effort to sell to an existing customer than to find a new customer.

Another common mistake of new businesses is to cast too broad a net for customers. They take the position that anyone who walks in the door is a potential customer—we will do business with anybody. That position is a mistake. Customers should be prequalified. You simply don't want to waste your time and effort trying to sell your products or services to someone who simply cannot afford them or really does not need them. You certainly do not want to actually provide products or services to someone who cannot afford to pay for them (unless you recognize from the beginning that it is a charitable donation or gift). The fact is that sometimes you are better off having no customers than bad customers. Not only can you fail to make any profit from a bad customer, you can miss opportunities and sometimes actually lose money.

LIFETIME VALUE OF CUSTOMER

Many business owners also miss the boat when it comes to understanding the value of each and every customer. They celebrate when they sell one product to one customer. True success comes when you have a community of customers who buy repeatedly from you. This loyalty and shared community creates a sustainable and successful business model. For instance, Carol, a local jeweler, sells a piece of jewelry to Joe. If Joe's wife enjoys the jewelry he will probably return to Carol to buy jewelry for other special occasions and turn into a repeat customer for Carol. Rather than a single purchaser, the jeweler now has a customer who has a much larger sales and profit potential. Carol understands the lifetime value of a customer. This is the goodwill that we referred to in the last chapter. Isn't someone much more likely to do business with someone they have a good history with than a stranger? If you have that good history—goodwill—with people, the word will get around, and soon you will have a solid reputation that will attract new business through referrals.

In fact, *it is much harder to find a new customer than to keep a satisfied customer coming back.* One of the greatest assets of a business is its customer list.

The customer cycle has the following stages:

1. Attract the customer (hardest part).
2. Make a sale.
3. Capture your customers' contact information.
4. Make your customer feel special (thank the customer for his or her purchase).
5. Keep in contact with your customer (send the customer advance announcements of new products, special promotions, or events).
6. Answer customer inquiries in a timely and friendly manner (turn complaining customers into happy customers).
7. Create a community or club for customers to join (give them value for free just for joining).
8. Ask your happy customer to "tell a friend" about your business or product.
9. Make a repeat sale to your customer.
10. Repeat the cycle.

Some of these steps are easier than others and some are more challenging based on the type of business you have. For instance, The Rich Dad Company attracts customers by selling books to them in retail bookstores. We knew it would be difficult to get their contact information. So within our books, we offer free additional information at our website, www.richdad.com. To receive the additional information, we simply ask the customer to give us his or her name and e-mail address. This allows us to provide the new customer with information about new Rich Dad products, special promotions, and upcoming events. We call these special offer placements "calls to action." Is this just a ploy to get contact information? We make sure that it's *not* just a ploy and that real value is received by the customer for joining.

Other companies that sell products through retail outlets offer customer rebates, in order to capture their customers' contact information. Or they build brand loyalty with their customers through promotion and advertising. For instance, a potato chip company may not have its customer contact information, but it does depend on its customers' making repeat purchases. For instance, it may choose to build its brand through "point of purchase" display promotions and brand advertising.

In the example of the jeweler mentioned above, Carol would be best served by finding out the dates of birthdays, anniversaries, and other special occasions for each of her clients when she sells them the initial piece of jewelry. Then a week or two before each of these dates, she sends a gentle reminder card indicating a special offer for a gift that may even be gift wrapped and delivered to the client's office. This not only generates additional sales, but it also supports the client. We can all use a reminder of those special occasions in our lives.

POSITION YOUR PRODUCT FOR THE TARGET

How do you target a particular group of customers? The process is the "product positioning" that we discussed earlier. You establish, through your marketing, advertising, and pricing, a particular concept or image of the product in the mind of consumers. That concept or image is tied to your brand (trademark). The trick is to pick a concept or image that is attractive to your target. You need to have something distinctive about you or your product. You need to be able to distinguish yourself from the competition. You want that distinction to be attractive to your target market.

Once you have established a position for your brand, you need to be careful that you do not dilute the message. You need to be particularly careful not to send contradictory or conflicting messages. This issue tends to surface when you have more than one product or more than one version of a product. Let's say you have an initial version of a product that you are selling very successfully to men in the twenty- to forty-year-old age bracket. You want to expand your market, and come up with another version of the product specifically designed to be attractive to women in the same age bracket. Do you market the new version of the product under the same brand, or develop a new brand for the feminine version of product?

The answer depends on two primary factors: the specific message used to position the masculine version of the product, and the nature of the differences between the versions of the product. For example, if the positioning message for the initial product was, "This is the product for a real he-man," then using the same brand for a feminine version of the product would be inconsistent and inappropriate. On the other hand, a feminine version of the product would not be inconsistent with a positioning message of, "This is the product for twenty- to forty-year-olds." If the masculine and feminine versions of the product are relatively similar, use of the same brand with both versions would probably not be inconsistent. However, if the masculine and feminine versions of product differed considerably, use of the same brand with both could cause confusion and would probably not be appropriate.

ANALYZE YOUR Ps AND Qs

So remember the five Ps of marketing:

1. Product
2. Person
3. Price
4. Place
5. Position

Now that you have your B-I Triangle in place, it is time to review your five Ps. You may come up with more questions (Qs) than answers. Bring your team together and create your business tactic and strategies while keeping your five Ps in mind. With your product, person (target customer), price, place, and position planned well and supported by a strong B-I Triangle, you will more easily find the sixth P. PROFIT!

In order to realize your business mission, your planning time is over. Take action on your new business today.

Know When to Quit.

Chapter 10

The Summary

Knowing When to Quit

That you do not like your job is not a reason to become an entrepreneur. It may sound like a good reason but it is not a strong enough reason. It definitely lacks a strong enough mission. Although almost everyone can become an entrepreneur, entrepreneurship is not for everyone.

There is an old saying that goes, "Winners never quit and quitters never win." Personally, I do not agree with that saying. It is too simple. In my reality a winner also knows when to quit. Sometimes in life, it is best to cut your losses. It is best to admit you have come to a dead end or to admit you have been barking up the wrong tree.

In my opinion, a quitter is someone who quits simply because things have gotten tough. I have been a quitter many times in my life. I have quit diet programs, exercise programs, girlfriends, businesses, books, studies, and so on. Every year I make New Year's resolutions and quit. So I know what quitting is and that I am a quitter.

One of the reasons I did not quit my process in becoming an entrepreneur was that I really wanted to be one. I wanted it badly. I wanted to enjoy the freedom, the independence, the wealth, and the ability to make a contribution to this world that a successful entrepreneur has. In spite of how badly I wanted to become a successful entrepreneur, the powerful concept of *quitting* was always right in front of me, holding the door open. It would have been easy to quit when I was out of money and owed a lot of money. It would have been easy to quit every time a creditor demanded payment. It would have been easy to quit when the tax department let me know that I owed more in back taxes. It would have been easy to quit when a project failed or a potential partner walked out of the deal. When things were tough, quitting was always lurking nearby, just a handshake away.

For me, becoming an entrepreneur is a process, a process I am still in. I believe I will be an entrepreneur in training till the end. I love business and I love solving business problems. There have been times I have cut my losses, shut a business down, changed directions, but when it came to the process of becoming an entrepreneur, I have never quit—at least not yet. It is a process I love. It is a process that brings me the kind of life I want. So although the process has been tough for me, it has been worth it. Also, that it was tough for me does not mean it needs to be tough for you. One reason for writing this book is that I want to make the process easier for anyone who is about to start the process or is already in the process.

Before ending this book, I thought I would leave you with one little thing that kept me going. It was the glow in the dark, even in the darkest of hours. I had a little piece of paper taped to the base of the telephone in my office at the wallet company. That little piece of paper came from a Chinese fortune cookie. It said, "You can always quit. Why start now?" There were many phone calls I had to handle that provided me with more than enough reason for me to quit. Yet after hanging up the phone, I would glance at the words of wisdom from the fortune cookie and say to myself, "As much as I want to quit, I won't quit today. I'll quit tomorrow." The good thing is, tomorrow never came.

Before You Quit Your Job We Offer These Tips

1. **Check your attitude**. Attitude is almost everything. We don't recommend becoming an entrepreneur just to make money. There are far easier ways to make money. If you do not love business and the challenges a business offers, then entrepreneurship may not be for you.

2. **Get as much experience as possible on five levels of the B-I Triangle.**
   In earlier books we advised people to work to learn, not work to earn.
   Instead of taking jobs for the money, take jobs for the experience. For
   example, if you want to gain experience in how business systems work,
   get a part-time job at McDonald's. You would be surprised at what happens the moment a customer says, "I want a Big Mac and fries." The
   moment that happens, one of the world's best-designed business systems takes over. It is a brilliantly designed system run primarily by people with only a high school education.

3. **Always remember that Sales = Income.** All entrepreneurs need to
   be good in sales. If you are not good in sales, get as much experience
   as possible before you quit your job. I heard Donald Trump once say,
   "Some people are born salespeople. The rest of us can learn to sell." I
   am not a natural salesperson. I did train hard to become one. If you
   want really great sales training, you may want to consider joining a
   network marketing business or a direct sales business.

4. **Be optimistic as well as brutally honest with yourself.** In his book
   Good to Great, Jim Collins does an excellent piece on this need to be
   brutally honest. He writes about his interviews with Admiral Stockwell,
   one of the longest-held POWs from the Vietnam War. When Jim Collins
   asked the admiral which type of person died in their cells, the admiral
   answered without hesitation, "The optimists." The POWs who did survive were those who could handle the brutal facts about their situation.
   On the flip side, know the difference between being brutally honest and
   being pessimistic. I know people who will tell you why something will
   not work even if it's working. I know people who store in their mind every piece of negative news possible. Negative people, or pessimistic
   people, are not the same as brutally honest people.

5. **How are you at spending money?** Too many people struggle financially because they *do not know how to spend their money.* Too
   many people spend their money and it never comes back. An entrepreneur needs to know how to spend money and have more
   money come back. It is not about being cheap, tight, or frugal. It's
   about knowing when to spend, what to spend on, and how much to
   spend. I have seen too many entrepreneurs go broke saving money.

For example, when business drops off, instead of spending money on more promotions the entrepreneur cuts back hoping to save money. When this happens business continues to drop off. This is an example of the wrong action, at the wrong time.

6. **Start a business to practice on.** No one can learn to ride a bicycle without a bicycle and no one can learn to start, build, and run a business without a business. Once you are familiar with the different parts of the B-I Triangle, stop planning and start doing. As I have always said, "Keep your full-time job and start a part-time business."

7. **Be willing to ask for help.** Rich dad often said, "Arrogance is the cause of ignorance." If you don't know something, ask someone who does know. On the flip side, don't be a pest and ask for too much help. There is a fine line between help and a crutch.

8. **Find a mentor**. Rich dad was my mentor. I have had many other mentors. Read books about great entrepreneurs such as Edison, Ford, and Gates. Books can be your best mentors. The Rich Dad Company has a mentoring program known as Rich Dad Coaching. The coaches on the other side of the phone are entrepreneurs, investors, and great coaches. Hire them to keep you on track to getting what you want from your life. One of my favorite entrepreneurs is Steven Jobs, founder of Apple Computer and Pixar. Not only do I like his style, I love the culture of his business. One of the most important things an entrepreneur can build is a business with a strong culture. As stated earlier, at The Rich Dad Company we work hard to foster and protect a culture of learning and free expression.

9. **Join an entrepreneur's network.** Birds of a feather do flock together. Every city I have ever lived in has groups or associations of entrepreneurs. Attend their meetings and find one that fits your needs. Surround yourself with fellow entrepreneurs. They are there for support as well as to be supported. Contact your SBA, the Small Business Administration, or your local chamber of commerce for a schedule of meetings and seminars. They are great sources of information as well as resources for entrepreneurs. One group I have been impressed with is the YEO, the Young Entrepreneurs Organization. Although I am too old to belong to this group of young men

and women, I have been asked to speak at several of their chapters. I have always been impressed with the quality of young person this organization attracts.

10. **Be faithful to the process.** One reason why many people do not quit their jobs and become entrepreneurs is that entrepreneurship can be extremely challenging, especially when first starting out. I suggest you follow the basics of the B-I Triangle and diligently do your best to master all eight categories of the triangle. It takes time, but if you are successful the rewards can be immense. As rich dad said, "Entrepreneurship is a process, not a job or profession." So be faithful to the process and remember that even when times are bad, the process will give you a glimpse of the future that lies ahead.

Over the years I have heard many people use the term BHAG, which stands for Big Hairy Audacious Goal. While having a big hairy goal is commendable, I believe the process and the size of the mission are more important than the goal.

Rich dad drew for his son and me a diagram that looked like this:

MISSION ➡ PROCESS ➡ GOAL

He said, "If you are going to have a big goal you need a strong mission to push you through the process. With a strong mission, anything is attainable."

Thank you for reading this book and we wish you the best of success if you should decide to become an entrepreneur or are already an entrepreneur.

Robert Kiyosaki
Sharon Lechter

Recommended Reading

"A Perspective on Entrepreneurship," Howard H. Stevenson, Harvard Business School Article, 1983
The Dollar Crisis, Richard Duncan, John Wiley & Sons (Asia) Pte Ltd, 2003
Good to Great, Jim Collins, HarperCollins Publishers Inc., 2001
It's Not About the Bike, Lance Armstrong, Penguin Putnam, 2001
Longitudes and Attitudes, Thomas Friedman, Farrar, Straus, Giroux, 2002
The War of Art, Steven Pressfield, Warner Books, 2002
The World Is Flat, Thomas Friedman, Farrar, Straus, Giroux, 2005
Your Marketing Sucks, Mark Stevens, Crown Business, 2003

Referenced Rich Dad Books

Rich Dad Poor Dad, Robert Kiyosaki with Sharon Lechter, Warner Business Books, 1997
Rich Dad's CASHFLOW Quadrant, Robert Kiyosaki with Sharon Lechter, Warner Business Books, 1998
Rich Dad's Guide to Investing, Robert Kiyosaki with Sharon Lechter, Warner Business Books, 2000
Rich Dad's Retire Young Retire Rich, Robert Kiyosaki with Sharon Lechter, Warner Business Books, 2001
The Business School for People Who Like Helping People, Second Edition, Robert Kiyosaki
with Sharon Lechter, TechPress Inc. in association with Momentum Media, 2003

SalesDogs, Blair Singer, Warner Business Boooks, 2001
Protecting Your #1 Asset, Michael Lechter, Esq., Warner Business Books, 2001
Own Your Own Corporation, Garrett Sutton, Esq., Warner Business Books, 2001
How to Buy and Sell a Business, Garrett Sutton, Esq., Warner Business Books, 2003
The ABCs of Building a Business Team That Wins, Blair Singer, Warner Business Books, 2004
OPM Other People's Money, Michael Lechter, Esq., Warner Business Books, 2005
The ABCs of Writing Winning Business Plans, Garrett Sutton, Esq., Warner Business Books, 2005

Rich Dad's Coaching

Working with a Rich Dad Coach will help you begin to change your
understanding of how the rich get richer and how you can start leveraging
your own resources to achieve wealth.

Your Rich Dad Coach will help you:

- **Expand your Context**
- **Achieve your Plan**
- **Write your own Rules**
- **Get what you want!**

Call today to receive a free introduction
to Rich Dad's Coaching
1-800-240-0434
ext 5021

About the Authors

Robert Kiyosaki

Robert Kiyosaki is an investor, entrepreneur, educator, and author of *Rich Dad Poor Dad*, the *USA Today* #1 business bestseller for 2003 and 2004.

The success of *Rich Dad Poor Dad* paved the way for the Rich Dad series of books - currently ten books in total. Most all of these books have earned spots on the bestseller lists of *The New York Times*, *The Wall Street Journal*, *Business Week*, *USA Today*, and others.

Prior to writing *Rich Dad Poor Dad*, Robert created the educational board game CASHFLOW® 101 to teach individuals the financial and investment strategies that his rich dad spent years teaching him. It was those same strategies that allowed Robert to retire at age 47. Hundreds of "CASHFLOW Clubs" - independent of The Rich Dad® Company - have sprung up throughout the world and thousands of people get together on a regular basis and play CASHFLOW 101.

Born and raised in Hawaii, Robert Kiyosaki is a fourth-generation Japanese-American. After graduating from college in New York, Robert joined the Marine Corps and served in Vietnam as an officer and helicopter gunship pilot. Following the war, Robert went to work in sales for the Xerox Corporation and then in 1977 he started a company that brought the first nylon and Velcro 'surfer wallets' to market. He founded an international education company in 1985 that taught business and investing to tens of thousands of students throughout the world.

In 1994 Robert sold his business and, through his investments, was able to retire at the age of 47. During his short-lived retirement, Robert wrote *Rich Dad Poor Dad* which has sold over 20 million copies worldwide and held a spot on *The New York Times* bestsellers list for over four years.

In Robert's words: "We go to school to learn to work hard for money. I write books and create products that teach people how to have money work hard for them. Then they can enjoy the luxuries of this great world we live in."

The Rich Dad Company is the collaborative effort of Robert and Kim Kiyosaki and Sharon Lechter. In 1996 they embarked on a journey to raise the financial literacy of people everywhere and carry the Rich Dad mission to every corner of the world. Today they continue this mission through the Rich Dad series of books and products, and live seminars, and educational programs.

Sharon Lechter

CPA, co-author of the Rich Dad book series, and co-founder of Rich Dad's Organization, Sharon Lechter has dedicated her professional efforts to the field of education. She graduated with honors from Florida State University with a degree in accounting and started her career with Coopers & Lybrand. Sharon has held various management positions with computer, insurance and publishing companies while maintaining her professional credentials as a CPA.

Sharon and husband Michael Lechter have been married for over 25 years and are parents to three children, Phillip, Shelly and William. As her children grew, she became actively involved in their education and served in leadership positions in their schools. She became a vocal activist in the areas of mathematics, computers, reading and writing education.

Today she remains a pioneer in developing new technologies to bring education into children's lives in ways that are innovative, challenging and fun. As co-author of the Rich Dad books and co-founder of that company she focuses her efforts in the arena of financial education.

"Our current educational system has not been able to keep pace with the global and technological changes in the world today," Sharon states. "We must teach our young people the skills - both scholastic and financial - that they need to not only survive but to flourish in the world."

A committed philanthropist, Sharon 'gives back' to the world communities as both a volunteer and a benefactor. She directs the Foundation for Financial Literacy and is a strong advocate of education and the need for improved financial literacy.

Sharon and Michael were honored by Childhelp USA, national organization founded to eradicate child abuse in the United States, as recipients of the 2002 "Spirit of the Children" Award. In 2004, Sharon joined the national board of Childhelp USA. Also in 2004, Sharon and Michael were recognized as an Arizona "Power Couple."

As an active member of Women's Presidents Organization, she enjoys networking with other professional women across the country.

Robert Kiyosaki, her business partner and friend, says "Sharon is one of the few natural entrepreneurs I have ever met. My respect for her continues to grow every day that we work together."

Spiritual Money

Rich Dad said, "Spiritual Money is not about money. It is about doing something that must be done and it disturbs you that no one else is doing it."

Rich Kid Smart Kid.com

Money is a life skill---but we don't teach our children about money in school. We are asking for your help in getting financial education into the hands of interested teachers and school administrators.

RichKidSmartKid.com was created by The Rich Dad Company as a free innovative and interactive Web site designed to convey key concepts about money and finance in ways that are fun and challenging… and educational for young people in grades K through 12.

AND, schools all across the world may also register at www.richkidsmartkid.com to receive a FREE download of our electronic version of CASHFLOW for Kids at School™.

Join Us

Play CASHFLOW® for KIDS™ and CASHFLOW 101 with family and friends and share the richkidsmartkid.com Web site with your local teachers and school administrators.

By taking financial education to our schools, together we can better prepare our children for the financial world they will face.

Thank you!

To learn more about Spiritual Money, refer to Chapter 6.

Get Started Today!

As a way of saying "Thank You" for reading this book,
we offer you the following free downloadable audio program.

"My Most Important Marketing Secrets."

Learn the marketing tips and strategies that I have found successful in
creating and building multi-million dollar businesses.

All you have to do to get this audio report is visit our website
www.richdad.com/beforeyouquityourjob
and the program is yours free.

In Addition:

You will find special resources to help you apply the principles from this
book. By actively applying the principles, you can make them a powerful
reality in your own life.

If you are serious about being a successful entrepreneur,
visit **www.richdad.com/beforeyouquityourjob** to find these resources now.

Thank you!

To contact Rich Dad *visit www.richdad.com*
or call 1-800-308-3585

To order books *visit www.twbookmark.com*

For more information:
CASHFLOW® Technologies, Inc.
4330 N. Civic Center Plaza, Suite 100 Scottsdale, Arizona 85251
TEL: (800) 308-3585 • Fax: (480) 348-1349 • E-mail: service@richdad.com

Australia/New Zealand:
Rich Dad® Australia™
4-6 Mentmore Avenue • Rosebery NSW 2018 Australia
TEL: 1300 660 020 • FAX: 1300 301 988 • E-mail: info@richdad.com.au